Your
Golden Retriever's
Life

Also Available from PRIMA PETS™

BETSY SIKORA SIINO

Joanne Howl, D.V.M., Series Editor

Your
GOLDEN
RETRIEVER'S
Life

Your Complete Guide to Raising Your Pet from Puppy to Companion

PRIMA PETS

An Imprint of Prima Publishing

Interior photos by Kent Lacin Media Services
Color insert photos © Isabelle Français
Chapter 6 illustrations by Pam Tanzey

Library of Congress Cataloging-in-Publication Data on File
ISBN 0-7615-2047-3

00 01 02 DD 10 9 8 7 6 5 4 3 2
Printed in the United States of America

How to Order

Single copies may be ordered from Prima Publishing, 3000 Lava Ridge Court, Roseville, CA 95661; telephone (800) 632-8676 ext. 4444. Quantity discounts are also available. On your letterhead, include information concerning the intended use of the books and the number of books you wish to purchase.

Visit us online at www.primalifestyles.com

Contents

Acknowledgments

I owe thanks to so many, both human and canine, for their inspiration to me in the writing of this book. Thanks goes first to the many individuals mentioned specifically within these pages, who so graciously shared their stories and experiences with me about their beloved, ever-inspiring, golden dogs. Indeed, if ever a dog were to claim the title "muse," it is the Golden Retriever, a dog who wields the power to change our lives. I have witnessed this miracle both from those Goldens I have known personally and those whose acquaintance I have never had the privilege of making. I thus thank Golden Retrievers everywhere—from the dearest family companions, to the most courageous search-and-rescue dogs, to the most magical therapy dogs, to the most diligent service dogs—for the benevolent gifts, endless patience, and tender loving care that they bring into our lives (whether we deserve such priceless gifts or not). And as always, I thank my family, my guys, whose enduring patience, support, and encouragement are my true inspiration every day of my life.

Introduction

My brother John once commented that people who live with Golden Retrievers tend to be rather cocky. "They think that Golden Retrievers are the greatest things since oxygen."

Now don't get him wrong. We're talking about a true dog lover here, one who through the years has surrounded himself with people who live with dogs—many of those dogs, not surprisingly, being Golden Retrievers. How interesting, then, that he would make this rather illuminating observation, finding it only natural to compare the breed not to diamonds, Mercedes convertibles, and other luxuries of life, but rather to oxygen, a fundamental component of life itself. Indeed, for those in the know, life is not possible without a Golden Retriever at the foot of the bed.

Throughout the pages that follow, you'll be meeting people who share this sentiment, people who equate the joy of living to the presence of a Golden Retriever. People like Michelle Soba of San Francisco, California, who states without shame that, "most people who know me think I need to seek psychological help regarding my attachment to my mutt." People whose dogs came to them from top flight breeders, from rescue groups, from the streets and vacant lots where they were abandoned—all sharing an identical devotion to a dog, a treasure, who transcends breeding, class or trappings of wealth.

You'll also be meeting these individuals' dogs, dogs who hail from an illustrious family of canine souls who possess, as a breed, the power to change lives. You can find them doing just that each and every day when you see a Golden Retriever leading a blind woman along a busy city street; a Golden assisting a man confined to a wheelchair with his grocery shopping; a Golden claiming every top honor at a local obedience competition, fueled by an insatiable desire to obey the every command of those she calls family; a Golden searching for, and rescuing, a child lost and frightened along a remote mountain trail, greeting the youngster with a tail wagging so vigorously you imagine the dog will take flight at any moment; or a Golden easing the physical and emotional suffering of a lonely senior in a hospital, who only in the presence of this dog will speak of his pain and his fears.

Oxygen, pure and simple. There is no other way to define this dog.

A Dog of Many Karats

Golden Retrievers, though occupying a niche within the American Kennel Club's Sporting Group—the breed's hunting roots often forgotten by those who find they have fallen under this dog's spell—are in truth some of the finest working dogs the world has ever known. Though the Golden Retriever breed is the result of carefully orchestrated breeding efforts, combined with a healthy dose of genetic luck, one is left to believe in divine intervention, as well. Only that could account for the creation of so beloved a creature, his golden coat shimmering like a halo as this dog lives up to all our expectations of what a dog can and should be.

Journey back with me for a moment to 1995, when America was jolted by a sickening blast that leveled an Oklahoma City federal building. Think hard enough and you may remember the dogs that made the accounts of that event somehow more bearable. Most of the search-and-rescue dog handlers who spent those heart wrenching days combing the rubble for the victims of this heinous act did so with Golden Retrievers by their sides. The dogs seemed to make it their personal mission to save lives and seemed to mourn when they discovered that the people they found were no longer living. When asked in television interviews if they felt the need to speak with therapists regarding the grisly task in which they were immersed, the handlers, exhausted, tattered, and covered in dust, would smile, hug their gentle canine partners, and proclaim without shame or hesitation that they had their therapists right there with them.

Indeed, the Golden Retriever has enjoyed a long and illustrious career as a therapist, and it is within the breed's natural predisposition for this vocation—a love of all creatures human—where the Golden's highest calling lies. The calling of family companion.

Throughout this book, I have attempted to get inside this dog's head through my own experiences and those of others who have chosen Goldens as their trusted companions. Once inside that lovely head, and the heart that guides it, we find this breed has plenty to tell us both about ourselves and the world in which we live.

Each breed of dog has a unique way of looking at the world, and the Golden is no exception. In fact, the Golden might be considered the rule, certainly the ideal. Though by no means the oldest breed of dog on the planet, few breeds have become as well-acquainted with the human species as the Golden Retriever. What began as a partnership in the hunting field in a mutual search for winged game, has evolved into a legendary bond between human and canine that pays tribute to why man chose this particular animal—the canine animal—as his best friend in the first place. This particular bond validates that concept and elevates it to legendary proportions. What an honor to discover that despite our considerable human weaknesses, this incredible golden animal has found us worthy of his affections, his loyalty, and the exalted position as his reason for living. Gosh, maybe there's hope for us after all!

Dog Ownership: The Many Sacrifices, the Many Joys

In the pages that follow we will be delving deeply into the bond that exists between humans and the Golden Retriever, but so will we also be visiting our own responsibilities in nourishing this relationship, what we must do to uphold our side of the bargain we have struck with this dog. I personally—and much to the chagrin or those who have never had the privilege of sharing their homes with dogs—have often compared the proper care of a dog to that of a child. I suspect there are some readers who are nodding their heads in agreement and smiling at this moment. Am I right?

Just think about it. Both require healthy food, fresh water, proper medical care and attention, regular exercise and grooming, even tooth care. But these are just the basics. Children and dogs also require ample nurturing of the soul, offered in the form of love, affection, intellectual stimulation, shared laughter, humane discipline, hugs, and cuddles. Combine all of these ingredients, and the object of your affection understands without question that he or she is a beloved member of the family. What a grand realization that is for anyone, canine or human.

Needless to say, then, the great responsibility of caring for a dog will not be taken lightly within this book. You will learn much about the sacrifice this entails in terms of time, expense, effort, and the lifelong commitment. I am not a believer in the ever-popular notion that dogs are disposable commodities, meant for us to enjoy for a few months, or even a couple of years, then discarded when they are no longer convenient or novel.

No, I believe in long-term —make that *permanent*—commitments. This magnificent species deserves nothing less. But so am I also a proponent of choosing a pet wisely, a task made just a little bit easier when the dog you are seeking is a Golden Retriever—and a task that I hope to have made a bit easier, too, with the guidelines and information offered up in this book. A wise choice in the beginning of the Golden/owner relationship is the first step toward ensuring that that relationship remains healthy, mutually fulfilling, and permanent for a decade or more.

A Golden Retriever in Your Life

Play the game properly and by the rules, and you will no doubt be amazed by the drastic changes that occur in your life as soon as a Golden Retriever crosses your threshold. Sure, success requires much work, time, effort, and overall commitment on your part, but what you receive in return is priceless. It is the Golden's mission in life, both as an individual dog and as a representative of his breed, to act as your guide through this miraculous experience.

To ensure you are ready to take on the grand adventure that is of living with a Golden Retriever, much honest soul searching is in order. Those who live with Golden Retrievers and regard them as family members do so because they cherish the Golden's legendary heart. In a sense they belong to a special club, linked by a common bond that comes from sharing life with this magnificent dog. They do not, in turn, suffer lightly fools who knock on the clubhouse door without the purest of intentions—particularly those fools who view this dog as nothing more than a status symbol or a temporary novelty. It is your job, then, to think deeply about just why you wish to invite a Golden Retriever into your home and heart, just why you wish to join this illustrious club.

Should you deem, after much of that honest searching of your soul, that your intentions are worthy—and the time in your life is appropriate for such a leap—you will learn the secrets of this breed shared by those who welcome you to the club. The Golden, you see, is more than merely a beautiful dog blessed with a luxurious coat of gold from which he allegedly takes his name. No, the quintessential Golden is golden because he lives by the Golden Rule, treating the humans he encounters each day as he himself wishes to be treated—as family.

Perhaps this adherence to the Golden Rule explains the true mystique and magic at the heart of the Golden Retriever. He is, in short, a phenomenon. Though he appears on the surface a big, friendly, floppy guy with nothing but play and dog kisses on his mind, don't let the exterior fool you. Within that golden mantle beats the heart of a genuinely spiritual creature, who loves us more, perhaps, than we deserve to be loved. Imagine a world where we all followed his example.

I now invite you to take a journey into the inner workings of the life-altering relationship that can exist between a family and this golden dog. Be warned, though. Choose to embark on this journey, to embrace it as your own, and life as you have known it will never be the same.

So, You Want a Golden Retriever

In This Chapter

○ What Makes a Golden Retriever Special?
○ Keys to Your Golden's Happiness
○ Where to Find the Perfect Golden for You

Close your eyes. Now think of the word "dog." What image appears in your mind's eye? Odds are, it's the sweet smiling face of a Golden Retriever.

Now open your eyes and look around. You may find a real Golden in your direct line of sight. Goldens, you see, are everywhere. They're in our neighborhoods, in our city parks, in the cars next to us at stop lights. They're on our television screens, gracing commercials for everything from fire insurance to contact lenses. The Golden Retriever is the quintessential dog. The dog that everyone knows. The dog that everyone adores.

Sure other breeds have ample claims to fame. You have your Lassie, your Rin Tin Tin, and your Old Yeller. But when the subject is Golden Retrievers, you think not just of a single dog, but of every dog. Many of the dogs you meet on any given day will be Golden Retrievers, and most people you meet—even those who know almost nothing about dogs—know these dogs.

For some people, breed choice is a status thing. You might want a certain breed of dog because everyone else seems to have one or because you keep seeing that breed on television. We might assume this keeping-up-with-the-Joneses mentality, coupled with the Golden's blond beauty, would account for this breed's vast popularity. On the contrary, the Golden's magic is anything but skin or status deep. Her popularity stems from the purity of her heart, her kind manner, and the fact that she just plain loves the human species. We in turn can't help but love her back.

What Makes a Golden Retriever Special?

Poll a group of Golden owners and you'll hear some of the most glowing dog stories you've ever imagined. For most people, the dream of owning a Golden is a lifelong ambition, typically sparked during the impressionable years of childhood. Many are inspired by the golden memory of a legendary Retriever encountered early on—either their own or the pet of a friend—and they carry that memory when it comes time to choose a dog of their own. The Golden must be some dynamic dog to inspire the long-term desire that carries through childhood and adolescence and into the days of adulthood. And yes, some dynamic dog this is.

Golden Retriever enthusiast Sharon Ralls Lemon, from Kansas City, Missouri, is a textbook case of how childhood encounters with Goldens can inspire one's adult longings for the breed. Asked what makes Goldens so special in a field of hundreds of special dog breeds, Sharon determines quite accurately, I believe, that it's the Golden Retriever's "uncritical enthusiasm for life and all it offers."

Equally charged by both the promise of wilderness adventure or an intimate afternoon at home, the Golden Retriever is eager to join her family wherever they happen to be. Goldens are content at horse shows, picnics, and impromptu baseball games at the park. Running alongside a trusted companion rolling around on in-line skates, a leisurely walk along a quiet lake, or just a game of fetch in the front yard are all proper activities for the Golden Retriever, who, above all, just wants to be with the people she loves. Simply put, the Golden Retriever craves companionship and approval. In seeking these from us, she makes us feel like the most important beings on the planet—quite an irresistible combination for often egotistical, yet frequently insecure, humans.

You might say the Golden Retriever is both quintessential dog and quintessential homebody. But she's a homebody with a twist. The Golden indeed loves to be home, but to this dog, "home" is wherever her family is at the moment. This democratic sense of home and "uncritical enthusiasm for life" explains why this dog is so in demand—not only as a pet and companion, but also as a serious working dog. It also explains why she is able to successfully combine the two seemingly opposing roles in whatever job she is called to perform.

Touching Human Hearts

Every morning, Golden Retrievers wake up and change the lives of those they live with and those they meet throughout their day. Few breeds can boast so vast a resume built upon such a wide variety of talents.

A *Golden Retriever Who's Who* would be a volume too thick and heavy for most of us to lift off the coffee table. In it we would find pages and pages about dogs who lead the blind and assist people in wheelchairs; dogs who perform their original task of retrieving game in the field; and dogs who search out and rescue people lost in mountains, deserts, and rubble from earthquakes, bombings, and other disasters. We would read about dogs who invite a collective chorus of *oohs* and *aahs* when they step into the conformation show ring; and dogs who provide therapeutic magic to children, adults, and those in hospitals or convalescent homes who need a friend. Finally, we would read about special-agent dogs who sniff out drugs and other contraband at airports and customs offices; and plain old pet dogs who wield their Golden magic in homes where the words "family member" have nothing to do with one's genetic composition or number of legs.

The people whose lives have been changed by the presence of this dog, even if only briefly, are too numerous to summarize. Golden Retrievers have brought voices back to traumatized children, renewed the faith of physically challenged individuals in what life has to offer, and expanded the capacity for love of just about every human heart that has been touched by that Golden glow.

The breed's diverse talents and the character of the dog tell us 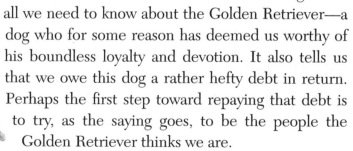 all we need to know about the Golden Retriever—a dog who for some reason has deemed us worthy of his boundless loyalty and devotion. It also tells us that we owe this dog a rather hefty debt in return. Perhaps the first step toward repaying that debt is to try, as the saying goes, to be the people the Golden Retriever thinks we are.

The Breed Standard

The Golden Retriever is of English and Scottish descent, and presumed to be a mix of water spaniel, setter, and even a bit of Bloodhound. The breed is the product of breeding efforts carried out by nineteenth-century alchemists to satisfy the growing demand for dogs who could retrieve their quarry—primarily birds—in icy waters. Those breeders succeeded in their mission, but along the way, both the breeders and the public at large in the United Kingdom and United States realized that the gold they had struck was 24 karat.

When you see a Golden, what you'll notice first is that lustrous coat. Wavy or straight, the dense, water-resistant coat can range from a deep, reddish-gold in one dog to a light cream in another. (The latter color is likely to lose points in the show ring but invite family affections equal to those of his deeper-hued brethren.) Light or dark, this dog is a powerfully built animal who celebrates his love of life and humankind with every move of his well-muscled physique. The breed isn't as large as we might imagine; males, at 23 to 24 inches tall at the withers, typically stand a couple of inches taller than their female counterparts. Most Goldens weigh between 55 to 75 pounds, though it's not uncommon to find Goldens who have reached the non-breed standard 90-pound (and beyond) mark.

Every inch an athlete who requires vigorous exercise every day, the Golden Retriever is a merry animal who carries his tail proudly and seems never to stop smiling. That gentle smile is the breed's trademark, accented by a kindness of the eye unmatched in the canine kingdom. The kind expression is the product of dark, soulful eyes, framed by somewhat short, endearingly flopped ears that are soft to the touch, alert to the world, and ever asking for a quick scratch. Like I said, the quintessential dog.

What's the American Kennel Club?

Founded in 1884, the American Kennel Club (AKC) is a non-profit organization dedicated to the advancement of purebred dogs. Composed of over 500 dog clubs from across the nation, the AKC's objectives include maintaining a registry of purebred dogs, promoting responsible dog ownership, and sponsoring events, such as breed shows and field trials, that promote interest in and appreciation of the purebred dog.

To be eligible for AKC registry, a puppy must be the offspring of individually registered AKC parents, and the breeder must obtain the proper paperwork before the puppy's sale. Once registered, a dog is eligible to compete in AKC-sanctioned events and, if bred with another AKC registered dog, to have his/her offspring registered.

The AKC approves an official breed standard for each of the 147 breeds currently eligible for registration. The standard is written and maintained by each individual breed club. An attempt to describe the "perfect" dog of each breed, the breed standard is the model responsible breeders use in their efforts to produce better dogs. Judges of AKC-sponsored events and competitions use the breed standards as the basis of their evaluations.

Because of the AKC's emphasis on excellence and high standards, it is a common misconception that "AKC registered" or "AKC registrable" is synonymous with quality. However, while a registration certificate identifies a dog and its progenitors as purebreds, it does not necessarily guarantee the health or quality of a dog. Some breeders breed for show quality, but others breed for profit, with little concern for breed standards. Thus, a potential buyer should not view AKC registration as an indication of a dog's quality.

Golden Character

So now we know all about what this lovely dog looks like and what he's accomplished throughout the decades. But to get even better acquainted with this dog, we need to look deeper into his character and personality. I think you'll like what you find.

It doesn't take a rocket scientist to figure out that a dog who boasts such an intimate partnership with humankind, a dog who consistently ranks within the top 10 of the American Kennel Club's (AKC) most popular breeds, and a dog who has attracted an almost-crazed following just has to be downright lovable. And that, my friends, he is. So universal are this dog's charms that he who can resist the soft dark eyes of the Golden Retriever has to be some kind of space alien who should be reported as soon as possible to the nearest conspiracy theorist!

The Golden Retriever is a bundle of love, pure and simple. Sure he's intelligent, but lots of dogs are intelligent. This dog combines wit with an insatiable desire to please people—both those he knows personally and those he is still waiting to meet. Therein lies the Golden's charms. How can we resist him? We just can't.

Goldens are described in their AKC breed standard as friendly, reliable, and trustworthy, and most do all in their power to uphold that tradition. As a whole, Goldens harbor a universal love for humankind and are not at all shy about expressing their emotions. Be aware, however, that mass popularity—the scourge of the purebred dog world— has resulted in overbreeding. This invariably leads to the production of dogs who don't quite meet the standard either in appearance or temperament because their often ignorant breeders are breeding for all the wrong reasons (usually just for the money). Such temperament defects caused by overbreeding may lead to the occasional Golden who doesn't love all humankind or who growls instead of wiggles when he sees a stranger at the front door.

Most Goldens, however, can be legitimately described as kids at heart, even when those telltale white hairs of age speckle that beloved muzzle. They retain that childlike—or rather, puppy-like—glow well into old age.

You might say that the Golden is blessed with a rather endearing oral fixation—a casebook study for Freud. The fact is, most of these dogs don't feel complete without something in their mouths, whether it be a ball, a Frisbee, or a stuffed bear. This is a trait that heralds back to his beginnings as a hunting retriever. Today, even those Goldens who don't hunt (most Goldens) retain this very prominent hunting characteristic. As his name implies, this is a retriever, and in the absence of hands, that means carrying whatever he is retrieving very gently in a "soft" mouth where the teeth barely leave an imprint.

> As a whole, Goldens harbor a universal love for humankind and are not at all shy about expressing their emotions.

Keys to Your Golden Retriever's Happiness

A successful relationship between a Golden Retriever and her family cannot be a one-way street. Sure, Goldens are easily pleased, but you can't in good conscience accept all that unconditional Golden love and loyalty without offering anything in exchange. When you bring a Golden Retriever into your home, you owe that animal a lifetime commitment fueled by responsible and consistent care and communication. The following questions will help you sort out the requirements and devise a plan that will help you be the very best partner possible to your golden friend.

How Will the Golden Retriever Fit into My Daily Routine?

You might be better off asking how you will fit into the Golden Retriever's daily routine. You see, every dog, even the easygoing

Golden Retriever, thrives best with a predictable daily schedule. She finds security in knowing that feeding times, grooming time, play times, exercise sessions, and bedtime will all occur at the same times each day. Needless to say, this places a rather heavy responsibility on you. Those who live with dogs are welcome to approach each day with a sense of fun and spontaneity, but they must also be creatures of habit.

You have to be honest with yourself, preferably before you bring a new Golden Retriever into your home. If you travel frequently and/or spend a great deal of time at work with no one at home to care for the dog, and if you're not big on walking, jogging, and exercising, perhaps this isn't the right time for you to get a Golden Retriever—or any dog for that matter. There's no need to feel guilty about this. Dog ownership is a major long-term commitment. In a perfect world, everyone would view it as such and the shelters wouldn't be full of the innocent casualties of insufficient forethought and preparation. But, unfortunately, ours is not a perfect world.

How Much Space Does a Golden Retriever Need?

A Golden Retriever is a rather large, decidedly powerful dog, yet she may not require as much space as we might assume is necessary for a dog of her size and background. There's a catch, though. Although a Golden can live quite contentedly in either city, country, or suburb, she will remain content only if she is afforded plenty of exercise and activity—and if she is allowed to be both an inside and an outside dog. Contrary to what many people believe, there is no law stating that larger dogs must automatically be outside dogs. All dogs enjoy time spent

outdoors, but they must also be offered ample time indoors with the family.

The family is the Golden's reason for living, so this breed's dependence on the optimum indoor/outdoor lifestyle coincides with her family's allegiance to it. The "indoors" in the equation can be the interior of anything from a small apartment to a lavish country estate. Whether humble or palatial, the home should include a private little corner that is the dog's own, where she can sleep, eat, and retreat whenever she feels the need for some privacy. The outdoors is where "space" comes in. This can be provided by a variety of venues: beach, park, or mountain hiking trail. And we're talking every day. Which brings us to our next question. . . .

> Contrary to what many people believe, there is no law stating that larger dogs must automatically be outside dogs.

How Much Exercise?

So glad you asked. The answer is simple: a lot.

Sure it's great to have a spacious fenced backyard for your dog, but you can't just relegate your pet to the backyard and assume she will get all the exercise and activity she needs. Such canine management techniques border on cruel and unusual punishment.

Goldens—and all dogs, actually—require two types of exercise: exercise of the body and exercise of the mind. These exercise needs can and should be met each day. If you enjoy cycling, in-line skating, or jogging, that's great. Your Golden would love to join you in these pursuits, assuming of course she is mature physically, properly conditioned, and the weather permits her safe participation. Just use your imagination. Goldens are typically ideal candidates for dog parks (enclosed parks where healthy, well-behaved dogs can run and play together in leash-free abandon). Or you might decide to start agility training—the hot new canine activity that keeps dogs fit, mentally stimulated, and increasingly bonded to their owners. (Agility training and other formal canine activities are covered in Chapter 8, Family Life.)

Another excellent exercise option, and the simplest one on the list, is walking. Goldens love being out in the air—soaking in the sights, sounds, and scents; exercising their bodies inside and out; and meeting fellow dogs and their owners. Walking is the ideal activity for dogs of all ages—and it's good for *you*, too.

The bottom line is that nothing—even your own long and stressful day at work—should keep you from getting your dog out and exercised every day. When you choose an athlete for your companion—and a Golden Retriever *is* an athlete—you commit to that responsibility.

How Much Training?

Every dog needs lots of training. Unfortunately, far too many dog owners don't take the issue of training seriously. I can't count the number of well-meaning owners I've counseled whose dogs ran wild, destroying furniture and dominating households. The owners had refused to even consider the simple remedy of obedience training. Too many people assume that dogs automatically read our minds and know what we expect of them. If they misread us, and fail to obey our every command and our every whim, then off to the pound they go.

A more humane approach to living with dogs is to recognize that dogs learn more efficiently and permanently, and bond more deeply with their owners, when the owners enroll their pets and themselves in several courses of obedience classes. Golden Retriever owners find this even more rewarding because their breed is one of the most talented obedience breeds ever created. The secret to that Golden success is the breed's desire to please its handlers and probably the trainers heading their classes, as well. Rarely will you find a dog so eager to please. He's not a show-off, he's just being himself, and that means doing all he can to do your bidding.

The results are in the titles. For example, the first three dogs to earn the Obedience Champion title from the American Kennel Club were Golden Retrievers. That's not surprising considering that each year, virtually every top obedience honor goes to a Golden. Even the AKC's Canine Good Citizen (CGC) program—an activity in which those without show and competition aspirations can participate—seems to have been custom-made for this breed. Many Goldens now proudly boast the initials "CGC" after their name.

The Golden Retriever was made to please and to learn. You don't need to compete in obedience shows with your dog at an international level, or at all, but why not take advantage of her natural talents and get her and yourself to a trainer? This is important whether your Golden is a puppy who with proper training will be

better equipped to become a well-adjusted member of his breed, or an older dog who will find security in understanding what you expect of her. You'll be amazed at how much both you and your dog can learn, how much stronger your bond grows, and how much your pup loves sharing this special brand of dog/human communion together. Everybody wins.

Can My Golden Retriever Stay Home All Day Without Me?

The answer to this question depends on the dog and the character of the person that dog lives with. Keep in mind that a Golden is happiest when surrounded by the family she loves—preferably all day or at least most of the day. Loneliness, anxiety, and even accidents on the carpet can all be consequences of leaving a dog home alone all day, every day. Puppies require frequent contact throughout the day for socialization and training purposes. This is especially true for their emotional well-being and for house-training. It takes a year or more for that puppy bladder to mature to the point where the pup can "hold it" all day. For these reasons, an older dog may be a better candidate for a latchkey lifestyle.

This is not to say that it can't be done. With a bit of creativity, you can make concessions to help your Golden make it through the day without you. This might include doggie day care, which is offered by some boarding kennels, or neighborhood dog walkers to fill in the gaps during your absence. You can also arrange to come home each day at lunchtime for a walk during which the dog can relieve her bladder and expend some energy. A workaholic might be better off choosing a pet like a goldfish whose social needs aren't quite as demanding as those of a Golden Retriever. This dog deserves more than life as a mere weekend companion.

One of the greatest plagues within the canine family is separation anxiety (a dog's panicky reaction based on his inability to cope with his owner's absence),

Did You Know?

The word for "dog" in the Australian aboriginal language Mbabaran happens to be "dog."

which can lead to destructive behavior (chewing, digging) and incessant barking (followed by nasty calls from neighbors). This anxiety can have a negative, possibly fatal, impact on the relationship between dog and owner. Far too many dogs land in the nation's animal shelters because their owners were unable to deal with the consequences of their pets' separation anxiety.

A successful latchkey Golden Retriever has owners who ensure that when they are home, they spend plenty of quality time with the resident pooch. Refer back to the former questions about routine, training, and exercise; those discussions can help you and your dog make this arrangement a success.

Separation anxiety is far less a threat when a dog has a reliable routine, plenty of exercise to expend all his pent-up energy, and consistent long-term training that builds and maintains the bond between dog and owner. Dogs want and need to know that they are important to their families, that their needs are a priority, and that they are loved and treasured. Simply put, they're not all that different from children. Remember this, abide by it, make the necessary commitments, and all can live happily ever after.

How Will My Golden Retriever Get Along with People and Other Animals?

Given what you know at this point about the Golden Retriever's friendly, outgoing nature, you probably have a good idea how most Goldens get along with others. Just keep in mind who you're dealing with—one of the world's premier service dogs for the blind and those in wheelchairs. In other words, Goldens enjoy spending their every waking and sleeping moment by the side of people they regard as family and partners. Puppies destined for greatness as service dogs spend their first two years of life with puppyraisers. These people tap into the breed's natural inclinations by taking them everywhere to introduce and socialize them to every realm of human life—a dream come true for a Golden Retriever.

So will a Golden get along with people other than those within her immediate family? She should, assuming she's not one of those unfortunate products of incompetent breeding practices. She should enjoy the company of other animals too, especially other dogs. The Golden is an ideal candidate for a multi-dog household, and in most cases, for a household with kids, too.

Although no dog, no matter how reliable, should ever be left

> Separation anxiety is far less a threat when a dog has a reliable routine, plenty of exercise to expend all his pent-up energy, and consistent long-term training that builds and maintains the bond between dog and owner.

unattended with small children, the bond that can develop between children and their beloved Golden Retriever is the stuff that classic dog stories, books, and movies are made of. This is not to imply that every Golden naturally adores children. A small human can take a little getting used to for a mature Golden who has never seen one. Every child should be taught how to approach and introduce himself safely to a dog, and every dog should be introduced to young humans during puppyhood (ideally before 12 weeks of age). In most cases, the communion between a child and a dog (or puppy) is a natural one. (Introducing children to dogs is covered further in Chapter 8, Family Life.)

Although I certainly can't recommend allowing dangerous or unkind interactions between kids and dogs, it's not unusual to see a big, benevolent Golden Retriever tolerating the attentions of children who are just learning to groom a dog, pet a dog, lay down on top of a dog, and ride a dog like a pony. Most Goldens think they're related genetically to people, so they tolerate these well-meaning ministrations with patience and love. However, it's dangerous and unfair to assume that every Golden will naturally embrace the role of nanny to every child who crosses her path.

Don't assume that your Golden will be a pushover for every adult she encounters, either. Though Goldens are legendary for their love of our species, they also have a pretty good sixth sense. Most can see the true character of a person, especially if that person means to harm their loved ones.

Many years ago, I was assigned to write an article on service dogs for a national pet magazine. I remember speaking with a lovely young woman in a wheelchair who was partnered with an equally lovely Golden Retriever service dog. During a break from her college classes one afternoon, she went out to an isolated open area to allow her dog to run a bit. While the dog was behind some bushes, a man approached the woman in a threatening manner. Before the guy knew what hit him, that lovely Golden—a dog who had never behaved aggressively toward a human being—leapt at the would-be perpetrator and pinned him to the ground. All those obedience titles that are heaped upon Goldens each year are matched only by the number of times Goldens perform heroic acts both in the line of duty and when least expected. They know when to get along with people—and when not to. These are smart dogs.

Surefire Ways to Make Your Golden Retriever's Life Unpleasant

Making your Golden Retriever's life unpleasant certainly isn't your goal here (at least we hope it's not), but by exploring these issues, you'll be less likely to make mistakes that result in Golden Retriever discontent.

It's difficult to imagine that the smiling Golden Retriever could ever feel unhappy or disillusioned, and hard to believe that people could do things, by accident, intent, or neglect, that might hurt or disappoint this very loving dog. But unfortunately, it happens every day. Betrayal and neglect are as natural to the human species as loyalty and unconditional love are to the canine. Given this fact, and all the mistakes we've made and harm we have caused them through the centuries, sometimes it's amazing that the Golden Retriever—and the dog family at large—hasn't just given up on us. Won't we be sorry if they ever do?

Things a Golden Retriever Simply Cannot Live With

Because we're talking here about a Golden Retriever, there's every possibility that even if one violates the trust this dog places in his owner and fails to make the full and necessary commitment to the relationship, the dog will still remain loving and loyal. That's just the way these dogs are. That does not mean, however, that we are within our rights to take advantage of his sweet spirit.

The Physical   The first area where trouble can brew for the Golden Retriever is in his physical care: neglect of his basic needs. Every dog requires fresh water and nutritious food, proper housing, regular grooming, and routine preventive veterinary care. But these are the areas in which even the most well-meaning owner can inadvertently fall down on the job. For example, leaving a water bowl out all day in the hot sun during a heat wave, or leaving it where it can freeze on a frigid cold day, means your dog can't drink his water. And regardless of the weather—he needs it.

Food is another issue. Malnutrition can stem from both under-feeding (or feeding poor quality food) and overfeeding. The latter situation typically occurs in a home where a dog is offered table scraps and "people" food out of a misguided demonstration of love. This usually results in an obese pet, who will not live as comfort-ably, or as long, as his more svelte counterparts. (Nutritional infor-mation is discussed in Chapter 3, Food for Thought) As for proper housing, even a dog with a water-resistant coat like the Golden Re-triever needs shelter from rain, sleet, wind, sun, and snow—prefer-ably shelter provided by being indoors with his owners during inclement weather and extreme temperatures.

A Golden can also do without owners who neglect mainte-nance of his physical health. Individuals who will not make the annual trek with their dog to the veterinarian for checkups and booster vaccines, and those who do not deem it necessary to brush that golden coat several times a week and get the dog bathed periodically need not apply. A filthy matted coat can lead to severe skin problems and discomfort, not to mention down-right pain made all the more intense when coupled with sore ears, gums, teeth, and overgrown toenails.

The Spiritual   Neglect of a Golden's physical health is bad enough, but neglect of his spiritual needs may prove to be even more painful for this dog. The quickest way to see that precious smile fade from the sweet face of a Golden who is so eager to demonstrate his love is to ignore what little he asks for in return for his loyalty and affection.

A dog so eager to please relies on clear and consistent han-dling, training, and direction from his family, and he trusts that his family will understand and respect this. Inherent in that trust is the belief that he will be offered ample companionship from his loved ones, protection from unruly children and rough han-

Just Say "No" to Chaining

No discussion about making a dog's life unpleasant would be complete without a comment about the controversial issue of chaining. "Chaining" is the short title for the all-too-common practice of tethering a dog with lead material (usually rope or a chain) to a sedentary object to prevent him from running away. I'm not talking about that once-in-a-blue moon occurrence when you're washing your car or playing tennis and you want to have your dog nearby and safe. I am referring to those people who chain their dogs out all day, everyday; a practice that is not only cruel, but downright dangerous as well.

No dog is immune from the long-term effects of chaining, and those effects can be devastating. A chained dog suffers from extreme boredom, loneliness, and often exposure to extreme heat and cold. He is also at risk of being tormented by passersby with cruelty on their minds. The chained dog typically barks incessantly and resorts to compulsive chewing and licking of his limbs out of sheer boredom. In time, even a friendly Golden Retriever could turn mean. His natural affection for people may be replaced by an aggressive, vicious nature borne of a lack of human contact and room to run. This is a simple and surefire way to ruin a dog.

dling, and training rooted in positive reinforcement and mutual respect. Eager to participate in all manner of activity and exercise, he trusts that his owners will commit to him for his lifetime; communicate with him clearly and fairly; and arrange an exercise regimen that is appropriate for his age, condition, and abilities.

This dignified, genteel dog can do without an owner who regards formal training and socialization as unnecessary; who views living with a dog as a matter of status or novelty; and who prescribes to old wives' tales about physical punishment and rubbing-his-nose-in-it house-training methods. (Proper training methods are discussed further in Chapter 6, Basic Training for Golden Retrievers.)

He can also do without an owner who will sentence him to a lonely exile in the backyard once he grows beyond the cute and cuddly puppy stage. The ideal Golden owner views the responsibilities as causes for celebration, not exasperation. So celebrate and enjoy your dog each and every day. You won't believe how enriched your life will be when blessed with the presence of this golden dog.

Maybe a Golden Retriever Isn't the Dog for Me

As we've seen, if you take on the care and nurturing of a Golden Retriever, keep in mind that this is a big dog with ample daily exercise needs. He will shed; demand lots of your attention and companionship; and run up hefty bills for food, veterinary care, grooming, and boarding.

An accurate description of this golden canine package sometimes comes as a shock to the well-meaning owner who had only the best intentions when choosing a Golden Retriever for a companion. This trusting animal assumes his owner knows what she's getting into from the start. How sad that many of these dogs suffer when they realize that wasn't the case after all.

Betrayal of a Golden Retriever's expectations, whether done intentionally or through well-meaning ignorance, can be avoided by thinking carefully and honestly about your lifestyle and the responsibilities of living with a dog before inviting that dog in. That honest evaluation may convince you that you're ready to take on the commitment for the next decade or more (as Goldens typically live into their early teens). You might also come to the legitimate decision that this isn't the right time for a dog—not to mention such a demanding dog as the Golden Retriever. Perhaps you're in college with an uncertain future, or you're in the military and must move every two years. Moving with a large Golden isn't always the simplest task, as all those Goldens who populate the animal shelters surrounding the nation's military bases can testify.

So what happens if, for whatever reason, you realize after the fact that you just made a mistake in your choice of a pet? There you are with a big golden dog who regards you as his reason for living, and whose heart you feel you will soon have to break. Well, don't give up yet. First, evaluate your lifestyle and try to pinpoint the root of the breakdown of your relationship. Perhaps you can set aside a little more time each day to spend with your dog—maybe by coming home for lunch (and some canine companionship) and by increasing your daily exercise time with your dog. Obedience training may also help. It creates a bond between you and your dog and builds your dog's confidence, but keep in mind, it also requires a commitment on your part.

If the problem is behavioral, stemming from your dog's chronic separation anxiety, a qualified canine behaviorist may be able to help you. These specialists are trained and experienced in dealing with serious canine behavior problems. Remember, canine behavior problems are typically the fault of a dog's owner, and are the results of miscommunication between that owner and her pet. Most can be remedied, especially when the pet is a Golden Retriever.

If, however, you're talking about a more serious problem—such as a move to a region where dogs are prohibited, financial problems, and such, there are legitimate circumstances under which people must give up their dogs. In such instances, Golden Retrievers are pretty fortunate because they are represented by a vast network of breed rescue groups

Did You Know?

The wolf, from which dogs are descended, was the first animal to be domesticated.

throughout the nation. Given their amenable natures, they usually have less trouble than some breeds adjusting to new families.

You might have neighbors or family members who know and adore the dog and are thrilled to welcome him into their family. In the absence of such an ideal remedy, you can contact your dog's veterinarian, the local Golden Retriever rescue group, humane society, and animal shelter, most of which can be located in the phone book and by word-of-mouth from other dog owners. Remember that no one but you can make guarantees about your dog's fate. Whatever you do, do not offer your pet "free to a good home." Such ads are often answered by disreputable people who collect free dogs. The dogs wind up in research laboratories or the hands of people who take pleasure in abusing animals.

The best option is to choose wisely and in a timely manner and avoid having to face the devastation of finding a new home for your pet. Do your homework ahead of time, evaluating yourself and the breed honestly. Look beyond the romantic image of running along the beach with a golden dog by your side, and make an equally honest commitment for the long haul. That's the best way to prevent broken hearts, both yours and the dog's, later on.

Where to Find the Perfect Golden Retriever for You

So you've been honest and forthright and now you're ready to make that commitment. As we've seen, you're likely to find Golden Retrievers wherever you look, but now you are faced with finding and choosing the right Golden for you. This is not a choice that can be made on impulse, for it involves choosing a member of your family whom you hope will be with you for the next 10, 12, even 15 years. Take your time with the decision, and weigh all the options.

Puppies Versus Older Dogs

When launching into your quest for your new Golden, your first question should be: What age Golden Retriever is best for me? Ignore that nagging impulse dictating that your new pet must be a puppy. Puppies are wonderful, but they are a huge and often frustrating responsibility. They require a great deal of training and attention and can drive you crazy as they learn all the rules of what it means to be a dog—and a dog within your home.

An older dog, on the other hand, who has matured into the calmer temperament that emerges during the second to third year of life, may come to you with some previous training (including house-training, if you're lucky) and an all-around understanding of the world. He might also come with some bad habits, but so long as these don't involve aggression or other behavior stemming from past abuse, the habits can usually be remedied with some obedience training and consistent handling. Adopting an older dog can be a true joy, so don't discount its pleasures. Be patient and positive. There will be a transition and a period of getting acquainted with the older dog, but a wisely chosen dog, coupled with the Golden's typically lovely temperament, can result in a long-term relationship identical to those that begin when a dog is a puppy.

Now on to an exploration of where you might find a Golden Retriever—puppy or older dog—with whom you can share this

> Throughout your search you'll be meeting many smiling Goldens along the way. Keep a sound head, and avoid impulse. Choose wisely, and you won't be sorry. And neither will your dog.

lovely relationship. But heed this warning: Throughout your search you'll be meeting many smiling Goldens. Keep a sound head, and avoid impulse. Choose wisely, and you won't be sorry. And neither will your dog.

Buying from a Breeder

Probably the most reliable source for healthy, well-bred Golden Retrievers are ethical, reputable show breeders. These are people who approach breeding as a vocation and devote their lives to the betterment of the breed. They seek to improve the breed in conformation, health, and temperament, creating champion show and working dogs and dogs that blossom into champion pets, as well. Whether show, working, or pet pups, products of a sound breeding program all reap the benefits of that magical combination of health, genes, temperament, and beauty.

The catch here is that anyone can say that he is a breeder. Your challenge is to ask questions that will help you determine whether a particular breeder fits the "ethical" and "reputable" mold. So-called "backyard breeders," who breed just because they happen to have purebred Goldens and would like to make a few bucks, will probably not offer the answers you seek. They will typically be more intent on moving their product than ensuring the pups land in the right homes. It's doubtful they'll demonstrate much in-depth knowledge about the breed. They might be able to mention a dog's papers and even drop the word "pedigree," but these alone do not guarantee a well-bred Golden.

The genuine ethical show breeder, on the other hand, will riddle you with questions about your living situation, your lifestyle, and your family, all in hopes of making a mutually satisfying and permanent match. This individual will run a clean facility and will willingly answer all the questions you ask. He will discuss health guarantees, the genetic health of his breeding stock, spaying and neutering requirements for non-show puppies, the importance of training and socialization, nutrition, vaccinations, and anything else pertinent to the long-term well-being of the puppies. This breeder's puppies will be sold with sales contracts that legally document all this information. If the contract also includes a "return to breeder" clause—meaning that the buyer promises to return the puppy at any time if he is no longer able to keep the animal—then you have probably found a good breeder.

And just where do you find this person? Word-of-mouth is a start. Poll local veterinarians, humane societies, and animal shelters. Hook in to the show network, too, by contacting your local kennel club and the American Kennel Club, and attend dog shows, which offer a great opportunity to meet lots of breeders and lots of dogs in one place.

Good breeders may also advertise in the newspaper and dog magazines, and on the Internet, but remember, a Web site or a published advertisement doesn't guarantee that a breeder is ethical or is producing quality dogs, no matter what claims you read. You need to do your own legwork to determine that, and it takes time and effort. Ask questions, evaluate the answers honestly, and trust your instincts—no matter how cute the puppies are, no matter how anxious you are to hear the pitter patter of Golden Retriever feet within your home.

When you work with a conscientious, ethical breeder, you may have to wait a little longer than you would like, which can be frustrating once you've determined that you're ready right now. If you find a breeder with whom you feel comfortable but discover there won't be an available puppy, or a retired show dog, for a few months, take a deep breath, and resolve to be patient. Good breeders don't typically churn out puppies

like a factory assembly line. They might also charge more for their treasures than your neighbor down the street who bred his dog so the kids could experience the miracle of life. Let this be your mantra: Good things come to those who wait; you get what you pay for. Ten years from now when you gaze down at your beloved golden friend lying peacefully at your feet by the fire, you'll remember those old cliches and smile.

> Anyone can say that he is a breeder. Your challenge is to ask questions that will help you determine whether a particular breeder fits the "ethical" and "reputable" mold.

Buying from a Pet Shop

Most puppies at pet stores come from puppy farms (known as "puppy mills"), and puppies from puppy farms (or mills) are taken away from their mothers at too tender an age. Those beleaguered mothers can be of questionable genetic health and temperament, and are bred at each heat cycle to produce as many puppies as possible until their weary bodies just give out.

Sure the pet-store puppies may be purebred, though, as I've mentioned, the word "purebred" is not synonymous with "quality." These puppies often lack proper socialization because of the sad way in which they come into the world. In most cases they are delivered into an environment of mass production that is deficient in sanitation, comfort, and nutrition. They are transported and sold at an age when they should still be basking in the warmth of their mother and their siblings. Ideally, a puppy should not leave his mother until he is at least eight weeks of age, yet many pet-shop puppies are much younger than that, because the younger the puppy, the cuter and more marketable he is. Even if the pet-shop puppy winds up healthy and well-adjusted, he is usually bred for profit rather than in the best interests of man's best friend.

So I am no fan of the pet-shop puppy. It's not the unfortunate little animal himself I dislike, but the mass-production system in which cute puppies are marketed in a pet-shop window with sometimes careless regard to their health, temperament, emotional well-being, and suitability to the owners who take them home. In most cases, pet-shop puppies are very expensive, and the price tag may increase dramatically several months down the road if genetic problems begin to crop up. At that point, the family has already bonded with their new pet and the tragedy can intensify. Though a convenient source of puppies, a prospective owner's convenience should take a back seat to a puppy's—and an entire species'—well-being.

I will, however, offer one positive nod to a type of pet shop as a source for a new pet. There is a recent trend in which an animal welfare group teams up with a pet supply store (a store that sells *only* supplies—no puppies or kittens), and the store provides a public venue from which the shelters may adopt out their animals to new owners. Contrary to what some may believe, the animals in need of placement are not solely mixed-breeds. Many a purebred—hence many a Golden Retriever—has found its fate resting in the hands of the volunteers who dedicate themselves to giving society's throwaway animals a second chance.

The animal welfare/pet-supply store partnership is beneficial to everyone involved. Unlike the traditional pet store where store employees indiscriminately sell puppies as commodities like socks or bananas, shelter and humane society volunteers at pet store adoption events screen prospective adopters according to the same system employed at their own facilities. Consequently, those who do not measure up, do not get a dog. This system ensures that only deserving souls are granted the privilege of taking home one of the homeless animals. The store in turn wins, because adopters are likely to choose that store for their future pet-supply shopping needs. This particular partnership is not only a positive and progressive trend, but one made possible by the existence of the pet supply store.

Adopting from an Animal Shelter

As we've seen, even the beautiful Golden Retriever is not immune to abandonment and neglect, and even the beautiful Golden Retriever is a frequent guest at the nation's animal shelters. The reasons they end up there more often than not rest with the dogs' owners.

When a dog's behavior is named as the problem, that's probably because her owners underestimated the importance of training and socialization. You may notice that many of the larger dogs in shelters are somewhere around one year of age. These are the dogs whose owners tired of them once their pets lost that cute puppy fluff and developed the increased appetite and exercise needs of the adult. Indeed no breed is safe from this phenomenon, especially a breed as popular and populous as the Golden Retriever.

Visit virtually any animal shelter in the country, and you'll probably find a Golden or two waiting patiently for someone to love. According to Robin Adams, co-founder of Delaware Valley Golden Retriever Rescue in Pennsylvania, "time, money, and divorce" are the top three reasons Golden Retrievers are surrendered to shelters. Robin's work as a rescuer has often left her disillusioned with the human species—for example, when she receives a dog 8 to 10 years old who is given up because the kids are off to college and the parents don't want the responsibility anymore. Despite the disillusionment, the bright and resilient spirit of the Golden Retriever keeps her going.

It is that bright spirit that typically makes second chances so viable for Golden Retrievers and the adopters who invite them to join their families. As Robin explains, "If these dogs had an anthem, it would be, 'If you can't be with the one you love, love the one you're with!'"

When you adopt a Golden Retriever from a shelter, first find out as much as you can about the dog (unfortunately, this can be difficult if the dog was found as a stray). Her health history, too, might be a mystery, but don't be turned off by the unknown. Approached with common sense, a shelter can be the very place where, for a minimal adoption fee, you find your canine soulmate.

The dogs you find here will most likely be young adults, and they will probably already have been spayed or neutered to prevent the production of more homeless dogs. Good shelters screen prospective adopters thoroughly and mandate contractually that if the animals are not already spayed or neutered, they must be within a designated period of time. Once you have found a likely candidate, ask to visit with her outside of her enclosure. This should give you a preliminary glimpse into your basic compatibility.

If you like what you see and decide to try adoption, remember that you're allowed a few weeks to see if the arrangement is a promising one. Your first stop should be your veterinarian's office for an examination and the various tests that can tell you what's going on with the dog

Did You Know?

The United States and France have the highest rates of dog ownership in the world, with almost one dog for every three families. Germany and Switzerland have the lowest rates, with just one dog for every ten families.

internally. Though it can take months for a shelter dog to settle in and feel completely comfortable within a new family, you should get a pretty good idea of her character during those first few days you spend together. By setting down rules and attending obedience classes right away to offer the dog a sense of security, you may marvel at the ease with which an adopted Golden Retriever can fill the dog niche within her new household.

But don't be naive, either. As I've mentioned, it's not wise or safe to assume that the "Golden Retriever" title ensures that this pup will be sweet, gentle, and all those wonderful adjectives that follow this breed around. Like any dog, Goldens can be bred with a screw loose, or can have a bad temperament due to abusive treatment and neglect. If you discover that this isn't a match, don't be embarrassed to take the dog back to the shelter. A sad turn of events, but you need to look out for the well-being of your household. The same holds true in the case of dogs that demonstrate fright and timidity that are the products not of momentary nerves, but of past abuse and ill-treatment. Though you might be sympathetically attracted to such a dog, resist the impulse to be a savior unless you are truly up to that responsibility. In truth, most people don't have the time, the energy, or the know-how to facilitate such heroic rehabilitation.

Adopting from a Rescue Group

These days, almost every breed of dog is represented by a breed rescue group, staffed by networks of volunteers who pick up unwanted dogs from shelters, streets, or the homes of owners who mistreat or no longer want them. These volunteers, many of whom are breeders, rehabilitate the dogs, if necessary, provide foster homes for them, and adopt them out to new owners. The adopters, assuming the rescue group is one of the good ones, must prove themselves worthy of providing a new home to this second-hand pup. On the bright side, the Golden Retriever is fortunate to be represented by an amazingly well-coordinated network of rescue groups coast to coast; on the not-so-bright side, how sad that the breed's vast popularity has made such a network necessary.

Few breeds boast so active and national a breed rescue network—a network connected all the more efficiently these days by the Internet. The enthusiasm with which the Golden Retriever's rescuers pursue their calling is a definite plus for the dogs they seek to place. The benefit to adopters is that in most cases, the foster-home housing of rescued dogs helps the rescuers get to know the dogs well and become familiar with their likes, dislikes, quirky habits, compatibilities with cats and children, and so forth. This knowledge helps to ensure that the dogs land in compatible homes.

> Approached with common sense, a shelter can be the very place where, for a minimal adoption fee, you find your canine soulmate.

Robin Adams' Delaware Valley Golden Retriever Rescue has been responsible for the placement of hundreds of second-hand Goldens since its inception. Along the way, Robin has been impressed by the demand for older Goldens. They are so in demand that would-be adopters have to sign up on a waiting list for them. That certainly testifies to the resilient nature of this dog's character.

Yet despite the wonderful intentions of rescue workers, even here you must be on your guard. It's not unusual to hear unfortunate stories of rescue groups that willingly match dogs and families who are obviously not right for each other simply to get a dog placed, or that in some way fail to meet the noble ideals of the rescue concept. Steer clear of groups that seem just a little too anxious to get a dog into your house, that don't mandate that all the dogs be spayed or neutered, that don't bother to vaccinate the dogs they place, and that do not agree to take the dog back for any reason should the arrangement prove not to work.

Despite the bad apples, most breed rescue groups are sticklers when it comes to ensuring that this time around, the arrangements will be permanent for their dogs. They go to great lengths to evaluate prospective adopters and to get to know the dogs in their care. If working with a rescue group, don't be insulted by the endless questions volunteers will ask or the in-depth evaluation they will make of your intentions and your living situation. You and the rescue workers have the same goal: a happy and permanent adoption of a new member of the family.

> If working with a rescue group, don't be insulted by the endless questions volunteers will ask or the in-depth evaluation they will make of your intentions and your living situation. You and the rescue workers have the same goal: a happy and permanent adoption of a new member of the family.

How Do I Choose the "Pick of the Litter"?

So, now you know all about where you might find your new Golden Retriever, but how, we must ask, should you go about choosing the dog who will be your companion for many years to come?

A Serious Mission

Whether seeking a puppy or an adult Golden for your companion, you will be evaluating the same basic factors. Granted, there might be some mystery to the health and family background of a rescue or shelter dog, but if you keep a clear head, you should be able to trust your instincts and determine whether a particular dog is a match. Remember that a clear head means ignoring that nagging voice in the back of your head that says, "Take the runt," or "Take the timid one in the corner." What you want is a healthy, well-adjusted, robust pup to whom you feel a natural attraction and whose exuberance makes you believe that the feeling is mutual. Anyone who has ever chosen a puppy knows that moment of communion, a moment that can be described only as "magic."

When San Francisco, California, resident Michelle Soba decided that it was time to make her dream of living with a Golden Retriever a reality, she did everything right. She began attending dog shows at which she met two breeders, partners with whom she felt immediately comfortable. She was on a waiting list for months, and when her puppy's litter was whelped, she visited the pups every week. At last the fateful day came for her to choose. Michelle remembers the moment when breeder June Smith asked, "if I wanted to take them into a room to see who I wanted and who wanted me. But the thought of choosing just one puppy was beyond me."

Michelle asked June for her opinion. Without hesitation, June, who had gotten to know Michelle very well by now, said the choice was obvious. One particular puppy had the perfect temperament and disposition to live in the city and accompany his owner to work each day, which was exactly what Michelle was looking for. And that's exactly what she got. Today, thanks to diligent socialization and training, Michelle and Trevor tool around together all day every day. He's welcome at the bank, city offices, local department stores, and even an occasional restaurant. He hardly notices city noises and as Michelle proudly proclaims, "Everybody loves him!" Chalk it up to a visionary breeder who knew her puppies and a wise puppy buyer who was willing to be patient and do her homework. If only everyone would take the choice so seriously.

Signs of Good Health

Not all prospective Golden owners can rely on a trusted breeder to play matchmaker. Your first task when faced with this mission is to look for signs of good health. You can usually tell when a dog or puppy is healthy and when he's not. Clear eyes, a moist (though not necessarily cold) nose, clear breathing, and a lively step are the first signs you'll notice. Look for a healthy lustrous coat, too, which in partnership with the skin, acts as one of the clearest indicators that all is well internally.

A healthy appetite is a good sign, and even though you may not want to hear this, so are firm feces that are free of blood or mucus (diarrhea can indicate anything from a minor infestation of internal parasites to a serious life-threatening infection, such as canine parvovirus). (Health conditions are covered further in Chapter 5, Common Health Concerns.) Check the ears, too. The flaps should be clean and free of parasites, and free of odor from inside the ear—odor that makes you want to run into the next room.

Although these are all obvious signs of health that you should evaluate when choosing a new Golden Retriever puppy or dog, some health indicators aren't so readily apparent. If you're purchasing a puppy or dog from a breeder, the breeder should provide you with documented evidence that your prospective pet's parents have currently tested clear for eye problems by the Canine Eye Registration Foundation (which, for proper certification, must be done annually), and have been x-rayed and deemed free of hip dysplasia, with a "good" or "excellent" rating, by the Orthopedic Foundation for Animals. This latter determination

Boy or Girl?

When Sharon Ralls Lemon of Kansas City, Missouri, was looking for a rescue Golden Retriever, she envisioned a lovely female on the petite side with flowing tresses the same red-gold color as her own. With great expectation, Sharon visited a local foster home and was greeted, not by her vision, but by a big, strapping male who was so intent on letting her know how thrilled he was to meet her, that he practically dislocated the arm of the diminutive woman at the other end of his leash. Several hours later, this dog crossed the threshold of his new home—Sharon's home—the home that would be his for the next decade. Though he was not the dog she imagined, Sharon has never looked back. Her Cricket, as she christened him, although not a petite female, lived up to every other expectation Sharon had of the Golden Retriever breed.

Male or female, Goldens in general make great pets and engender equal love and devotion from their owners. Technically there are gender differences, but those differences end as soon as a dog is spayed or neutered, as all pet Goldens should be. Females tend to be a bit smaller than males, and both genders, when altered, make better, even more attentive, companions. But what all Goldens share is that great capacity for love, and a talent for surprising us, delighting us, and living up to, and even exceeding, our expectations.

cannot be made until a dog is at least two years old, so if you're purchasing an older dog, he may have already been x-rayed. Unfortunately, hip dysplasia, a hereditary malformation of the hip joints, is a problem in Goldens, so it's wise to arm yourself with the information ahead of time.

Of course, there may be no way to know a shelter or rescue dog's genetic predisposition for hip dysplasia, but a veterinarian can help you determine whether a dog is affected, and if so, how severely. In some cases, the condition can be controlled or corrected. Of course, no dog is perfect, and even a dog with a mild case of a genetic condition (which should of course be spayed or neutered), can live a life of contentment and comfort. Find out all you can, and you'll be more comfortable in your relationship with your pet, because in knowledge, as we know, there is power.

You can further exercise this power after you evaluate the prospective pet's health and make your choice, by following up with a visit to your veterinarian as soon as you bring your new pet home.

Evaluating Golden Temperament

We hear much these days from some experts about the important role temperament testing plays when it's time to choose a new canine companion. At the same time, we hear from others that these tests—for example lifting a young puppy into the air or rolling him on to his back to see if he struggles—in no way tells you whether he will be dominant or submissive in the years to come. The truth probably lies somewhere in the middle. The puppy who wiggles and doesn't care to be rolled over on his back is indeed probably more of a leader among his littermates, he's more dominant in character, but that does not mean he won't be a cooperative member of your household and an attentive and enthusiastic student in obedience classes with you. We're talking Golden Retrievers here, after all.

The best way to "temperament test" a puppy is to meet his mother—and dad, too, if he's available. Much of temperament is inherited, but the puppy's character is also molded by the style in which his dam mothers them. A mother who is calm, friendly, and diligent in her maternal duties is far more likely to raise well-adjusted pups, especially if they are afforded the luxury of spending the critical and very impressionable period of their development—the first seven to eight weeks of life—with a mother who obviously en-

joys being a dog and a mom. Such lessons will stay with the young-sters into adulthood, especially if they are fortified by owners who are of similar minds as the mother.

So, go ahead and roll the puppies on their backs, lift them into the air, and observe the interactions of the littermates. All of these are tests for temperament, but because there's no such thing as a formal temperament test, you should use your common sense, too. Pay attention to how the pup responds to (and plays with) his littermates. Just as in human families, the youngsters take on cer-tain roles. If you spend just a little time watching them, after a while you will probably be able to figure out who's the boss, who's timid, and who's the peacemaker. This will indeed give you some idea about the temperament of each pup, though the full fruition of their temperament and character will depend on the people with whom they live and their mutual compatibility.

While flipping a puppy over on his back is harmless enough, trying this with a large, unfamiliar (and possibly aggressive) adult dog puts you in a potentially dangerous situation. You can, how-ever, observe how both adult and puppy respond to you, to the people who are taking care of them—breeder, foster mom, shel-ter staff—and how they respond to their environment. Has the dog had any obedience training? If so, does she respond to your basic commands? Does the dog or puppy seem enthusiastic about exploring her surroundings? Is she shy upon meeting you? (Re-member, shyness is not unusual in a shelter or rescue dog, so in these cases, don't hold it against the dog until you get to know her better.) Did she growl and snarl at you the moment you walked in the door? Or did she make you feel that you were long-lost friends who should now be together forever? If the answer to this last question is yes, this just may be the Golden for you.

Welcome Home!

2

In This Chapter

❍ Preparing for Your Golden Retriever's Arrival
❍ Golden-Proofing Your House and Yard
❍ Which Supplies Do You Really Need?
❍ The First Night with Your Golden Retriever Puppy

There are few events in life more wonderful and more memorable than that divine moment when you drive up to your house with a new puppy in your lap or a lovely new dog in the back seat. It's a moment we dog lovers dream of from the time we are children. The idea pops into our young minds, and we begin the classic cajoling for a puppy—even if there already happens to be a dog in the house. For some children, the dream comes true. Others must wait until adulthood, when the power to make that dream come true is in their own hands.

What follows is a guide to the necessary preparation and the get-acquainted period with your new pet. It's an exciting time, a nervous time, sometimes a frustrating time. The better prepared and informed you are, the better equipped you'll be to cope with the inevitable questions and problems that can and will arise. Consider it a long-term investment. Prepare now and you'll have more time to enjoy the special moments that will become treasured "remember whens" years down the road, when as a family you reflect on the happy memories you have shared with that very special dog.

Preparing for Your Golden Retriever's Arrival

The amount of time you will have to prepare for your new Golden Retriever will depend on the circumstances under which he joins your family. From a timing standpoint, a long wait on a breeder's waiting list will differ widely from finding a stray Golden Retriever on the street who you sense might be your canine soul mate. In the former case, you can do your homework at your leisure and relish the anticipation; in the latter case, you won't be afforded that luxury. You'll have to get prepared fast.

The preparation process of welcoming a new Golden Retriever (or any dog, for that matter) into your family is not unlike preparing for a marriage or the arrival of a new baby. In fact, many who have been through both believe that raising a dog on your own is great preparation for raising a child someday. Both involve families grappling with training and discipline issues; remedying sleep problems; dealing with separation anxiety and house-training; and shopping for age-appropriate toys. Those who have children, but haven't experienced these issues with a dog may find the comparison insulting. However, if you ask most dog people, they'll tell you: Kids and dogs—they're *all* family! What's insulting about that?

So let's find out how we can make our new golden friend's arrival a pleasant event for everyone involved. And remember, the advice you find here may also come in handy should you find yourself faced with the prospect of welcoming a new little human into the fold. But don't tell anyone where you heard that.

Getting Ready—Heart, Mind, and Home

Every once in a while you experience a major transition that forever changes your life. Bringing a new dog into your home qualifies as one of those transitions. That new dog walks in, wags his tail, and life as you know it will never be the same—nor would you want it to be.

Those who have lived with dogs before should find their first experiences with the very amenable and eager Golden Retriever a joy. If, however, you've never lived with a dog, or even if you have never raised one on your own, you have an even greater adventure awaiting you. Remember: When you embark on any adventure, preparation is the key.

Prospective Golden Retriever owners should acknowledge that they must prepare for the newcomer's arrival on two distinct levels: the emotional and the physical. The first of these, the emotional preparation, involves seeking a balance between the dog's tugging on the heart—one of the breed's great talents—and the common-sense messages from the mind. The two don't always agree.

> Remember: When you embark on any adventure, preparation is the key. Prospective Golden Retriever owners should acknowledge that they must prepare for the newcomer's arrival on two distinct levels: the emotional and the physical.

San Franciscan Michelle Soba was inspired by the memory of the pet dog her family had when she was a child. When she turned 30, she decided it was time to get a dog of her own. She always loved Golden Retrievers and knew that when the day came to get a pet, that would be the breed for her. Her life was now suitable for a dog, so she took the plunge.

Michelle found a reputable breeder and put her name on the breeder's waiting list for a puppy. This afforded her ample time to make arrangements, which included gathering the essential supplies and reading up on Golden Retrievers. She not only did her research, she went even further, by trading in her two-seater sports car for a more Golden-friendly sport-utility vehicle, and switching her studio apartment for a spacious flat with a backyard. When one goes to such great lengths to accommodate the needs of the new canine member of the family, somehow you know the arrangement will be long-term—and a success. Today, Trevor accompanies Michelle everywhere she goes, from work, to play, to family gatherings. The two have formed a very special bond made possible by Michelle's preparation.

Michelle and Trevor's experience demonstrates the great benefits of preparing emotionally and physically for your dog's arrival. If you prepare similarly, you'll be rewarded greatly. Not only will you forge a strong foundation, you'll also realize your dog recognizes your concessions in lifestyle, housing, time management, and even transportation. Dogs have a sixth sense programmed to pick up the appropriate signals from those who love them and are willing to sacrifice for them. They may not understand the mechanics of the sacrifice, but they can recognize the gesture and sense its significance. You can see it in their eyes and feel it in the sloppy kisses on your cheek.

Decisions to Make Before Bringing Your Golden Retriever Home

Some of the most heated marital and roommate arguments in history have been waged over differences of opinion about the care and management of the family dog. Only by consistent practices, which all family members agree to uphold, can you attain a harmonious dog-owning household. Agreeing to this consistency is an integral component to the preparation process. If you've already ironed out the kinks and differences of opinion ahead of time, then you won't have to argue in front of the dog. Goldens are sensitive critters. They don't like to hear their family members argue. It makes them nervous.

> Your goal is to make sure that everyone in the household understands the rules and agrees to abide by them. Dogs thrive on consistency.

Your goal is to make sure that everyone in the household understands the rules and agrees to abide by them. Dogs thrive on consistency—Golden Retrievers are especially attuned to it—and they greatly appreciate a family who acts cohesively. Dogs, like children, feel far more secure when they have limits set for them. Setting boundaries, then, is extremely important.

Setting Boundaries

Surprisingly, setting boundaries has more to do with the behavior of the people in the family than with the physical boundaries for the dog. This is because the dog's physical boundaries—and hence his sense of security and safety—can only be set with proper and consistent enforcement from his owners.

Before his arrival is the time to determine where your dog will be allowed in the house and where he won't be allowed. Inviting a dog in and allowing him to run wild through the house all day when you're home and when you're not, is to invite trouble in the pet/owner relationship. A dog has to earn free rein, and that can take months or even years. You should figure out where the dog will be allowed when he is indoors with the family, and where he will be confined when no one is at home.

It's time for a meeting of the minds. What follows are questions you should address. Discuss them and any others you deem pertinent to your household. Then make the necessary decisions that will keep peace within your house—and help ease the transition you'll experience when your new pooch comes home. Here goes—and no arguing, ya hear?

Will Your Dog Be Allowed on the Furniture?

If the dog won't be allowed on the furniture, enforce the rule—positively and gently—from the beginning. A successful "no dog on furniture" policy begins with a "no puppy on furniture" policy. While you're at it, why not buy your pet her own furniture: a dog bed or pillow for a corner of the family room so that she can feel like part of the family, too. If your dog will be allowed on the furniture, be prepared to share the furniture for life.

Where Can Your Dog Retreat?

It might be the kitchen, it might be the laundry room, it might be a corner of the master bedroom, but wherever it is, your dog needs a place to retreat for peace and quiet whenever she feels the need. Once you decide where that spot will be, get that area ready with the necessary decor and accessories before your

Golden comes home. This spot will do double duty when you are not at home and need to confine the dog in your absence.

Which Rooms of the House Will Be Open Territory and Which Will Be Off-Limits?

In most Golden Retriever households, the dogs are allowed to roam anywhere they want because the families want their dogs with them at all times. But the wise caretaker approaches this freedom gradually, keeping control over the dog and where she will and will not be allowed. Make the decision and vow to make enforcement a priority. You might choose later to extend the dog's boundaries when she proves herself reliably house-trained and mature in her chewing compulsions. But that decision should be made communally so that everyone—dog and family members alike—understand and respect the rules. (Notice here that the assumption is that the dog will be indoors at least part of the time. You won't find any "outdoors-only" policies here.)

> In most Golden Retriever households, the dogs are allowed to roam anywhere they want because the families want their dogs with them at all times.

Where Will Your Dog Sleep?

Determining where the dog will sleep is another issue and often a controversy. Most trainers and behaviorists believe that allowing your dog to sleep in your room (especially on your bed) will lead your dog to assume that he is equal to or dominant over his owner. However, many dogs spend each night sharing their owners' bedrooms peacefully and happily—and have done so for centuries. In the beginning, it is best to abide by some more conservative rules. If your dog will be sleeping in a crate, then a spot beside your bed might be the perfect location. If not, your dog should sleep in a more neutral location, such as a clean laundry room or cozy corner of the kitchen to prevent his assuming that he is equal to or dominant over his owner. As time goes by and your Golden proves to be a humble soul who doesn't snore too loud, maybe you can bend the rules.

What Veterinarian Will You Use?

Just as parents-to-be screen pediatricians before the arrival of their little bundles of joy, so too, should you check out veterinarians before your new dog arrives. Poll fellow dog owners, breeders, and local animal welfare groups for recommendations. If you are uncomfortable with the veterinarian you choose—perhaps he doesn't answer your questions as clearly as you would like or there seems to be a personality conflict—feel free to try someone else. The ideal veterinarian is one who loves dogs, who respects the bond between dog and owner, and who will sensitively care for your dog well into the dog's golden years.

What Type of Food Will You Feed Your New Pooch?

Today there are many excellent commercial dog foods on the market, and choosing which might be best for your pet can be a bit daunting. You might want to use a food you have used before or get recommendations from friends who own healthy dogs, veterinarians, or a reputable dog breeder. Choose a high-quality commercial product and stick with it. Switching foods back and forth makes for a finicky appetite and tummy aches, although sometimes a particular food does not sit well with a particular dog. When that is the case, by all means try something new. Purchase a moderate amount of food and have it ready when your new pet comes home. (Dog foods and nutrition are discussed in Chapter 3, Food for Thought.)

To prevent digestive upset, you will first want to feed the pup whatever she has been fed by her previous caretaker. If you intend to switch to something different, after a few days feed her a combination of the old food and the new, gradually replacing the old-food ration with the new until you are feeding her the new food exclusively. (Nutritional information is discussed in Chapter 3, Food for Thought.)

Who Will Take Care of Your Dog?

That's a rather broad question, isn't it? But you'd be surprised at how many people don't take the time to ponder this rather obvious issue before they decide to get a dog. They neglect to consider this cornerstone of the dog/owner commitment, and they end up contributing to the heartbreaking problem of unwanted, homeless, and abandoned pets.

The answer to this question depends on the composition of the dog's family. If you are a single person, the answer is you. If this is to be a family affair, you may want to divide up the various feeding, grooming, yard cleanup, and walking details, but remember that children won't necessarily stick with their assignments, despite the promises they make. Indeed they should be encouraged to participate, but when all is said and done, it must be an adult who bears the true responsibility.

How to Talk to Your Golden Retriever

Golden Retrievers are very sensitive dogs, alert and eager to understand what you want from them. It is thus vital that everyone in the dog's family, and ideally, everyone with whom she will come into contact on a routine basis, speak the same language. Get together and agree that the dog's teaching will be guided by the tenets of positive reinforcement and consistency. Then decide precisely which words and hand signals you will be using as commands. It's not fair for the dog to have to figure out that "come" from one person is identical to "here" from another, or when playing ball, that "drop it" means the same as "give."

Cohesive language, coupled with the house rules governing the dog's boundaries, will give the dog clear messages of what you expect of her and how she can most efficiently please you. And that, as you know, is what life is all about for the Golden Retriever.

What Sort of Household Routine Do You Foresee for Your New Pet?

It's wise to discuss just how the addition of a new canine companion will change your current lifestyle. A cousin of mine, for example, mandated that in her household, someone had to come home at least every four hours to take the dog out and give her some exercise. What may have seemed extreme in one household was the rule in this one, and everyone respected it. The dog was a family member and her needs were no less important than those of any other family member.

Discuss ahead of time the need for frequent canine bathroom breaks, two or three feedings a day (multiple meals are better than a single mealtime), training sessions, dog-walking times, play time, and exercise. Let everyone participate, and everyone will feel a personal investment in the new pet and will recognize the responsibility that comes when you invite a member of another species to share your home.

Who Will Train the Dog?

Ideally, everyone in the household should train the dog. A good professional dog trainer relishes the chance to train everyone in the family and welcomes everyone, even babies, to participate in formal training class sessions. Check out the local classes and get your new pet enrolled as soon as possible—puppies in puppy kindergarten, older dogs in more traditional obedience classes—and get working on the bonding and the behavioral foundation of your relationship right away. (Training issues are discussed further in Chapter 6, Basic Training for Golden Retrievers.)

> Most "behavior problems" are really just misdirected behaviors that are natural to a dog. For instance, dogs need to chew, but they should be encouraged to chew on acceptable chew toys rather than the living room furniture or your shoes.

What Behavior Problems Will You Tolerate?

Most "behavior problems" are really just misdirected behaviors that are natural to a dog. For instance, dogs need to chew, but they should be encouraged to chew on acceptable chew toys rather than the living room furniture or your shoes (the latter of which shouldn't be left within the dog's reach in the first place). Dogs need to bark, but train your dog to bark only when appropriate—to announce that someone is at the door, for instance—and to stop on your command. (A dog who gets lots of exercise is less likely to have incessant barking problems.) Most dogs love to dig, so you might want to designate a place in your yard that is the dog's own digging spot, or, if at all possible, take her to the beach now and then. Every cloud has its silver lining—and every behavior a legitimate motivating factor!

Golden-Proofing Your House and Yard

Walk into the homes of most people who own dogs and you can usually tell right away that this is a "dog" house. I don't mean that the place has that telltale "doggy" odor, but that there's a comfortable, rumpled, lived-in, homey look and feel to the place. A look that says "a dog lives here."

We'd like to think that everyone who lives in that house is happy with the arrangement, and the best way to maintain that communal contentment is to make sure that you provide a living situation in which your pet can't get himself into trouble. Dogs are not creatures who are driven by vindictive impulses, but they can be world-class troublemakers if their owners allow them too much freedom. Golden Retriever–proofing your home involves training yourself to be a world-class safety monitor for the good of your house, your yard, and your dog's safety. That way, if something happens or if something is destroyed, you must blame the safety monitor and not the dog.

How Your Golden Retriever Sees Your House

The first step toward Golden Retriever–proofing your home—and home-proofing your Golden—is to acknowledge and accept that because your pet loves fun and games and spending time with you, he sees your house and yard—and anywhere else you happen to be—as one big playground.

The second step is to acknowledge and accept that you are 100-percent responsible when it comes to the preservation of your home and the safety of your dog. Anyone who has ever lived with a dog or puppy can testify to finding expensive books chewed to smithereens, gnawed-on $100 leather running shoes that can never be worn again, and shards of glass Christmas ornaments that we pray did not find their way into the dog's esophagus. And, we don't even want to think about the consequences of electrical cords or the television cable as the target of a dog's chewing impulses!

And what do all these items—or what's left of them—have in common? They were all left out where the dog could get to them. We thus find another reason why the dog should not have free and unlimited access (especially unsupervised) to the giant playground. It also shows you why even when you are home, you should know where your dog is and what he's doing at all times. At least with the Golden Retriever, keeping track of his whereabouts shouldn't be too difficult—chances are he's at your side and trying to get into whatever *you're* doing.

When accidents happen—and trust me, they will—don't misread your dog. Yes, he may crouch down and hang his head when you return home and find he has demolished your first-edition Hemingway. But he is responding to the anger in your body language, not the memory of what he did hours ago and his shame about doing it. Contrary to what many dog owners believe, dog's don't feel bad about chewing up your belongings. This is because the canine mind doesn't operate according to the tenets of shame and guilt. The bottom line: Don't leave first-edition Hemingways or other tempting chewable items out where your dog can get to them. And don't punish the dog for things destroyed while you weren't around. Unless you catch him in the act, your punishment will be meaningless.

Safety and Sanity: It's in the Details

The well-being of house and dog is a two-way street. You want to protect your home from the dog and the dog from potential dangers in the home. Protecting your home means managing your dog and his behavior responsibly. Give him the tools he needs to be a decent citizen and a pleasure to have around the house. House-train the dog and offer him ample opportunities to "do his business" outdoors, and you won't have to worry about how to remove stains and odor from the carpet. Hardwood floors will fare better if you keep your dog's nails trimmed. Your upholstery will last longer if you resolve to keep the family pet off the furniture, or at least restricted to only those sections of the couch that have been covered with a sheet.

> If you have a swimming pool, don't assume that your pup will be safe just because he happens to be a water dog. If you can't be there to supervise, make the pool an off-limits area for your dog, just as you would for a child.

How you position your furniture can also help. Golden Retrievers are large, powerful dogs with lots of energy. It's probably not wise to display your delicate antique collectibles on a flimsy three-legged table in the hall that could easily topple with one swish of the dog's tail.

As I've already mentioned, confining your dog while you're not at home will help prevent the massive household destruction that can occur when a dog is feeling the pangs of separation anxiety. Obedience training will also help preserve your household—in general, a well-trained dog is more pleasant to have around the house, is a better citizen of the neighborhood and community, and is more easily controlled when his head and his energy do not get the better of him. In return, this well-trained animal enjoys more freedom and more time with the family. Sad and all-too-common is the story of the dog who is sentenced to full-time exile in the backyard because "he's a bad dog." Whose fault is that?

The steps you take to protect your home will also help protect your dog from more than just permanent backyard exile. The Golden Retriever is an indoor/outdoor dog, and the dangers he may encounter can be found in both environments. Look at your home and yard and imagine a curious toddler coming for a visit. You now have a good idea about what you might need to do to keep your pet safe. Potentially dangerous items that most people have around the house include, but are certainly not limited to: toxic cleaning materials, tiny toys that might be swallowed, all those delectable materials lurking in garbage cans, and virtually anything that can be chewed and eaten. Remember, think as a toddler and get to work.

Electrical cords should be a primary concern, especially when puppies are present. One run-in with a cord that is plugged in, and the joy of living with a puppy becomes a horrible nightmare in the form of a seriously injured, possibly dead, pup. Obviously you can't dispose of all your electrical cords and resort to heating and cooking with fire, but you can hide them behind furniture, restrict your dog's access to certain rooms (for example your computer room) and monitor his activities carefully. Prevention is always the best medicine.

Yard-Proofing

Take the same precautions outdoors. Antifreeze is a deadly poison, and one with a sweet aroma and taste that attracts a curious canine nose. There may be more electrical cords outdoors, too,

Did You Know?

The penalty for a killing a Greyhound in ancient Egypt was the same as the punishment for killing a man.

Common Household Hazards

"Beware of Dog" signs are pretty commonplace in our society, but in many cases, it's the dog who needs to beware of household dangers. Take stock of your home. Make sure that the following are kept out of the reach and vicinity of the Golden Retriever and look around for anything else you think might be dangerous for your pet.

❍ Antifreeze, either spilled on the ground or stored in its container. Antifreeze appeals to dogs because of its sweet taste and aroma. If you catch your pet drinking some, call the National Animal Poison Control Center immediately (888) 426-4435. (There is a $45 charge per case.) Even a small amount can prove toxic and deadly.

❍ Raw meat, which can carry salmonella and parasites, and, poultry, pork, and fish with splinter-prone bones that can lodge in a dog's throat.

❍ Plastic-wrapped foods that could be swallowed, plastic and all.

❍ Live electrical cords.

❍ Delicate glass Christmas ornaments and similar decorative items that can shatter within even the soft-mouthed grip of a Golden Retriever.

❍ Glues, cleaning solvents, and other toxins, which can poison dogs just as they can poison children.

❍ Open gates, front doors, or back doors, which can lead to a lost or stolen Golden.

❍ Vinyl pool covers that can trap even a competent canine swimmer under the water.

❍ Vegetation treated with toxic pesticides.

❍ Oncoming cars or other vehicles (the best reasons to keep even a well-trained Golden on a leash).

as well as poisonous plants (see Appendix A) and toxic pesticides on the vegetation. Try to use only non-toxic materials and hide those cords.

If you have a swimming pool, don't assume that your pup will be safe just because he happens to be a water dog. As a hunting retriever, Goldens are typically regarded as natural swimmers and water lovers, though not every Golden shares this characteristic. If your particular pet does love the water, conduct some practice swimming sessions to ensure that he not only can swim proficiently, but that he can get himself out of the pool, as well. And be careful if you have a vinyl pool cover designed to keep debris out and heat in. If your dog falls or jumps into the water while the cover is on—not out of the question if your dog loves to swim—he could drown if he becomes trapped under the cover. If you can't be there to supervise, make the pool an off-limits area for your dog, just as you would for a child.

Which Supplies Do You Really Need?

Now the fun starts! The date is set for you to pick up your new puppy from the breeder or retrieve the lovely two-year-old from the shelter or foster home. It's time for the pre-arrival shopping spree! Do your new pet a favor, and get the shopping done ahead of time. You'll have enough to think about during your first days together. Walk into just about any pet supply store and you'll be amazed at today's variety of pet products, all part of what has become a billion-dollar industry. Or, perhaps you'd prefer browsing through the thousands of products (many of which are personalized) offered in the many pet-product mail-order catalogs. Either way, you needn't empty your savings account to keep your pet in grand style. As we'll see, you may deem some products worth paying a little extra for (leather collars as opposed to nylon, for example), but most essentials are not expensive—a welcome fact for dog owners on fixed budgets. Now, let's look at what you'll be needing.

Dinnerware for Your Dog

A dog has to eat and drink, and he needs his own set of dishes for doing so. These need not be Waterford crystal or Lenox china. Choose instead stainless steel, ceramic, or heavy plastic dishes. Ideally, the dishes should sport weighted bottoms to prevent an enthusiastic eater from toppling them over and sending kibble and water across the floor. A puppy may do better with smaller, lower-sided dishes than those of an adult Golden. All dishes should be kept clean to prevent illness and odor. Wash dishes every other day (every day if feeding canned food) with mild dish soap, and be sure to rinse thoroughly.

Collars, Leads, and Leashes

From puppyhood into adulthood, a young Golden will require a progression of collars to keep up with his swift growth. Opting to forego the collar until his growth stabilizes is not a wise decision. You want the young dog to grow accustomed to the sensation of the properly sized collar around his neck. Additionally, connected to that collar should be an identification tag that will be his ticket home if he is lost. Collars are available in a rainbow of colors and materials—the most comfortable being a traditional leather or woven nylon mesh collar with a secure (preferably buckled) fastener.

Examine the collar periodically to make sure it is in good condition and remains smooth and free of rough edges that might irritate the dog's neck. Make sure it fits properly too: You should be able to fit two fingers between the neck and the collar. Team that collar with a sturdy leather or nylon mesh lead (leash) that has a secure clasp mechanism, and you're in business. (I'd steer clear of chain leads because they can pinch and injure the neck.) An-

May I See Some I.D., Please?

One of the most important gifts you can give your pet is identification. Should a dog be lost, clear and proper identification is the quickest—and sometimes only—way of ensuring he will get home again.

The classic collar and tag is still the most reliable identification method. It's the first thing people look for when they find a lost dog. Today, there are a variety of tag styles from which to choose, and you can even get a collar with your name and phone number embossed in the nylon mesh or engraved into the leather. So keep it current and keep it secure.

While the ID tag is reliable, it's not necessarily permanent, so you may want to supplement the tag with a more contemporary method. Tattooing is a popular identification method whereby the dog is tattooed with a distinct number inside the ear or, preferably, on the groin. The number is then recorded with one of several national tattoo registries.

Even more high-tech (and even a bit controversial), is microchip identification. A tiny microchip containing a distinct number is implanted under the animal's skin, and the same number is recorded with one of several national registries. Although suspicious types claim that there is something Orwellian about this method, its genuine drawback is that many people don't know about microchip identification, so they don't know to take the dog to a shelter or vet who has the equipment necessary to read the microchips. I suggest you stick with the tried and true (and feel free to try a new method, too), but most of all, know where your dog is and what he's doing at all times, and he won't get lost in the first place.

other option is the extendable leash that allows a dog to wander 20 to 40 feet from his owner while still remaining "on lead." These are appropriate only for dogs trained not to pull on the leash—and trained to mind their manners during encounters with other dogs and people.

Also available are specialized collars for training purposes only, the most common of these being the chain choke collar and the far-too-popular pronged pinch collar. These should not be used on puppies younger than six months of age, and the latter style is probably not necessary at all for the amiable Golden Retriever unless being used for unusual circumstances and *only under the direction of a qualified trainer.* For walking, jogging, cycling, and other such activities with a Golden, many owners prefer the H-shaped harness to a neck collar. The harness, which fits almost like a jacket around the dog's chest, back, and shoulders offers the well-trained dog a sense of security and comfort, and it appeases those owners who don't like the idea of pulling and tugging a dog around by the neck. The one drawback of the harness is that it may inspire some dogs to pull. The remedy? Training.

Crates are Great!

A dog crate is essentially a box, typically composed of sturdy plastic or stainless steel wire (similar to a cage) that can be used as an effective and cozy confinement device. A dog crate can be a miracle tool (especially for house-training), as long as it is not abused. A crate-trained puppy, and later crate-trained dog, will regard his crate as a safe haven, a cozy bed, and his own private domain. The crate should not, however, be used to confine your dog for hours and hours a day, only taking him out to play and then putting him away again as though he were a gerbil or a hamster.

> Reward the pup with treats for entering his crate and spending time inside. His association with the crate should be positive, so never send your dog to his crate as punishment.

Furnish the crate with soft, flooring such as towels and blankets. Reward the pup with treats for entering his crate and spending time inside. His association with the crate should be positive, so never send your dog to his crate as punishment.

Size-wise, the crate should be large enough for the dog to walk in, stand, and turn around. An adult Golden will require a crate far larger than he needed as a puppy. If you have a puppy, but you'd rather not buy a small crate now and a large one later, pad the sides of an adult-size crate with pillows, towels, and blankets to reduce the interior space (excess space could make the puppy nervous). In time the puppy will begin to develop a positive association with the crate that will make it a valuable addition to your dog-care accessories in the years to come.

Most dogs regard their crates as their private dens. When the crate is used humanely, most won't soil their dens and will actually enjoy them. The crate can even act as your dog's bed in your room and a familiar haven when you are traveling (a dog who travels by air must do so in an FAA-approved crate). A crate is not, however, a substitute for a dog house, and is best used indoors for brief confinement periods, training, and bedtime.

Baby Gates and Exercise Pens

In your quest to keep your dog confined when you are not at home and denied access to certain rooms when you are, you may need some equipment to facilitate this endeavor. This is where doorway baby gates and wire exercise pens made for dogs can come in handy.

Baby gates are readily available in a variety of sizes and materials where baby and toddler supplies are sold. They can be used to block the dog's access to rooms and stairways. The wire exercise pen, which is much larger and airier than a dog crate, is available at most large pet supply stores and through mail order. (Mail-order catalogs are advertised in dog magazines and over the Internet.) The pen permits you to confine your dog anywhere—indoors or out—while still affording him room to stand up, stretch, and walk around. This is a marvelous invention—essentially a spacious, well-ventilated playpen or corral for puppies and dogs—that no dog owner should be without. When designing your dog's private corner of the house, the "ex pen" provides excellent fencing material, plus you can use it anytime you need to confine the dog in the garage, the basement, the kitchen, the park, the family room—anywhere. It folds flat for storing and travel, and it won't leave your dog feeling cramped and deprived.

Bedding and Shelter

Your dog should have bedding in a specified area inside your house. If you have a crate, you'll need bedding inside the crate as well. Blankets and towels make for inexpensive, comfortable, and easy-to-wash bedding. If you'd like to spend a little more, you can buy one of the many large pillow-style dog beds, which are made of synthetic fibers and cedar, the latter of which helps to repel fleas.

The dog who will be spending time outdoors may also need a doghouse, especially in rainy, muddy, cold, and snowy areas (although indoor accommodations are preferable during any extreme weather conditions). Here, too, you will find a vast array of available styles, ranging from traditional wood to the popular heavy plastic igloo-style house. The doghouse you choose should be water and wind resistant in construction, material, and design, and the floor should sit elevated somewhat above the ground for insulation and to prevent floor leakage. The house should be comfortably appointed with clean bedding, as should the dog's favorite corner of a shaded patio (if you have one).

Grooming Supplies

It's never too soon to start grooming your pet, a process that should proceed gradually, introducing procedures one step at a time, and in the most positive way possible (keeping the sessions short and giving lots of treats helps). Your grooming kit should include dog shampoo (only puppy shampoo for puppies because it's gentler on puppy hair and skin), nail clippers, slicker brush (to control shedding), pin brush (for general brushing), comb, canine haircoat conditioner (optional), toothbrush and toothpaste made for dogs, and blood-stopping powder (in case you clip a nail to the quick). All of these products are available at most pet-supply stores. An ample supply of treats will help you make grooming sessions as enjoyable as possible, so keep those handy too. (Grooming issues and supplies are discussed further in Chapter 7, Grooming.)

The Joy of Toys

Several years ago I reported on a survey conducted by a national dog magazine on dog toys. On it's face this wouldn't seem the most exciting topic in the world, but sorting through all the responses from devoted dog owners all over the country was actually a pleasant and illuminating experience. I was surprised to learn that the number-one toy was not the squeaky toy or the rawhide bone, but the stuffed animal—an item that I realized my own dog fancied above all others.

So, have a well-made stuffed animal handy for your new pet right away—the fleece-style stuffed dog toys tend to be favored by many dogs. It's not unusual to see a Golden Retriever carrying a stuffed bear or bunny around in his mouth for hours at a time. His

So, How Much Is This Going to Cost?

The basic supplies for your new dog can come with a hefty price tag depending on size and quality, and often it's a price you'll be paying more than once. Remember to factor in these costs when making the decision to get a dog. Prices likely will vary depending on where you live, but the following should give you a good idea of what to expect.

Item	Low Price	High Price
Crate	$40.00	$200.00
Food and Water Bowls	3.00	60.00
Collar	4.00	40.00
Leash	4.00	50.00
ID Tag	3.00	15.00
Pet Stain/Odor Remover	4.00	10.00
Brush	4.00	20.00
Toys	1.00	40.00
Food (8 lb. bag)	4.00	9.00
Bed	15.00	200.00
TOTAL	$82.00	$644.00

soft mouth helps to ensure that you won't have to replace it with new stuffed animals every two weeks. If your dog is uncharacteristically destructive, she will require more supervision, and a safer, sturdier selection of toys.

Although dogs may love their stuffed animals and regard them as symbols of security, they also crave a variety of toys for all their playtime whims. You will need: a collection of safe (heavily constructed) squeaky toys for fun and fetching (examine them regularly for tears or loose squeakers which can be a choking hazard);

rawhide bones (or the new rawhide composite bones); Nylabones; and various specialized chew toys and balls for retrieval practice. Rope and other tug-o-war toys can also be favorites, but if your dog tends toward aggression or dominance, these tendencies may come out when playing with such toys. It's still okay for these dogs to have the ropes and tug-o-war toys, but they should be reserved as chew toys only.

Dogs of all ages need toys for fun, security, chewing, and expending energy. Toys can serve as gum-relief devices for teething puppies, boredom alleviators for latchkey pups, and anxiety relievers for those moments of stress that can affect any dog. You may even try rotating the toys occasionally—bringing out new toys and putting away the old—just as parents sometimes do with toddlers to retain the toys' luster and excitement-value. Anything to keep playtime interesting. Anything to keep it safe, too. And remember: Inspect toys periodically for safety, and replace them as necessary.

> Dogs of all ages need toys for fun, security, chewing, and expending energy. Toys can serve as gum-relief devices for teething puppies, boredom alleviators for latchkey pups, and anxiety relievers for those moments of stress that can affect any dog.

The First Night with Your Golden Retriever Puppy

Anyone who has ever raised a puppy remembers that first night. Over the years, the memories blend together and the good times outshine the bad. But what remains most vivid is the memory of the first night your new puppy spent in his new home. Why? Because rarely does it pass smoothly and without incident. You remember the dog's whining and crying. You remember your complete lack of sleep. And, you remember that profound sense of panic as you began to question why you decided to get a puppy in the first place. Relax. A rough first night is normal and expected, especially if your new dog is a puppy.

Culture Shock

If you think about it, how could it go smoothly? You take a puppy eight weeks of age or so away from his mother and siblings. You bring him into this strange house with unusual smells and a bed so unlike the only bed he's ever known. It may look the same and feel the same, but where's Mom? Where's the sister whose ear he always chewed before bed? And in the midst of his confusion, there are new two-legged creatures oohing and aahing over him.

Be sensitive to your new puppy's confusion and insecurity, but don't fawn. From the beginning, you want to be affectionate but firm. There should be no yelling and no hysteria. You must be the voice of reason, handling the puppy firmly and gently, with an overriding sensitivity to what he's going through. From your first moments together, you want the young dog to understand that you have certain expectations in regard to his behavior, but that he can also depend on you to be fair, nurturing, and willing to abide by a predictable routine.

The Arrival

When asked what their Goldens love best in the world, most owners will without hesitation respond with a single word: "people." But that does not mean you should have a crowd waiting to greet your pup when she enters her new home for the first time. Sure your friends and family may be excited to meet the new addition, but ask them to wait a few days until she has settled in a bit and become accustomed to her new surroundings. Don't confuse the pup with a bunch of faces who won't be part of the immediate family.

Plan the newcomer's arrival at the start of a weekend so you'll have several days to get acquainted and so it won't matter if you miss a little (or even a lot) of sleep.

When you arrive at your house, allow the pup to sniff around and explore. Watch for the telltale crouching and sniffing that indicates she might be seeking a spot to relieve herself. Begin house-training right away, taking the pup outside immediately after she eats, drinks, or wakes up from a nap. Praise her for eliminating and bring her back inside. If you catch her in the act of soiling the carpet, scoop her up, whisk her out to the designated spot, and praise her for finishing outside. Successfully house-trained puppies are the products of positive reinforcement and consistency, not negative—and often frightening—punishment and yelling.

> Be sensitive to your new puppy's confusion and insecurity, but don't fawn. From the beginning, you want to be affectionate but firm.

Feel free to play with your pup, but make the sessions short and not too wild. Throw a ball and see if she's interested. Introduce her to her new teddy bear or other stuffed toy that she can take to bed with her for security. Offer the puppy small meals every few hours, preferably consisting of the food she has already been eating, even if that is not what you intend to feed her in the future. You don't need to add digestive upset to the list of challenges facing you tonight.

Bedtime

Eventually, that fateful moment will come—bedtime. You can't put it off any longer. Now the true adventure begins. This is one night when you might have to bend the rules a bit—not in how you will deal with the puppy, but where. Even if you don't plan to let the dog sleep in your bedroom later, positioning your puppy's crate on the floor next to your bed for the first night might be the easiest way to get a good night's sleep. Place the pup inside the crate with a comfort item or two (such as a stuffed teddy bear).

> Plan the newcomer's arrival at the start of a weekend so you'll have several days to get acquainted and so it won't matter if you miss a little (or even a lot) of sleep.

Now pray that she'll snuggle in and sleep through the night—but don't hold your breath. She may be tired and settle down to sleep, but odds are she'll wake up in a couple of hours and cry out of loneliness or simply a desire to play. If this occurs (and it probably will), don't immediately lift her up and cuddle her. That only reinforces the behavior. What you can do is comfort her by quietly placing a finger in the crate to remind her that you are there. Again, try your best not to take her out of the crate while she is crying. When she quiets down, you might offer her a cuddle or two to reward her for settling down, and perhaps take her outside to relieve herself, but keep the atmosphere quiet and dimly lit. She needs to learn that this is not a time for play. Do what you must to get through the night, but try to stick as well as you can to the rules.

The next day you'll be tired, but you will realize that you have already begun to establish a routine. Your puppy will realize it too. It may take a few days for the pup to begin sleeping for longer periods of time and to decide that there's no need to cry anymore. She will begin to accept you as her new family. Memories of her mom will fade. That's how it should be. She has now embarked on her own journey as a Golden Retriever in the company of a human family. If you, her new mom or dad, remain calm, cool, consistent, and firm, your puppy's trust in you will blossom. In the days to come, she will grow increasingly peaceful within this house that is quickly becoming home.

Making an Older Golden Retriever Feel Welcome

You've been warned about overwhelming a puppy with crowds of people anxious to meet him during his first few days adjusting to his new home. The same holds true for the older Golden Retriever coming home for the first time. Yes, these dogs love people, but they need to get acquainted with their people before meeting the neighbors, your coworkers, your friends, and your entire extended family.

The First Night and Beyond

In general, the welcoming scene shouldn't be quite as intense for the older dog as it is for a puppy, and this is one reason many people prefer bringing an older, more settled dog into their lives. Nonetheless, there will be some adjustments for the more mature Golden. This is not only a new family for him, but a new environment and a new routine, as well.

Though the puppy had to grapple with the trauma of leaving his mom and littermates, the older dog may have his own separation issues. By the same token, he could just enter the house, settle right in, and adjust as if he were simply away on an extended vacation (mature Goldens tend to make themselves at home wherever they are). If the dog you've brought into your home is fairly well adjusted, he may look around and then curl up on the pillow you provided for him and drift off to sleep. After a few days of this, he will realize that "Hey, maybe this is where I live now. And ya know what? It's pretty nice."

The greatest pitfall facing you in this situation is the temptation to succumb to the "pity syndrome." This is no time to feel sorry for your dog even if he came from a rescue group and his first go-round as a pet didn't work out. Just as you do with a puppy, you need to remain gentle but firm, calm, and consistent. Resist the temptation to reward neurotic behavior (such as incessant whining). On that first night, prepare a confined and cozy spot for the dog, tuck him into his crate or bed for the night, and there's every possibility that you'll all sleep soundly.

Handle with Care—and Common Sense

The steps you take to make the older Golden feel welcome will help everyone else in the household adjust to the new family member, too. Even if the dog comes to you house-trained, assume she could use a refresher on the protocols. Offer her ample opportunities to relieve herself outdoors—and thus to succeed in your eyes. Be generous with the treats and praise. Make sure she has plenty of chew toys, which will help her deal with anxiety and stress. As with puppies, feed her what she has been accustomed to eating. You'll have plenty of time to switch later if that is your plan.

> Even if the dog comes to you house-trained, assume she could use a refresher on the protocols. Be generous with the treats and praise.

Get yourself and the dog to an obedience class right away, too. This affords you the opportunity to start working together to build your communication patterns and the foundation of your relationship. Eager as the breed is to please, your Golden will probably be grateful for the opportunity to get to know you through this particular channel—and vice versa. Find a good trainer who shares your vision on humane training and who is sensitive to the fact that you and your dog are going through a transition. The trainer should be able to facilitate the transition by optimizing the training opportunity, and, if need be, by helping you work on any bad habits your new pet may have brought with her.

Be sensitive to your pet. Make sure she gets plenty of exercise every day. Carry on according to the parameters of a daily routine. Allow the dog to get acquainted—on a leash of course—with the contours, scents, and sights of her new surroundings and the people who live there. Before you know it, you'll be wondering how you ever got along without this dog. You'll hardly remember what life was like without her. And your Golden? There's no question how she'll be viewing the situation. You're her reason for living, and as far as she's concerned, you always have been.

3

Food for Thought

In This Chapter

○ Choosing the Best Food for Your Golden Retriever
○ Goldens and Their Food Allergies
○ Is It Okay to Share My Food?
○ What's All the Fuss About Supplements?

Golden Retrievers—and dogs in general—are not people. That seems obvious, right? It's obvious until you consider all the people who just can't resist that temptation to feed their dogs steak, fried wontons, double bacon cheeseburgers, and cake—all the same foods we humans adore. Gorging on such fare is bad enough for humans, but offer them to a dog, and you lead the pooch down the path of chronic canine discomfort, failing health, and hefty veterinary bills.

But feeding dogs is so enjoyable, especially when the dog in question is a big, gentle, oh-so-grateful Golden Retriever who could charm anyone with her sweet smile.

Who doesn't love to dangle a treat in front of a dog and watch the dog perform a ballet of sits, downs, begs, and rollovers, all in anticipation of the tasty morsel in your hand. Feeding dogs is part of what makes living with them so enjoyable. Rarely will you feel so important and appreciated each and every day.

Feed a dog incorrectly, however, and you betray the pact you made with that dog the moment he entered your household. Sure, the dog will make you feel like you're betraying him when you refuse to share with him what's on your plate, but you must resist the guilt. Feeding your dog properly requires that you vow first to choose a high-quality food for your pet, and second, that you feed him only that food (supplemented occasionally with equally healthy treats), in an appropriate manner, for as long as your dog lives. This second vow is more difficult for some people to keep than others. Perhaps the information that follows will serve as inspiration to those who have difficulty with this.

Why Good Nutrition Matters

A properly fed Golden is easy to spot by her bright eyes, lustrous coat, and jaunty step. However, the impact of nutrition runs far deeper than a dog's outward appearance. Overall health, too, is determined by the food—the fuel—that enters her body each day. Poor-quality fuel (or inappropriate fuel such as cake, candy, leftover lobster, and such) can lead to malnutrition, resulting in a dull coat, eyes devoid of luster, a lack of energy, and inferior organ function.

Food As Love

To many dog owners, food is love. However, contrary to popular belief, it is not loving behavior to indulge your pet by succumbing to his pleadings for junk food—or too much food. Undermining a dog's energy potential—his comfort, and his longevity simply because of what or how we choose to feed him—is not loving.

Pursue nutrition the right way, though, and you are paying the proper tribute to your pet. You are enriching and probably prolonging his life. By following what you know to be right and best, you are honoring your dog

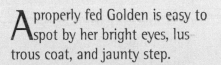

A properly fed Golden is easy to spot by her bright eyes, lustrous coat, and jaunty step.

and his trust in you as his caretaker. And yes, when food is viewed in this light, it does indeed become love. When feeding is based on a philosophy and practice of sound nutrition, food becomes the foundation upon which the healthy dog and every cell in his body is built. It's a matter of basic biology, pure and simple.

Nutrition Concerns Are Vital for Goldens

Proper nutrition is vital to every dog, but the issue takes on even greater significance for Golden Retrievers. That is because Goldens tend to be prone to obesity and food allergies. Not every Golden, mind you, but many.

Experts say there is a reason for this tendency. Though today he lives happily as one of the most beloved pets, the Golden was bred originally as a field dog—a hunting dog. The energy levels, activity demands, and no doubt metabolisms of a field dog are quite different from those of a pampered pet. It's only logical that somewhere along the line, this radical change in vocation would take a toll on the dog's constitution. This has resulted in Golden Retriever metabolisms that—coupled with the mass overbreeding that comes from breed popularity—have had no chance to evolve naturally to complement the dogs' contemporary role.

Ignored or inadvertently fostered, obesity and food allergies can detract from a Golden Retriever's quality of life—hardly the intent of those who have fallen under the spell of this magical dog. Nutrition, then, plays a pivotal role in ensuring that we do proper justice to this animal who offers us his undying loyalty. And that, my friends, is why nutrition matters. Let's take a look at ways in which owners can combat and even prevent problems caused by poor nutrition.

Vitamins, Minerals, and All That Jazz: Nutrition's Building Blocks

Given the importance of nutrition in the care of our Golden Retrievers, the choice of food and the methods of feeding are crucial decisions facing those who choose to live with these dogs. Before you attempt to make these decisions, it's wise to take a quick refresher course on nutrients.

This isn't meant to be an end-all dissertation on all things nutritious, but it will help you in your quest to choose the right package in a sea of brightly colored packages marketed toward the animal in your life. Keep in mind that even veterinarians are taking nutrition more seriously these days and acknowledging the powerful link between nutrition and health. A consulting veterinarian at a major pet-food manufacturer once told me that this is no longer a subject that students can afford to sleep through in veterinary school. So on to the nutrients.

Water

You may be surprised to find water included in this section, let alone the first nutrient listed, but this is exactly where it belongs.

The Importance of Water

Water is important to every living creature, and your Golden Retriever is no exception.

Water makes up around 65 percent of your adult dog's body and even more of your puppy's constitution. Dogs need water to help their cells function properly and to aid in proper digestion. Basically, dogs need water to live. Without water, a dog will die within only a few days.

The water in your dog's body needs to be replenished on a regular basis, because it is routinely lost through respiration, digestion, and urination. On hot days or when exercising heavily, your dog needs even more water to keep his body running smoothly.

To keep your Golden Retriever at optimum health, provide him with constant access to plenty of cool, fresh water.

Water is the one nutrient, the absence of which can result in immediate death (from dehydration). As the major component of the dog's body, water is critical to proper cellular function and blood composition. Always, always, always ensure that the water bowl is filled with fresh, clean water (especially if served outside in severe weather conditions where it might freeze or become too hot to drink).

Proteins

Proteins are the primary components within hair, blood, muscle, and bone. They are also important players in the dog's immune system. Once ingested, proteins are broken down into amino acids, which go on to construct the primary structural tissues in the body. Whether from animal or plant sources, the proteins within a dog's diet must be of the highest quality to ensure that they do the job intended for them and are both palatable and easily processed.

Fats

Though the dog world is populated by far too many overweight or "fat" dogs (many of them Golden Retrievers), dietary fat itself remains a vital component in the canine diet. Moderation is the key. Fats are best and most easily ingested by the dog solely through a high-quality, appropriately balanced commercially sold dog food, and not as leftover Chinese food or the cheese omelette from a Sunday brunch. An appropriate complement of fatty acids in the diet helps maintain the health and resilience of a dog's coat and skin, and assists in the absorption of such fat-soluble vitamins as A, D, and E. Fats are also excellent sources of energy, but if a dog is not burning up excess fats through activity, the result will be a fat, and very uncomfortable, pup.

Carbohydrates

Most commercial dog foods include a combination of meats and grains, the latter typically including rice, barley, wheat, or corn. Those grains, as well as non-grain ingredients such as potatoes, provide the dog with carbohydrates, which are essentially strings of sugars that provide quick energy for the animal's day-to-day activities. Fats pack twice the energy power of carbohydrates, but as with fats, if carbohydrate intake (and, by the same token, sugar intake) exceeds activity requirements, the result is a dog who stores fat and ultimately reaches an uncomfortable and unsafe weight.

Vitamins and Minerals

The vitamins and minerals are where the chemistry of dog food formulation enters the picture—and explains why pet-food companies maintain armies of scientific researchers to get their formulations just right. For starters, vitamins are critical to almost every function of the body, yet if a dog's diet is either deficient or overloaded with vitamins, the dog's health will suffer. The same holds true for the minerals, which typically work in tandem. Phosphorus, for example, teams with calcium for bone growth and maintenance, while iron relies on copper to foster blood health. Throw one of these mineral teammates off balance, and the dog's tissues—and the dog—will suffer. This is why most experts recommend that dogs be fed a high-quality commercial food. Such foods include everything the dog needs, and they contain the correct chemical configuration as well.

> Dogs now live longer than ever before, many enjoying healthy lifestyles well into their teens.

Choosing the Best Food for Your Golden Retriever

With all the talk of the millennium and lists of the great leaps of progress enjoyed throughout the twentieth century, you're not likely to see the advancement of pet food quality included on those lists. However, for those who love dogs, the recent advancements in pet food quality are truly revolutionary. The proof is the life span of dogs. Dogs now live longer than ever before, many enjoying healthy lifestyles well into their teens. Much of the credit for this lies in the advancements of canine nutrition.

Reading Those Labels

Your choice of dog food will be all the easier if you know how to read the small print—those labels on packages and cans.

First, check out the ingredient list. In addition to a guaranteed analysis of its protein, fats, fiber, and moisture, the label must include a list of ingredients, with the most prevalent ingredients listed first, going down to those ingredients that are not so plentiful. Those first few ingredients will typically include such items as "lamb," "chicken by-products," and "rice meal." Your goal is to choose a food rich in high-quality sources of proteins, carbohydrates, fats, and other vital nutrients. If you can, try to avoid unnecessary ingredients such as sugar and artificial colorings. Products from reputable manufacturers will typically be offered in the proper balance.

Look for a phrase that in some way states that this food is "complete and balanced" for a specified life stage (puppy, senior, or even "all life stages"), and that it has been tested according to the protocols set by the Association of American Feed Control Officials (AAFCO). This means that the food has been proven to be "complete and balanced," preferably by the animal feeding trial method, in which real dogs are fed the food according to AAFCO protocols. The food is evaluated in areas such as palatability and its ability to promote proper development and overall health. The highest quality foods will proudly make the "complete and balanced" proclamation, and unfortunately, so will some of lower quality, so be on your guard. Choose foods that have passed the feeding trial test, and look to your dog's health to evaluate how a particular food is meeting his nutritional needs.

During the last half century, dogs have gone from munching on bones and raw meat to eating commercial foods designed to satisfy every species-specific function and tissue. Additionally, we now find a vast array of foods designed for the various stages of life—from the high-energy, high-growth stage of puppyhood to the more sedentary days of old age. We also find foods for overweight dogs; for active, high-energy, athletic dogs; and even for dogs with health problems such as food allergies and urinary tract troubles.

Given this revolution and the resulting enhancement of canine health and longevity, what should you feed your Golden Retriever? The answer to that question is quite simple: There is no one perfect dog food for Golden Retrievers.

Before you throw up your hands in exasperation, allow me to explain. Each dog, as you know, is unique, and so are each dog's nutritional needs and metabolism. Age is a factor. Puppies should be fed puppy food to enhance their growth, while senior dogs may fare best with foods designed for the physical needs of an aging dog. In this latter case, the theory holds that older dogs may be inclined to gain weight and suffer from protein-related urinary problems, so senior foods are formulated with fewer calories and reduced amounts of high-quality protein. Also available are puppy foods designed to facilitate slow growth in large puppies, which can benefit Goldens who come from exceptionally large lines or are prone to hip dysplasia or other orthopedic problems.

In addition, to age-related considerations, remember that dogs have taste buds, too. Although health is your first priority when selecting a dog food, consider that some dogs find certain foods more palatable than others. Golden Retrievers cannot, however, afford to be too finicky, as this is a breed commonly affected by food allergies.

When it comes to food allergies, remember that what works well physically for one dog, may not agree with

Did You Know?

Houston topped the 1998 list of cities with the highest number of postal workers bitten by dogs, with Chicago a close second.

the system of another. Plenty of Goldens can eat any type of food and never exhibit an itch, a rash, or an upset stomach. However, pesky food allergies do tend to plague many lines of Goldens, so don't be surprised if there are only two or three foods that your dog can tolerate. (Food allergies are discussed below.) Allergies or no allergies, remember that above all, your dog deserves a high-quality diet.

That high-quality food may change as your Golden ages, so you must remain ever-vigilant to what he may require at a given stage of his life. The wise caretaker pays attention to all the factors linked to nutrition: age, activity level, overall health, and skin and coat condition. Know your dog well and understand that what you see on the outside of the dog—the condition of his skin, coat, and bowel movements—is often a clear indicator of what's going on inside. This way you'll be able to determine just what the best food is for your Golden—and what isn't. The power is in your hands. Use it wisely.

Goldens and Their Food Allergies

Your Golden scratches, he licks himself constantly, his stools are stinky and runny, and almost every food he ingests seems incompatible with his system. Welcome to the club. Your dog may be like many other Goldens out there and be suffering from an allergy to his food. Nutrition specialist Alfred J. Plechner, D.V.M., co-author of *Pet Allergies: Remedies for an Epidemic,* describes such an allergy as a critical condition that can cause not only widespread canine discomfort, but also serious systemic illness. If you find yourself faced with this challenge, the following tips might help relieve your pup's misery.

Veterinary Assistance

When you notice the signs of canine food allergies, which can range from skin rashes to gastric upset (vomiting, diarrhea, etc.) to behavioral problems, consult your veterinarian, who we hope takes nutrition seriously. The veterinarian can evaluate the dog and test her for thyroid problems, which can be linked to food allergy symptoms. If appropriate, he can prescribe topical remedies, allergy testing, allergy shots, and dietary remedies.

Diet

With canine food allergies gaining more attention and credibility, pet food manufacturers have attempted to formulate foods to help allergy sufferers. A hypo-allergenic diet may include one of the many popular lamb and rice formulas—the ingredients of which are presumed to be more compatible with and easier on the system. Allergy diet therapy may require so-called "all-natural" foods that are lacking in preservatives and/or unnecessary additives. Or, it may require a prescription diet specially formulated for allergy relief. Sometimes just a switch to a food composed of ingredients your dog has never tried before, such as venison or barley, is what the dog needs to relieve her allergy suffering.

A vegetarian diet might also be helpful. Though vegetarian diets are not widely recommended for dogs, some dogs—especially food-allergic dogs—can fare well with them. Dogs are far more omnivorous than they are true carnivores,

Did You Know?

Dogs and cats in the United States consume almost $7 billion worth of pet food a year.

so assuming it is properly formulated, a vegetarian diet can maintain a dog's health and activity level. Many veterinarians actually prefer vegetarian diets to home-cooked meals (which we'll discuss shortly) because of the commercial vegetarian diet's complete and balanced nature. But do consult with your veterinarian before taking this step.

Got Allergies? Just Say No to Treats

Lay off treats, table scraps, and people food, especially while you are investigating the cause of your pet's allergies. These outside elements can only complicate your search for the cause of your dog's allergy. Indeed, their very presence can amplify the allergic reaction and obstruct the positive effects of a new hypo-allergenic diet. (If your pup is a bit overweight, this might also be the ideal opportunity to help her shed a few excess pounds.)

Switch Gradually

Switching foods can be upsetting to the dog's gastrointestinal system. When trying a new food, introduce it gradually by combining it with the old food. Over time, increase the amount of the new food until the entire ration is the new variety. Do not switch around haphazardly, one food this week, another the next. Constant switching makes for a finicky dog—and a dog who hasn't a chance of overcoming his food allergies.

Please Don't Breed

Though all pet Golden Retrievers should be spayed and neutered for the good of both their health and behavior, any Golden Retriever—even one of show quality—who experiences chronic food allergies should be altered for the good of the breed. Dr. Plechner and others believe that there is a genetic component in the widespread allergies that occur so prevalently in some breeds, and indeed the evidence seems clear given the number of affected Goldens. So, do your allergic companion and her breed a favor, and protect future Goldens and their owners from the same uncomfortable, exasperating fate.

Premium Foods Versus Grocery Store Foods

Once upon a time, it was assumed that the so-called "premium" foods procured from the local pet supply store were superior to the foods one could pick up at the local supermarket. But those times have changed somewhat. Today, quality foods are available at both the pet supply store and the grocery store, yet there are some differences between the two, and one must remain committed to being a conscientious consumer.

This mission begins by avoiding the generics. I cringe when I'm in line at the grocery store and I notice in the basket behind me a large bag labeled simply "dog food." I see that generic bag far more often than I care to, and it depresses me to think of the dogs who find the stuff in their dishes every day—especially Golden Retrievers who may have a predisposition to food allergies. Those allergies are only exacerbated by poor-quality ingredients, additives, and excess sugars and salts, the latter of which are typically intended to enhance palatability of lesser-quality foods at the expense of nutrition. Living

> Living with dogs means taking their nutrition seriously and knowing what you are choosing as your pet's fuel.

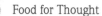

with dogs means taking their nutrition seriously and knowing what you are choosing as your pet's fuel.

Cost Differences

The first difference you're likely to notice between what we will call "premium foods" (those available solely at pet supply stores and through veterinarians) and what we will call "grocery-store foods" (some of which may also be available at pet supply stores) is cost.

To illustrate this difference, I have conjured up an imaginary premium food, derived from a poll I took of premium foods available at a local pet supply superstore. The average price of a 20-pound bag of this fictitious dry food is $17.50. Next I conjured up a fictitious grocery-store counterpart, weighing in at $7.80 per 20-pound bag. (Canned foods can command anywhere from 50 cents to $1 for a 13-ounce can. Because they are best used as flavoring rather than the sole component of the diet, their cost is not an issue for many owners, nor for our purposes here.)

But one cannot evaluate cost differences by price alone, for all is not what it seems on the surface. We may wonder, for example, just what is behind this price disparity. It doesn't necessarily mean that the quality of the ingredients in one is rancid,  while the other would be equally acceptable for humans. No, in most cases it has to do with the nature and content of those ingredients. Our premium food, for example, may contain a higher amount of actual meat or poultry as opposed to meal or by-products (the latter of which may be perfectly acceptable for canine consumption). The grocery-store food may boast a higher and less-expensive grain content than its premium counterpart.

Either one of these foods may be perfectly healthy and palatable for your dog, although there is one more factor to consider. In most cases, the dog needs to eat less of the premium food than he does of the product purchased at the grocery store. Depending on a Golden Retriever's size and weight, he may require four or five cups of dry premium food a day, while a nutritionally equivalent ration of a grocery-store brand might be five-and-a-half to seven cups or more. And that's okay. If the food is of high quality, the dog likes it and it agrees with his system, if his skin and coat remain in top condition and his energy levels remain high, then you can feel confident feeding the food to your canine companion, regardless of where you happen to buy it.

Calling Card Differences

Another difference you may notice between premium and grocery-store dog foods—and one that isn't all that pleasant to ponder—is the difference in the stools those foods produce. Wrinkle your nose all you want, but part of being a responsible, conscientious dog owner is getting acquainted with your pet's bathroom habits.

Once your puppy or dog is settled in, it won't take long if you're paying attention—and you really should pay attention—to get to know your pet's bathroom rhythms. Although an adult dog's patterns will change from those of puppyhood, you'll soon figure out that your dog's daily bowel movements average two or three a day, that they typically occur at certain times of the day (in conjunction with feeding times), and that they are of a certain color and consistency. This is not fun to think about, but it is so necessary. Such intimate knowledge is the key to evaluating what is going on within your dog's body. Normal healthy stools that suddenly emit a foul odor or are of a watery consistency (diarrhea) and perhaps tinged with blood or mucus, are profound indicators of illness or poor-quality food. In either case, action on your part is essential, beginning with a visit to the veterinarian.

And just what does this have to do with the food you feed your dog? Many owners find that the premium foods are likely to produce smaller, firmer stools. They may also emit less of an odor and be easier to clean up. But whether you feed your dog so-called premium foods or those from the grocery store, this is a rather large dog, and her calling cards will also be rather large, no matter what you feed her. Even a slight reduction in size or firming of their consistency won't change that, nor will they change your responsibility to clean them up every time they are left in your pet's wake.

Home Cooking: Preparing Your Golden Retriever's Meals Yourself

Another option for feeding the Golden Retriever—one not for the lazy or faint of heart—is playing in-house chef for your dog. Although the idea may enchant and inspire the domestic nature of the dog's owner, be warned that this is no easy task. Think about it long and hard before making the commitment. Frankly, most owners just aren't up to it.

Think, for example, of the basic responsibilities of feeding a dog properly. First, you will have to be willing to commit to preparing the food on a routine basis. Dogs, after all, must eat every day, and this large animal must have ample supplies of her rations to satisfy her equally ample nutritional requirements.

Then there is the question of your competence to do the job correctly. Unless you are an expert in the art and science of canine nutrition—a field in which experts make new discoveries every day—then you could actually endanger your pet's health by failing to provide her with all the nutrients she requires, in just the perfect balance. Although you may be able to prepare the food in the necessary mass quantities, the food must be compatible with your pet's internal system (taking into account, of course, those food allergies). You'll need to figure out the precise amounts of each ingredient to ensure that your pet receives the proper balance of nutrients without gaining weight. You must also be willing to store the food properly—a challenge more daunting than keeping a 20-pound bag of dry kibble in a cool, dry place.

If all the negatives have still failed to dissuade you, there are books and resources available that will help you get started. What you will find as you enter the world of home-cooked diets for dogs are recipes that are rather omnivorous in nature: combinations of meat, grains, and vegetables. The ingredients—particularly meats and possibly eggs—should be cooked, not just thrown together raw. Raw meat can contain parasites and disease to which dogs are just as susceptible as people.

Though commercially prepared diets are typically complete in vitamins and minerals and require no supplementation, a homemade diet will also require supplements to ensure the dog receives the required nutrients that may be lacking in the home-cooked ingredients. You will also be faced with the challenge shared by pet food manufacturers worldwide: to make it palatable.

Most dogs take to home-cooked meals readily, for dogs seem to have a natural affinity for "people" foods. But in time, many owners tire of the task of cooking for their pets every week.

Did You Know?

The world's heaviest, as well as longest, dog ever recorded was an Old English Mastiff named Zorba. In 1989, Zorba weighed 343 pounds and was 8 feet 3 inches long from nose to tail.

Feeding Larger Dogs

The Golden Retriever is not what we would call a "giant" dog, and its standard calls for a dog a bit smaller than the 90- to 100-pound wonders that occupy so many of our homes and hearts. Yet when you find yourself the caretaker of a puppy who will grow into a large dog, you may feel inspired—once that puppy-growth pattern kicks in—to enhance the process in hopes of "creating" a really big dog. This misguided philosophy, one fueled by feeding high-energy, nutrient-packed foods, is a mistake. Speedy growth leads to joint problems, muscle problems, and a mature physique that may never be as sound and strong as it was meant to be.

A better approach is to exercise patience. Feed the puppy as directed and feed only foods designed for reasonable puppy growth. Resist the temptation to supplement the diet with high-power vitamin/mineral supplements that can throw the balanced diet and the dog's growth patterns off kilter. Gradual growth is healthier, resulting in stronger, more resilient dogs. Appreciate your pup, no matter what size he blossoms into as an adult. With so wide a size differential within this breed, you never know where your pup will ultimately fall on the spectrum, but larger size does not mean a larger heart, and heart is what the Golden Retriever is all about.

Should this occur in your household, don't be ashamed to give up the responsibility. It was a valiant effort and an educational experience. The dog enjoyed it, and you probably did, too—for a while. It was something you pursued out of a genuine love for your dog and a concern for her well-being. From then on, when you reach for the kibble and simply pour it into your pup's bowl, you can think back on the grand experiment and smile.

If those fond memories inspire your continued wishes to cook for your dog, why not try your hand at homemade dog treats? Here again, you'll find recipes galore—even whole cookbooks devoted to the subject—and you can allow your creativity to run wild. You can bake dog biscuits of all flavors and shapes, and you never need to worry that your pet's entire nutritional well-being will suffer if you fail to live up to your domestic culinary duties.

How Often and How Much Does My Golden Retriever Need to Eat?

The answer to the first part of this question is simple enough. How often does a Golden Retriever need to eat? Why, every day, of course. But as you should expect, the answer is deceptive. It's not as simple as you might think. We'll explore why in the sections that follow.

As for the part of the question regarding quantities, that too can be a bit tricky. As we have seen, a Golden Retriever can range in size from 60 pounds or so to 100-plus. Needless to say, dogs of two such vastly differing sizes will not require the same rations each day to maintain their healthy, svelte physiques. Unfortunately, given the number of overweight Goldens running around, it would seem that not all Golden Retriever owners are exercising the proper dietary management and restraint techniques. To avoid that very easy pitfall, read on.

The Importance of a Feeding Routine

Dogs are creatures of routine, and this extends to their feeding regimen just as it does to virtually every other aspect of their existence. They are more likely to thrive both emotionally and physically when they know when and where their food will be served each day. It's no secret that dogs in general are rather fixated on food, and the Golden Retriever is no exception. A dog who is nourished according to a set feeding regimen is more confident and relaxed, secure in the knowledge that he never needs to worry about where his next meal is coming from—a sad concern of far too many dogs out there.

This brings us to the subject of rescue dogs. If your pup came to you as a rescue dog, especially one who was ill-treated by a former owner, he may enter your home with some food-related baggage. He may have come from a home where dogs were fed only when someone thought about it—and they thought about it rarely. Or he may have lived in a home where feeding was the sole responsibility of a six-year-old child who tended to forget the promises she made in order to get a puppy. Or the dog may have lived in a free-for-all multi-dog household where those who did not scramble at mealtimes ended up hungry.

> A dog who is nourished according to a set feeding regimen is more confident and relaxed, secure in the knowledge that he never needs to worry about where his next meal is coming from.

You'll understand, then, if this dog is a bit worried about mealtimes and a bit overprotective of his food when it is served. Most Golden Retrievers are, however, the most adaptable of dogs. If you remain committed to instituting a reliable feeding routine every day, in time, even the formerly mismanaged pup can learn to relax and trust that the food will be there without fail. This leaves him more energy to focus on the more pleasant pursuits of life, like carrying a teddy bear around in his mouth all day or playing house with the neighborhood kids. Unpredictable mealtimes shouldn't stand in the way of these very natural Golden Retriever callings.

As an added benefit, the routine also assists you in managing your pup's bathroom regimen. A dog who is fed at the same basic times every day will probably also need to go out and relieve himself at the same basic times every day, and that makes life easier for everyone.

Puppy Feeding Schedules and Amounts

Adult Golden Retrievers can vary dramatically in size, and the same is obviously true for puppies. Consequently, there is no set ration that will sustain all puppies equally. That is all contingent upon the puppy. To determine just what your puppy requires, begin by following the guidelines for serving amounts listed on the package of the food you have chosen (remember that dry food is cleaner and better on the teeth). Divide the daily ration into preferably four feedings a day, and make any necessary changes based on how your puppy flourishes and grows—or how he doesn't.

What is standard for all puppies is the fact that they must be fed throughout the day—those four formal feedings considered the ideal—to fuel both their active awake hours and the dramatic growth their bodies experience during their first year of life. Also standard is the fact that a puppy requires more protein and calories than does a mature adult dog. Puppy foods are formulated to satisfy these nutritional needs. This does not, however, mean that an unbridled flow of food and nutrients is better. Far from it. Malnutrition and overnutrition are equally dangerous to the growing puppy (and the mature adult, as well).

What you seek, remember, is slow and gradual growth that allows all the body tissues, joints, and structures to develop in concert and to strengthen appropriately before making the next growth leap. Watch your pup carefully to make sure that he seems to be growing the way he should, gaining the appropriate number of pounds at the appropriate rate, maintaining a healthy activity level, and certainly not losing weight. Ask for your veterinarian's evaluation of your pet's growth whenever you take the pup in for his puppy vaccines. Work to institute sound eating habits in your pet (and sound feeding and treating habits in yourself) at the earliest age. Serve your puppy's meals in a clean, roomy, low-sided dish, and for your own sanity, place it on a washable placemat, newspaper, or towel. Puppies can be some of the messiest eaters.

Keep in mind, too, that feeding time is also a valuable house-training aid. Most pups need to relieve themselves following every meal, so when mealtime is over, whisk your pup outdoors for a bathroom break. His very natural cooperation in this area offers him the ideal opportunity to learn and succeed, and it offers you the opportunity to praise him for his performance.

By six months of age, your puppy has now reached approximately half his adult size, so you may begin to reduce the number of daily feedings, first by reducing the daily ration from four to three feedings a day. At around your pet's first birthday, you may reduce it to two, with the daily ration divided into the number of meals a day you intend to feed. Just keep it to a routine. Instill the routine from the time your Golden is a puppy, and you'll find feeding times, and life in general, far more peaceful and uneventful in the years to come.

Feeding Your Adult Golden Retriever

When the Golden Retriever reaches about 18 months of age, you can assume that she has probably attained the bulk of what will be her full adult size. This is the time when the adult feeding schedule should be set in stone. It's all part of the routine.

Although puppies must be fed small meals throughout the day, a multiple-feeding regimen is a routine that is best maintained when the dog is an adult, as well. The adult need not be fed as frequently as she was during puppyhood when her tummy was small and her energy levels and growth requirements needed constant fueling. Health is also a consideration behind the multiple adult feedings.

An adult Golden Retriever (or any dog) is best fed several times a day, her daily ration divided into two or three small meals that prevent her from feeling deprived once the initial burst of carbo energy has subsided, and prevent the potentially fatal condition known as canine bloat, or gastric dilatation-volvulus. (This condition is discussed further in Chapter 5, Common Health Concerns.) If your Golden could afford to lose a few pounds, the multiple-meal method can make the diet regimen a bit easier for the dog to tolerate, providing her with a daily ration upon which she can munch at various times throughout the day.

Some dogs can be free-fed, meaning they can be offered a full bowl of food (preferably dry kibble; canned food will spoil) throughout the day from which they may nibble whenever they feel the need. But the Golden Retriever is not typically the ideal candidate for this method. This dog doesn't always have the self-discipline to heed the "full" signals from the stomach.

We have already discussed what your Golden should be fed, but there is more to contemplate in terms of the form the food should take. Dry kibble, canned food, and semi-moist foods are all options. Experts typically dismiss semi-moist foods, especially for allergy-prone dogs who may easily react to the semi-moist food's colorings and additives. Many owners find that their dogs enjoy a combination of dry and canned foods. In this case, the bulk of each meal consists of dry kibble, with a spoonful or two of canned food thrown in for flavor. If, as I do, you prefer sticking to a dry-only diet, that's fine too (and preferable in terms of

Did You Know?

Dogs are mentioned 14 times in the Bible.

convenience), and it's also good for the dog's teeth. The same cannot be said for a soft canned-only diet, which is messier and more fragrant than dry kibble. The soft canned food will affect the odor and consistency of the resulting bowel movements in the same ways.

The amount of food you feed your dog will depend on the food you have chosen, so as you do with puppies, use the recommended serving amounts on the package. These can range from about four to seven cups for an adult Golden, depending on the particular food and the size of your dog. Then evaluate the situation. If the dog's coat, skin, and all-around condition remain healthy and her weight is maintained, then whatever amount you are feeding her is probably doing the job. If, however, your skinny dog is getting skinnier, then you may have to increase the daily ration a bit. On the other hand, if your overweight dog is growing more so, cut out the treats and reduce the daily ration— or perhaps try one of the "lite" foods that contain fewer calories and less fat.

Serve your dog's meals in a sturdy, spacious plastic or stainless steel feeding bowl with a weighted bottom to prevent toppling by a voracious eater. The bowl should be cleaned at least every other day, uneaten food removed after mealtime is over. Offer your dog a big bowl of fresh clean water along with the food, also served in a pristine, topple-proof bowl. Check the water throughout the day to ensure that your dog has constant access to this important

component of her diet. This is especially critical when winter's chill turns the water into a giant ice cube, or a hot summer sun transforms it into a mouth-burning liquid.

Other than the basic guidelines on how you should feed your dog, there is no set formula for content or amount that will nourish every dog equally. Every dog and every Golden Retriever is unique. Pay attention, do your homework, observe your pet closely, and choose her diet with common sense and forethought, and your dog will tell you everything you need to know.

Is It Okay to Share My Food?

You should already know the answer to this one. We humans tend to pity our dogs, considering it cruel and unusual punishment to sentence them to the same food, day in and day out. Why not spice things up a bit for them with a table scrap or two? This is where treating your dog as a human is treading on dangerous ground. Dogs can both emotionally tolerate and physically thrive on the same standardized daily ration, assuming it agrees with their systems, maintains a healthy weight and overall health, and is appropriate for their particular life stages. They don't need our misguided notions of love and charity to lead them and their nutritional balance astray.

> Pay attention, do your homework, observe your pet closely, and choose her diet with common sense and forethought, and your dog will tell you everything you need to know.

Sharing your food with your dog teaches the dog bad manners as he learns to beg at the table whenever the scent of food wafts down to the floor. It also invites obesity and allergic reactions and obstructs that all-important balanced diet. A nutritionally fit dog will probably live longer and more comfortably—a long-term benefit superior to the momentary pleasure of watching your pet munch on a morsel of filet mignon or a spoonful of macaroni and cheese. So resist your pup's pleading eyes, and show him love in other ways. Table scraps are not the answer.

Healthy Treats, Toxic Treats

Every dog loves treats, and life is more pleasurable for both of you if treats can be a special—though sporadically offered—part of your relationship. All foods should not be regarded as a treat. Keep the treats healthy, and offer them only for training and as rewards. The following will give you some guidelines as to what is acceptable, and what's not in the treat department.

Healthy

○ Dog biscuits (commercially prepared or homemade)

○ Canned dog food meatballs (a special treat for dogs who receive only dry kibble)

○ Carrots, zucchini and boiled green beans (great for dogs on a diet)

○ Edible chew bones

Dangerous

○ Chocolate

○ Poultry and pork bones (splinter easily)

○ Raw meat

○ Onions

○ Rich, fatty table scraps

What's All the Fuss About Supplements?

Each year, pet food companies spend small fortunes on research into canine nutrition. So competitive are they in their quest for the perfect food that they guard their formulas like national secrets and hardly acknowledge one another's existence at pet supply trade shows.

It's a competition borne of economics of course. Though to be fair, the cynics among us must step aside and allow for the possibility that it is also driven by the desire to see the world's dogs properly nourished. We might also acknowledge that sometimes the economic motive can lead to discoveries that are profitable while also being beneficial to the subjects at the heart of those discoveries. Such is the case with the symbiotic relationship between dogs and the manufacturers of the countless dog foods formulated to keep their bones strong, their eyes bright, and their organs operating efficiently.

What is the point of this economics lesson? To demonstrate that these great investments have resulted in an almost endless variety of foods—at least one of which should be able to offer your pet the complete and balanced nutrition he requires. Yet despite the "complete and balanced" claims that grace dog food kibble bags, some owners still believe that the healthiest dog is one who receives nutritional supplements as well as the dietary products created by those pet-food-company chemists and consulting veterinarians. To date, the evidence has yet to give supplements the stamp of approval.

Does Your Golden Retriever Need Supplements?

The answer to this question is "probably not." Assuming your pup is eating a high-quality commercial diet that meets the "complete and balanced" criteria, then supplements are not only probably unnecessary, but potentially dangerous, as well. The exception, of course, is if your dog has a specific health condition that might benefit from a nutritional supplement prescribed by a veterinarian.

Consider the vitamins. Both dogs and humans need vitamins to keep our bodies functioning properly. Some vitamins (such as the Bs) are water-soluble, which means the excess is flushed easily from the system. But excess fat-soluble vitamins (such as A and D), can accumulate and lead to toxic reactions and severe side effects. A dog with too much vitamin D in her body (not uncommon among dogs receiving a high-powered vitamin supplement) may begin to accumulate calcium deposits that ultimately lead to kidney stones and related organ failures. This is obviously not the intent of those well-meaning owners who are seeking to foster optimum health in their canine companions.

When Supplements Are Necessary

Supplements are often what the doctor orders, however, for owners who prepare home-cooked meals for their pets. Though the basic carbohydrates, fats, and proteins may be present in such diets, the vitamins and minerals may be lacking in the proper balance. These latter elements may then be supplied via nutritional supplements.

Many dog owners also swear by the "neutral" dietary supplements, such as garlic and brewers yeast, claiming they perform miracles in everything from enhancing overall vitality to keeping fleas at bay. Although there has yet to be scientific evidence substantiating these claims, these are basically harmless dietary additions. Keep in mind, however, that brewers yeast is featured prominently on allergy expert Dr. Plechner's list of dietary allergens.

Where supplements are concerned, then, most dogs don't need them. Those who do use them should receive them only under the direction of a veterinarian who understands and respects the power of nutrition and is well-versed in the chemistry of it all. Not every practitioner has such understanding.

Supplementation is best viewed in a big-picture sense, where each dog food is a unique entity, its own nutritional universe designed to supply a dog with all he needs to remain healthy and active. If you determine that a particular food isn't right for

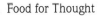

your pup, or that he has progressed into a new stage of life with a new set of nutritional needs due to age or medical condition, it's time to make a change. How fortunate today's dogs are that their owners have the freedom to switch—and have so many options from which to choose—all because society cares about the well-being of the canine species.

Medical Care Every Golden Retriever Needs

In This Chapter

- ○ Going to the Veterinarian
- ○ Preventive Medicine
- ○ Spaying and Neutering
- ○ Sick Calls and Emergencies

As a rule, veterinarians love Golden Retrievers. There are some breeds—whose names we need not mention—that some practitioners would rather not see on their daily patient roster. And most veterinarians have the scars to remind them why they feel that way. It's understandable, then, that when a veterinarian discovers that her next patient is a Golden Retriever, her mouth spontaneously curls into a smile.

Just place yourself in the veterinarian's shoes for a moment. You've had a tough day, riddled with diagnosis-defying cases, growls from disgruntled patients, and grumbles from frazzled owners. Then, late in the afternoon, weary and tired, you walk into the exam room. Sitting there is a big smiling Golden Retriever who behaves as though you are this dog's long lost adoptive parent—even though the two of you have never met before. His tail wags furiously, his eyes sparkle, his feet dance, and he squirms uncontrollably at the mere prospect of basking in your presence. In an instant, your spirits soar, and your day is salvaged.

This is a scene repeated every day in veterinary clinics throughout the nation. It's no wonder, considering that the dog at the heart of this scene is the sweet-faced, pure-hearted Golden Retriever. What makes the scene even more remarkable is the dog's resilience. It's not unusual for a Golden Retriever who has been through a gamut of health problems (even when those problems were caused by human neglect or abuse), to remain undaunted in his devotion to the human species, ignore his "baggage," and still offer that same golden greeting to the veterinarian. In light of such a warm and loving greeting, even the most jaded veterinarian is reminded just why she became an animal doctor in the first place. The Golden Retriever harbors the magic to make it so.

While not every Golden Retriever is so enthusiastic when it comes time to visit the veterinarian, the fact that so many are certainly makes life easier for everyone involved: the dog, the owner, and the doctor. How nice it must be for the veterinarian to examine a dog—even a dog who is in pain—confident that while the dog may try to lick her to death, he will not be inclined to bite the hand of the doctor who treats him.

The Golden's medical cooperation is a definite positive, because, like all dogs, that big friendly Golden isn't likely to be a stranger within his veterinarian's office. He will visit for preventive maintenance, unexpected emergencies, or simply to accompany his owner to pick up a heartworm preventive refill. Read on and learn more about your Golden's ongoing relationship with the veterinarian, and how to keep any potential fears of the vet's office to a minimum.

Going to the Veterinarian

When it comes time to visit the veterinarian—and it will come again and again—count your blessings that the dog who will be accompanying you will be a Golden Retriever. Lots of dog owners out there (because of past negative experiences or their own fear of all things medical) dread the prospect of packing the pooch in the car and trekking to the office that the dog remembers by sight and smell as that frightening place where people stick needles into her. When the owner is hesitant, the dog will be, too. But it doesn't have to be that way. The owner is in control. He can set a mood that can prove contagious to the dog, especially a dog like the Golden Retriever, who is always looking to her owner for clues about the situation at hand.

> You can take advantage of your dog's natural affection for people, and use that to help build a positive relationship between your pet and the veterinarian.

As the Golden's caretaker, you can take advantage of your dog's natural affection for people, and use that to help build a positive relationship between your pet and the veterinarian. This mission requires that you remain calm and clear-headed. If you model a positive attitude, your Golden will be more likely to follow your lead.

Selecting the Right Vet

The first step toward building your dog's positive medical experiences is choosing the right veterinarian. Keep in mind that you are choosing this doctor for both your dog and yourself. Your dog will benefit from the tender loving care of a doctor who possesses a genuine love for dogs, a "way" with animals, a sharp diagnostic mind, and a vast array of knowledge. You will benefit from such qualities, too, but you will also need someone whom you can talk to about your dog's condition. Your pet can't do that herself. Look for a veterinarian with whom you share a rapport, one who is willing to answer your questions clearly and completely, and one who won't mind if you wish to seek second opinions about serious health conditions. Obviously, this decision involves more than simply going with the least expensive contender.

And just how do you find this all-important person who will care for your dog? If you're lucky, you have already established a relationship with a good veterinarian because of other dogs and animals you have lived with. If dog ownership is new for you, or you have moved to a new area, begin by talking to people you know who have healthy dogs. Poll your friends, neighbors, and family members. You'll find that those who are working with wonderful vets won't hesitate to sing their doctors' praises. Take that to heart. Other potentially sound sources for recommendations are your dog's breeder (if your dog came from a breeder), local animal-welfare organizations, and local dog rescue groups, all of whom should be familiar with the community's better practitioners.

Having collected some names, it's time to make an appointment and give one a try. Once you enter the office, put on your evaluator's hat and start absorbing information. Is the waiting room clean? Is the reception staff friendly and conscientious? Are there patients in the waiting room who have obviously been there before and who the staff seem to know? When it's time to meet with the doctor, pay attention to how he communicates with you, handles and talks to your dog, and proceeds with the examination. You can usually tell pretty quickly when you're dealing with a practitioner who will simply not work for you or your dog.

Beware, too, of the veterinarian who reminds you more of a used car salesman than a concerned practitioner. Such a doctor will begin talking about all the "services" you should purchase for your dog even before he has gotten to know the animal on the examination table. In my experience, such practitioners are the exception, not the rule. With all the excellent veterinarians out there—people whose passion for animals and their well-being spans back to their childhoods—do the legwork to ensure that the care of your beloved companion is entrusted to someone who really cares.

One visit will usually tell you and your dog whether or not this particular veterinarian is for you. Sometimes, however, signs of incompatibility don't click in until you have made several visits to a particular practitioner. Should this occur, don't let embarrassment prevent you from trying someone new. Sometimes it's simply a case of conflicting personalities, or you realize that the veterinarian doesn't answer your questions as thoroughly as you would like, perhaps believing that laypeople just can't understand the details.

By the same token, what a joy it is to discover the veterinarian who shares a true communion with your dog, who respects her pain and discomfort, who is genuinely concerned about her condition, and who is attuned to the nuances

Did You Know?

Shelters in the United States take in nearly 11 million cats and dogs each year. Nearly 75 percent of those animals have to be euthanized.

of her behavior. Such a veterinarian understands that the health of a dog rests on a strong partnership between the doctor and the owner. The veterinarian can't do his work alone. Dealing with a patient who can't speak can be difficult, so you need to be the liaison for your dog. Be comforted when the veterinarian riddles you with questions about the dog's behavior, bathroom habits, diet, exercise routine, and skin and coat condition—and be honest with your answers. Sometimes just a tiny change in behavior or habit is the only clue the veterinarian needs to make a diagnosis. It's your job to gather that information about your dog, information that can be gathered only by someone who lives with the animal 365 days a year.

> Once you find the "right" veterinarian, you've taken an important step toward managing and maintaining your pup's long-term health and well-being.

Once you find the "right" veterinarian, you've taken an important step toward managing and maintaining your pup's long-term health and well-being. If all goes well, you may be seeing this individual for the next decade or more, in your dog's sickness and in health, so it's important to make sure you share the same concerns for the dog and a similar approach to how she should be cared for.

Your Golden Retriever's First Visit

Your Golden Retriever's first visit to the veterinarian should occur as soon as he comes to live with you, whether he is a puppy or an adult dog.

You have two goals when taking your dog in for such routine visits: to ensure that your dog is healthy (and will remain healthy)

Questions to Ask Your Veterinarian

When you are looking for a new veterinarian, here are some questions you might want to ask to see if this is the type of practitioner you would like to have caring for your dog. The answers will vary, of course, but you are looking for a pattern that reflects a well-trained, experienced staff with a genuine concern for your dog's well-being.

○ What made you want to become a veterinarian?

○ How long have you been in practice?

○ Are you a member of the American Animal Hospital Association (an organization that sets standards for veterinary clinics)? What sort of training or licensing does your support staff have?

○ What sort of cases or animals do you find the most challenging? The most rewarding?

○ What are your clinic's hours?

○ Who should I call in case of an after-hours emergency?

○ In case my dog requires an expensive procedure, do you offer payment plans?

○ Are you supportive of alternative therapies, such as acupuncture or chiropractic treatment?

○ What are the average fees for checkups, spaying and neutering, vaccinations, etc.? Do you offer a wellness program or a multi-pet discount?

and to establish in your dog's mind, through positive experiences, that the veterinarian's office is a pleasant place to be.

First impressions mean a lot, to dogs as well as to people. Because of this, I cannot stress enough that the first visit to the veterinarian must be as positive an experience as possible. Many animal behavior experts and pet owners have witnessed how just one negative experience can stick in a dog's (yes, even a Golden's) memory and make that animal fearful or even aggressive from then on.

Sad is the story of the dog who walks into the veterinarian's office for a routine visit as a happy-go-lucky soul and leaves—perhaps because of rough or unskilled handling—frightened and hunched, and determined never to enter such an establishment again. How can you prevent this? Let's look at a few preventive measures.

Keeping the Visit a Pleasant One

As we've discussed, one preventive measure you can take to ensure a pleasant visit is to choose a good veterinarian—one who understands the protocols of positive patient/veterinarian introductions and who keeps the treats handy as bribes and rewards. Your demeanor, too, is critical. It's your job to put on a happy face, to set the stage, to adopt a contagiously positive attitude. So, what else can you do? Well, if you can work it into your schedule, you may even want to make your dog's first visit just that: a visit. No vaccines, no examinations, just a visit with treats and joyful greetings from the staff. This may not be necessary if your Golden is a puppy or a well-adjusted adult, but if he is a refugee from bad experiences, then give it a try.

For the first "real" visit, again make your positive attitude paramount. Fill your pockets with dog biscuits and speak to your pet beforehand (and once you enter the office) as though you are embarking on the most magnificent adventure imaginable. If your Golden has a beloved security blanket—a tennis ball or a fleece teddy bear—that he enjoys carrying around, allow him to bring that along. Allow him to relieve himself before you walk in to the office. This helps to reduce the chance that he might do so inside, although such events are commonplace in veterinary offices. Keep your demeanor light and lively as you wait to be called. If you're lucky, the reception staff will greet your pet with

Questions the Vet Might Ask You

A good sign is a veterinarian who is anxious to learn all about your dog's home life, habits, and behaviors. Such a practitioner is honoring the owner's role in the maintenance of the dog's health. What follows is a sample of the types of questions you may be asked, which may give you a new perspective on what you should be looking for at home.

○ How old is your dog?

○ Has your dog had any past health problems?

○ What do you feed your dog?

○ How much and how many times a day do you feed your dog?

○ Has your dog exhibited any subtle changes in behavior lately?

○ Have there been any changes in your dog's bowel movements? Any blood or mucus?

○ Does the dog strain while urinating? Any increases or reductions in the number of times he urinates or defecates each day?

○ Has the dog been eating and drinking normally? Have you noticed excessive thirst or a lack of appetite?

○ Have you noticed any new or unusual lumps or bumps on your dog's body?

○ Is your dog walking, running, and playing normally?

○ Is your dog sleeping more than usual?

a friendly attitude, reinforcing that "magnificent adventure" message to your dog.

What to Expect When You Get There

During the first visit, you will most likely be asked to fill out an information sheet about you and your dog. Once you are called into the exam room, the conscientious veterinarian will probably wait a few minutes before getting down to business. He will make the necessary introductions with the dog—a moment perhaps bolstered by the offer of a treat—chat with you about the dog's health history, and of course ask about the reason for the current visit. If the reason is more than just vaccines and a routine checkup, the veterinarian will also want details on what seems to be troubling the dog. Be prepared with every bit of information you can offer, both physical and behavioral. All will help give the veterinarian a clearer picture of what's going on with the patient.

To be fair, if yours is one of those rare Goldens who doesn't like visiting the veterinarian and has been known to turn violent, you must inform the doctor about this as well. Then, armed with all the pertinent information, the veterinarian will begin to examine the dog, preferably from head to tail.

What to Expect During the Examination

Regardless of whether you have a young puppy or an older dog from a rescue group or shelter, your dog's first examination should be a thorough one. The examination should involve a complete evaluation (with both instruments and hands) of the dog's eyes, teeth, nose, ears, heart, lungs, groin, feet, and tail—the whole dog. During the exam, the veterinarian may ask you to help hold the dog still, or a veterinary assistant might help. Either way, your dog should not be handled roughly.

Use this opportunity to ask the veterinarian any questions you may have about your dog's health. Because this is your first visit, you will probably have certain concerns. If you have a puppy, this may be the first in a series of four or five visits over a six-month period during which your puppy will receive his series of puppy vaccines and accompanying physical examinations. Or perhaps your three-year-old Golden, just adopted from a rescue group, has come to you with an unknown health history and you are worried about his hips. Ask the veterinarian if the dog should be x-rayed for hip dysplasia. Discuss your concerns about hereditary conditions in Golden Retrievers, and ask if your dog's weight seems to be compatible with his bone structure.

Don't hesitate to ask any and all questions you may have. In fact, you may wish to write your questions down ahead of time so you won't forget them. Make sure the doctor is sensitive to your concerns and willing to answer your questions with equal concern for your pet's well-being.

If your puppy or dog needs vaccinations or a blood test for heartworms, these will usually come toward the end of the visit. If your dog is a senior citizen (past his seventh birthday), the veterinarian may also want to have other blood work done as a baseline for future potential age-related conditions.

Like pediatricians, some veterinarians prefer that an assistant administer vaccines and take blood so that positive associations surrounding the doctor remain intact. This isn't typically a problem for dogs. If they have been treated gently in the past and throughout the visit, most will tolerate the vaccine well and will hardly seem to feel the stick. Nevertheless, a treat reward following that minor prick is always welcome.

As for your behavior during the vaccination, don't stand with a look of dread on your face or hide in the corner. If you feel inclined to respond that way, just concentrate on the fact that the vaccination will help protect your dog from illness and suffering. Smile, be positive, and be strong. Remember, you are the one setting the stage. You are the one responsible for building that strong foundation

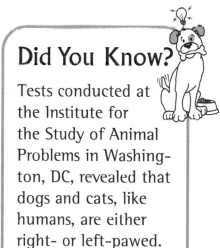

Did You Know?

Tests conducted at the Institute for the Study of Animal Problems in Washington, DC, revealed that dogs and cats, like humans, are either right- or left-pawed.

and forging a positive experience at the veterinary office that should remain with your dog throughout his life.

The routine veterinary visit is typically short and sweet, and your pup should emerge relaxed and invigorated. Most dogs can't wait to get out the door and into the car once they get their walking papers, but the Golden may have the opposite impulse. He may want to stay a while and visit with the staff. If that's the case, then by all means indulge him. The better the experience, the easier time you will all have in the future. Before you know it, your dog may be one of those who loves going along for the ride to the vet's office when all you need to do is pick up a new bottle of flea dip. If that is the case, consider yourself fortunate.

Preventive Medicine

It's as true for dogs as it is for people: Preventive medicine will keep you healthy and keep you living longer. Preventive medicine is the cornerstone of a sound medical care program.

More specifically, preventive medicine is a philosophy rooted in the scientifically proven belief that routine tests, vaccines, and early intervention at the first signs of health problems can dramatically reduce patient suffering (in humans or canines) and actually stave off illness and disease altogether. The opposing philosophy would be to wait until a problem grows too painful to bear before one finally calls the doctor. Follow this latter philosophy either for yourself or your dog, and you're at risk of discovering it's too late to reverse a condition that could possibly have been stopped in its early stages. Now, which philosophy would you consider more practical and more humane?

Of course an adherence to the practice of preventive medicine requires that you visit a doctor more frequently than you might care to—and that you take your dog to the veterinarian more frequently than she might want to go (unless of course yours happens to be a Golden who is a people addict). But those routine visits and a commitment to this philosophy are some of the greatest gifts you can bestow upon your pet, and upon the family who loves her.

Annual Visits

Dogs just seem to know when they're going to the veterinarian. It must be a universal nuance in human body language, or perhaps a scent we dog owners emit. Whatever it is, the moment you pick up the keys and prepare to pack up the pooch for a visit to the veterinarian's office, your dog knows exactly where you're going. His suspicions are proven correct the closer you get to your destination. He may accompany you in the car every day of your life, but he always knows that this trip is different. It's time for that routine trip to the veterinarian—the key to a sound preventive medical program and a must for every dog.

Poll a group of pet owners and you may be led to believe that the only reason for making annual visits to the veterinarian is to have your pet vaccinated. But that is only part of it. Keeping that appointment each year is your opportunity to take an active step in providing your pet with proper care for his health and well-being, just as we hope you would do for every member of the family. This is the time each year when you can make sure that your dog who seems healthy really is healthy inside and out, and to discuss any problems or concerns you may have. The annual visit involves communication

> It's as true for dogs as it is for people: Preventive medicine will keep you healthy and keep you living longer.

Rehabilitating the Fearful Patient

You know your dog must see the veterinarian every year, but what do you do if you live with a dog who, for whatever reason, cannot tolerate his annual visit? Here arc some ideas that could help your pet overcome the fear.

○ Discuss your dog's fears with the veterinarian and recruit the doctor and her staff to help you work with the dog. You might plan "visit-only" visits, during which you go to the office simply so that the entire staff can love your pup and shower him with treats. Positive associations can work wonders with dogs.

○ One creative practitioner I know is willing to see fearful patients in the parking lot of his animal hospital. This way, the dogs are more comfortable, the veterinarian is safer, and the dogs may ultimately learn that there is nothing to fear from the man in the white coat. Another option might be house-call veterinarians who, in the spirit of James Herriot, of <u>All Creatures</u> <u>Great and Small</u> fame, still bring their services door-to-door in their home towns.

○ Don't pity your dog or reinforce his fears. When he behaves in a fearful manner within the veterinary office, resist the urge to baby him. Remain gentle but firm. Keep treats handy and reward him for obeying basic obedience commands, the knowledge of which tends to build a dog's confidence.

○ If your dog happens to be fearful of a specific gender because of past negative experiences, choosing a veterinarian of the opposite gender might help. For example, a dog who is frightened of men might find it easier to tolerate the attentions of a woman veterinarian, and vice versa.

between the veterinarian and owner, both of whom we hope share an interest in the dog's ongoing health.

The first part of each annual visit will be a thorough examination. The physical examination will gauge the overall physical condition of the dog. Additionally, veterinarians tend to rccommend that dogs be given an annual blood test for heartworms. A clear test paves the way for the administration of a heartworm prevention program.

This is also the time each year when your pet receives boosters of his vaccinations to ensure that he will not contract any of the devastating illnesses that once ravaged the canine population. Although you may be able to purchase vaccines (with the exception of rabies, in most states) to administer yourself, don't discount the importance of the contributions of a doctor who is an expert on canine health and is skilled in assessing the long-term well-being of your dog.

After your initial visit, once-a-year exams should suffice, until the pup celebrates his seventh birthday. At that point, he has crossed the geriatric threshold, and your veterinarian will probably want to increase the annual visit to two visits a year. Though he may live on, spry and healthy, well into his teens, changes can occur quickly in an older dog, and it's wise to have him checked regularly for invisible signs that may be noticed only through the routine diagnostic blood and urine tests performed on elderly dogs. This way you will be better equipped to combat a condition that may be easily treated or managed in its early stages.

Vaccinations

One of the key players in preventive medicine is the vaccine—a few drops of fluid injected into the body through a syringe. What a gift those few drops of fluid are to the canine family. We vaccinate our dogs to protect them. Leave them unvaccinated and unprotected, and we send them into the world, ripe for attack by one of the countless viruses or bacteria that can cause

unspeakable suffering to any creature whose system has not been bolstered by these simple, though miraculous fluids.

How does a vaccine work? A vaccine is actually made up of the very disease from which you're trying to protect your dog. By injecting your dog with a very small amount of the disease agent—in a dead or neutralized form—the immune system in turn develops antibodies to fight off the agent. Armed with these antibodies, the body is now protected against future potential invasions. Today, dogs are living longer, healthier lives thanks to vaccines.

Your pet's vaccine protection begins during puppyhood. At about eight weeks of age, she should receive her first "puppy shot," typically followed by three more thereafter, administered every three weeks or so. This series ensures that the vaccines "take." Because maternal antibodies from the puppy's mother's milk, which is the pup's initial protection from disease, can render vaccine agents null and void, the series method allows the maternal antibodies time to dissipate, paving the way for the establishment of vaccine-based immunity, which will continue to develop for years to come.

The puppy shots and the subsequent adult booster vaccines, the latter of which are typically administered annually after the initial puppy series, contain the serum of five or six vaccines within a single syringe, offering the pup his much-needed protection in one quick and relatively painless shot. Not included in that syringe is the vaccination against rabies. Rabies vaccinations cannot be administered until the puppy reaches four months of age, and boost-

ers are administered anywhere from every one to three years, depending on the vaccine and the policies set by regional public health departments. Remember: Bacteria and viruses are out there just looking for an unprotected target, so protect your dog. Vaccination schedules are an area of great debate in the veterinary community, so it is critical that you discuss this issue with your vet and set up a schedule that makes sense for your dog.

Recommended Vaccinations

During the past few decades, the standard canine vaccines have changed. Every few years it seems a new vaccine is added to the mix, each one protecting the canine species to an even greater degree. While all dogs should be vaccinated, active, outdoor dogs like Golden Retrievers may be special beneficiaries, because the time they spend outside exposes them to all manner of potentially infectious agents.

The first vaccine that most puppies receive is the combination vaccine that protects a dog from canine distemper, canine infectious hepatitis, leptospirosis, parainfluenza, parvovirus, and sometimes coronavirus. This is the vaccine we refer to as the "puppy shot," and it requires an initial series of four shots (with the exception of coronavirus, which requires only an initial series of two) followed by annual boosters thereafter. Some veterinarians are also now recommending that puppies receive an additional parvovirus vaccine between five and eight months of age. It appears that the maternal antibodies that protect the infant pup from the disease may remain in the growing puppy's system longer than those for other diseases, thus neutralizing the initial vaccines and leaving the young dog vulnerable to this deadly virus.

Did You Know?

In 1957, Laika became the first dog in space, riding aboard the Soviet satellite Sputnik 2.

Sample Vaccination Schedule

This chart shows a typical vaccination schedule. Contact your vet as soon as you bring your puppy home to schedule his first checkup and to set up the perfect vaccination schedule for your pet.

8 Weeks: Distemper, hepatitis, leptospirosis, parainfluenza, and parvo (DHLPP), usually combined in one injection.

12 Weeks: DHLPP, possibly Lyme disease and bordetella

16 Weeks: DHLPP, rabies, Lyme (if given at 12 weeks)

20 Weeks: Parvo for pups considered at high risk

1 Year after last vaccination: DHLPP, rabies, and bordetella and Lyme, if given previously

The rabies vaccine cannot be administered until the puppy is four months old. This is the one vaccine that is typically mandated by public policy. Because rabies is always fatal to those unfortunate animals who contract it, it is in the best interest of every community—and every pet and pet owner—to keep it under control.

If you board your dog with a veterinarian or at a boarding kennel, the facility should require the bordetella vaccine designed to prevent canine cough (formerly known as kennel cough). If this is not mandated, then find another kennel. Though canine cough is usually not dangerous, it is highly contagious and can cause weeks of discomfort and sleepless nights for an affected dog and her owner. The vaccine, which is administered nasally or by injection once or twice a year, should protect the dog. If you enjoy hiking with your dog and tend to venture into tick-infested areas (or live in such an area), you might also want to look into the Lyme disease vaccine. Though it may not be 100 percent effective, and it does not replace the need to examine your dog carefully for ticks and to watch for the signs of the disease, it can be a valuable vaccination tool.

Spaying and Neutering

No discussion of health and preventive medicine would be complete without mention of spaying and neutering—the surgical removal of a dog's reproductive organs. When performed, these procedures promote just about every aspect of responsible ownership—from canine health to a dog's quality as a pet. And in the midst of these issues emerges the simple fact that spaying and neutering is one of the greatest gifts we can offer our dogs. Breeding dogs isn't for all but spaying and neutering is without a doubt for most. Let's examine why this is true.

Breeding and Overpopulation—Just the Facts

An estimated 5 to 10 million dogs are euthanized in the nation's animal shelters each year. Despite what some would like to believe, these dogs are not all simply animals who would have made unacceptable pets because of age or behavior problems, nor are they all mixed breeds. In fact, many are young, people-loving dogs—and some of them are purebred Golden Retrievers.

Some people find it hard to believe that a purebred dog could possibly end up in an animal shelter, especially so sweet and beautiful a dog as the Golden. But just ponder the many Golden rescue groups that exist across the country and the many Goldens who find their owners by way of those groups or shelters. Remember, breed popularity is no insurance against abandonment and neglect—it actually contributes to those problems because it inspires unbridled breeding and, as we'll see, some very damaging consequences.

Though spaying and neutering can help to prolong and enhance canine life, they also play key roles in the overall health of a breed. There is a reason that Golden Retrievers are no longer universally friendly, loving, and healthy. Too many are being bred without regard to health and temperament—dogs who should instead be altered and spend their days as companions. A responsible pet owner spays and neuters his or her dog (and good breeders, shelters, and rescue groups mandate they do so), both for the good of the Golden and the good of her breed.

Health and the Altered Dog

"You should breed her. She's so sweet." Golden Retriever owners hear such comments made about their pets every day. Yes, there is some merit to the notion that temperament has a genetic component, but that does not mean that every sweet Golden Retriever should be bred. What about hip dysplasia? What about eye problems, epilepsy, and hypothyroidism—the breed's genetically transmitted conditions you'll find discussed in Chapter 5? If your dog has any such conditions, you certainly don't want them being passed on to future generations! And what about the fact that there are not nearly enough good homes for the Golden Retrievers who are already here?

Today's Golden Retriever is, for the most part, meant to be a pet—the highest calling for a dog. Breeding has no place in the pet Golden/owner relationship and can actually diminish it. The altered Golden (one who has been spayed or neutered) is generally healthier and longer-lived than the intact Golden (one who hasn't been spayed or neutered). Scientific evidence demonstrates that altered female dogs are less likely to develop uterine diseases and mammary cancer, the latter of which is especially true when they are spayed before their first heat cycle at about six months of age. Altered male dogs, too, are healthier and less prone to such conditions as anal tumors and testicular cancer.

Healthier and a Better Pet?

Freed from the pesky hormones that prevent the intact dog from focusing completely on her human family, the altered Golden is a safer pet, no longer enslaved by sexual urges and tempted to run off in search of mates and any other new adventure that might catch her fancy. The result? Fewer lost dogs and fewer unwanted puppies.

Let's see: better health and longer-lives; better, more attentive pets; fewer euthanasias; and healthier breed lines for all Goldens. The answer is clear: Just say yes to spaying and neutering.

Myths About Breeding, Spaying, and Neutering

The myths about breeding dogs, spaying dogs, and neutering dogs are a source of constant frustration among those who work for the cause of animal welfare. These myths are embraced by those who look for any excuse they can find not to spay or neuter their dogs. We will now dispel those myths, and perhaps improve the lot of all those intact dogs out there who should be altered.

○ **Myth:** Breeding a dog is the perfect way to teach the kids "the miracle of life."
Truth: In our era of spaying/neutering enlightenment, this misguided notion still exists. Most who subscribe to this outdated philosophy

quickly change their tune after the puppies arrive and begin growing larger, more destructive, and more expensive by the day. The owners also realize they aren't as easily placed in new homes as the family anticipated. How sad the fate of puppies whose existence becomes not a miracle-of-life lesson for the kids, but rather a hard economic/ ethics lesson for the parents and a tragedy-of-life lesson for the kids.

○ **Myth:** A female dog will be healthier if she is allowed to have at least one litter.

Truth: A female dog will be healthier if she is spayed before her first heat cycle, safer from such deadly maladies as mammary cancer and various life-threatening uterine diseases.

○ **Myth:** An intact dog is a better athlete and less likely to become obese.

Truth: Any dog can be svelte and athletic, and every Golden Retriever should be. This has nothing to do with the presence of reproductive organs, and everything to do with an owner who offers the animal a healthy, junk-food-free diet and a sound exercise regimen every single day.

○ **Myth:** Spaying and neutering is dangerous and cruel.

Truth: It would seem that whoever came up with this idea might be projecting a bit. Most of us don't relish the notion of going in for major surgery or the thought of having ourselves spayed and neutered, so we decide that the same must hold for our dogs. We thus negate the many positive long-term and socially responsible effects of spaying and neutering and the fact that veterinary anesthesia and surgical techniques have never been safer.

○ **Myth:** There are plenty of homes available for purebred Golden Retrievers—and plenty of money to be made from breeding them.

Truth: If this were true, we would not find Golden rescue groups scattered throughout the country, nor would we be discovering so many Goldens in the nation's animal shelters or running abandoned

along freeways or in remote rural areas. As for the money consideration, if you checked the financial records of ethical breeders who
breed top-flight dogs as a vocation and who invest all they must
to breed the best dogs possible—you'd find that the alleged profits
are financing steady streams of quality nutrition, veterinary care,
grooming supplies, everything their dogs need. And that's how
it should be.

Sick Calls and Emergencies

At some time in every dog's life—especially in the life of a big active dog like the Golden Retriever—sickness or an emergency
enters the picture. Assuming you are an observant, conscientious
owner, you will be the first to notice when something doesn't
seem right with your pet. It could be a symptom as dramatic as
blood-tinged diarrhea, or one as subtle as a slight increase in
water intake. Or it might be an emergency situation such as a
piece of glass lodged in a paw pad during a hike or the onset of
heatstroke on a hot summer day. Whether you're dealing with a
life-threatening accident or the first signs
of an illness, the time will come when
you must remain calm and get the help
your dog needs as soon as possible.

When to Call the Vet

The first lesson in the discussion of when
it is appropriate to call the veterinarian is
that you must never be ashamed to make
that call. Pediatricians are accustomed to

Did You Know?

A dog's heart beats
between 60 and
120 times per minute,
compared with 60 to
80 times per minute
for humans.

How to Take Your Dog's Temperature

This is one of those indignities that your Golden Retriever won't enjoy, but it doesn't take long, and you can reward her with a treat afterward. It can be helpful to have an assistant to hold the dog so that she won't squirm. Lubricate a digital rectal thermometer using petroleum jelly or a water-based lubricant. Gently insert it into the rectum, where it should remain for one minute. The normal canine temperature ranges from 100 to 102.5 degrees Fahrenheit. Call your veterinarian if your dog's temperature is approaching 105 degrees Fahrenheit.

constant calls from new parents, and veterinarians expect—and even hope—for the same from their patients' "parents." Contrary to the beliefs of skeptics who think that most veterinarians are just out to make as much money as possible, most practitioners choose this profession because they love animals and care deeply about their well-being. They prefer being called before a potentially dangerous or painful health condition spins out of control, causing suffering to the animal and perhaps reaching the point where treatment is no longer possible.

You should feel free to call your pet's veterinarian whenever you notice something different in the animal's condition or behavior, whenever you suspect there could be a problem, whenever you feel a nagging concern, and of course, in the wake of a trauma like an attack from another dog or a car accident. If you find you are not working with a veterinarian who welcomes such calls, even when the condition being discussed turns out to be nothing, then perhaps it's time to find a new doctor for your dog.

I once made a call when my dog was walking with a slight limp. The veterinarian suspected an embedded foxtail in the soft skin between the toes. What we discovered was a massive infection inside the toenail that began to ooze a horrible green substance. If I had waited to call, the infection would have moved up into the bone, and who knows what pain and suffering my dog would have endured?

Yes, the sudden onset of a limp is definitely a reason to call the veterinarian, as are several other signs that may mean trouble is on the way—or may have already arrived. The classic "call-the-vet" symptoms are:

> Whether you're dealing with a life-threatening accident or the first signs of an illness, the time will come when you must remain calm and get the help your dog needs as soon as possible.

- ○ Loss of appetite (including a sudden disinterest in favored treats)
- ○ Excess thirst and/or urination, which could mean urinary tract problems
- ○ Straining during urination, perhaps with little fluid produced
- ○ Blood and/or mucus in the feces, which could mean a case of parvovirus or some other serious intestinal disease
- ○ Pale gums and mucous membranes
- ○ Unproductive vomiting, which could indicate bloat, an emergency situation
- ○ Listless demeanor, lack of interest in family and daily activities
- ○ Vomiting that lasts for more than a day
- ○ Loss of consciousness
- ○ Excessive salivation
- ○ Heavy bleeding
- ○ Severe diarrhea, or diarrhea that lasts for more than one day

Let me add a note to the last item on this list. You're likely to hear that you should only suspect a case of diarrhea that lasts for more than two days (or maybe even three), but again, my experience begs me to differ. When one of my dogs contracted parvo years ago as a puppy, it was the diarrhea one morning that clued me in, then the lack of appetite. He received immediate treatment and survived, but had I waited even a few more hours, there's every chance he wouldn't have reached his first birthday.

So use your common sense, and call whenever you feel even the slightest twinge that a vet's opinion is warranted. It never hurts just to check in and see what the doctor has to say. That's what he is there for. Making that call is your job and your responsibility in the partnership. To make your job easier, keep the veterinarian's number posted by the telephone along with those of other family doctors. It doesn't hurt to post the number of the National Animal Poison Control Center (888-426-4435, calls to which cost $45 per case; follow-up calls for each case are free). Make sure the pet sitter, the boarding kennel, or anyone who will be taking care of your dog while you're away has these numbers, too.

What to Expect If Your Golden Retriever Is Sick or Injured

When your dog is sick or injured—and I use the word "when" here rather than "if" because it probably will happen—there's every chance he will be anxious to let you know. Though cats can suffer stoically for days before finally deigning to inform their owners that they are in incredible pain or discomfort, dogs tend

Emergency Instructions for the Boarding Kennel/Pet Sitter

What if your dog becomes sick or hurts himself while you are away? If you leave your dog at a boarding kennel, ask if they have a vet on staff or if they use a veterinarian in the area for emergencies. Either way, it's a good idea to give them the name and number of your dog's veterinarian, especially if your Golden has a specific medical condition. If you have hired a dog sitter, leave an emergency list that includes your veterinarian's phone number, the phone number of the local emergency clinic, and the phone number for the National Animal Poison Control Center. Also leave information on any medications your dog needs or any special medical conditions to watch out for. Prepare for the unexpected to ensure your dog gets the care he needs should an emergency occur.

to take the opposite approach. And as linked as Golden Retrievers are to their families, it's the rare Golden who won't immediately let his human family know that something is wrong.

Dogs communicate their pain and their acknowledgment that all is not well in a variety of ways. Sometimes the trouble is obvious, as in the presence of a bleeding wound. But in the absence of such signs, the dog has to be more creative. An ailing dog may attempt to get the necessary attention by staring intently at you; by following family members around as if glued to their legs; by panting loudly (out of pain and/or fear); by behaving in an all-around restless, uncomfortable manner; and perhaps even by leaping into the lap of an unsuspecting owner, hoping that 100 pounds of Golden Retriever on the legs will convince Mom and Dad that he needs help.

Of course there are plenty of cat-like dogs out there, too, who will behave in a stoic manner, pretending that everything is all right, but the observant owner who knows her pet well can recognize the act fairly quickly. Some dogs may hide, which should be another sign to the family that something is wrong. And finally, the dog may exhibit a dramatic change in personality—a normally friendly dog, for example, suddenly growling and threatening to bite. Rather than punishing the dog or banishing him to the backyard, take this sudden change in personality very seriously. Remember when Old Yeller began to turn on his family? Rabies was the reason. There is always a reason for such dramatic shifts in behavior and, although rabies probably won't be the cause, chances are, the reason probably requires veterinary attention.

When you realize your dog needs help, just as always, remain as calm as possible. Remember, he will look to you for guidance on how he should be responding to the pain or strange feelings he is experiencing. If you panic, he will too. Call the veterinarian and tell her everything you can about the dog's condition. Listen carefully to what the doctor says. Again, the calmer you are, the better equipped you will be to act and respond effectively.

Once your dog has visited the veterinarian and problems have been diagnosed and treated through surgery or other forms of treatment, then you need to play dog nurse. The veterinarian will send you home with follow-up instructions for the patient, perhaps involving medications, dressing changes, or the need to keep the dog quiet and still. Follow those orders to the letter, keep a close watch on the patient, and keep in close touch with the doctor. Call if you have any questions, and for your dog's sake, please keep those critical follow-up appointments. In other words, keep up your end of the partnership.

How to "Pill" a Dog

Most dogs will require medication at some time or another—medications that must be administered over the course of a few days or weeks. Amenable animals that they are, Golden Retrievers aren't typically difficult to medicate.

Canine medications are typically in pill form, and the easiest way to administer that pill is to hide it in some type of coveted treat—even a people-food treat for this special situation. Cheese is a simple medium for such purposes as it can be squished effectively around pills of any shape. The cheese ball may then be gobbled up quickly by the enthusiastic Golden patient who is so excited by the scent of cheese that he fails to recognize the faint medicinal odor within. You can hide pills in anything that your dog loves that is squishy, malleable, and dog safe, such as peanut butter or canned dog food.

If, your dog won't take the piece of cheese or the spoonful of peanut butter, you might be able to crush the pill and hide it in your pet's dog food, although most dogs catch on to this pretty easily and may opt to fast that day. If all else fails, you may have to take a more forceful approach. This involves prying the dog's jaws open, and placing the pill on the back of his tongue near the center so that he has no choice but to swallow it. At this point, tilt the dog's head up until he begins to lick his lips, which is usually your sign that he has swallowed the pill. Whether you have to resort to this method, or use the more pleasant cheese-ball method, follow it up with a non-medicated treat, both as a reward and as a chaser for any medicinal aftertaste.

The Costs of Veterinary Medical Care

Veterinary care isn't free. In fact, it can be downright expensive. You want a veterinarian who is highly trained, deeply dedicated, and anxious to keep up on the latest advancements in his field. This individual plies his skills in an office with instruments, equipment, staff, and all the trimmings—all of which cost money to maintain. Most of these doctors don't make the kind of money "people doctors" make, yet we expect them to be just as flawless in their skills—more so, actually, because veterinarians are trying to diagnose problems in patients who can't tell them where or how their bodies hurt.

Although benefiting from the services of such a dedicated practitioner shouldn't break you financially, paying the vet bills is a part of pet care that you should anticipate before you invite a dog into your home, and that you should budget for just as you do for dog food and toys.

How to Discuss Finances with Your Vet

You will be better equipped to budget efficiently for your dog's veterinary care if you first educate yourself about the basics of routine preventive medical care and about the potential problems that could affect your dog, given her breed and personal history. The next step is to choose a veterinarian whom, because of your research, you believe charges reasonable rates for his services— and whom you trust to deal with you honestly and fairly.

Most veterinarians respect the fact that finances are an issue with their clients. Unless they are independently wealthy, most pet owners cannot afford to pay thousands of dollars for ongoing veterinary treatments that may or may not be successful. If you are faced with a tough treatment decision, a veterinarian who is sensitive to these issues will probably broach the subject with you first. If he doesn't, he should be willing to discuss costs honestly when you ask questions, and should not be offended if you wish to get a second opinion.

Let's delve into the fictional world and imagine that the veterinarian has just determined that your Golden Retriever has hip dysplasia (hip dysplasia is discussed in Chapter 5, Common Health Concerns). Discuss the severity of your pet's particular case, the pain she may be experiencing now, and how it may change in the future. If the condition is not severe, but is causing some discomfort, the sensitive veterinarian will probably suggest that you deal with the condition incrementally; a tactic that makes sense and is usually more economical. "Start out with medication, massage, and light exercise," suggests the doctor, "and we'll see how it goes from there." Eventually, surgery may be recommended, or it may be the doctor's first recommendation for a severely affected puppy or dog. Each case is different and requires open communication between pet owner and veterinarian. You can see how fundamental trust will help you through such discussions, which will help you make decisions that you consider practical, humane, and affordable.

It's sad that we have to think of our finances when dealing with an ailing dog, but that's just a fact of life. Many veterinarians are willing to work up payment plans for clients who don't have the immediate cash to pay for treatments or medications with high price tags. Be honest about your desire to help your pet and your ability to pay on a monthly basis. And honor your debts. As much as they'd like to, veterinarians cannot treat every patient *pro bono*, no matter how much they love animals.

And finally, once you've had your honest discussions, you can't feel guilty if the recommended treatment is too expensive for your budget. Most people, as much as they may wish they could and as much as they love their dogs, simply can't afford to pay for major surgery or for treatment of a catastrophic canine illness or injury. This may be further compounded by worry that the treatment or procedure itself will be too painful and traumatic for the dog.

Did You Know?

Big dogs have larger litters than smaller dogs, but smaller dogs generally live longer.

How to Make an Insurance Claim

It's your responsibility as a policyholder to make the best use of your insurance plan. Take these steps to get the most for your money:

1. Designate a file for pet insurance forms.

2. Always take a claim form with you to the veterinarian's office. Many companies require a veterinarian's signature.

3. Make copies of receipts. A receipt must accompany every claim form. Some companies require only copies; others require originals. Keep a copy for your records.

4. Make copies of completed claim forms. If a question or payment issue arises, a copy to review on your end of the phone line will be reassuring.

5. Note an acceptable payment period on your calendar. Reimbursement may slip your mind, and it may be delayed in cases where a problem is encountered and you forget to inquire about the payment's status.

6. Mark claims paid and date received. Leave a paper trail that's easy to understand. Looking back a year later, you'll be glad for the notations.

© 1999 Solveig Fredrickson

Both concerns, that of finances and that of the dog's overall suffering, deserve equal consideration. As the dog's owner, you must determine how these considerations play in to your pet's well-being. Sometimes treatment is the answer. Sometimes simply managing the pain is as far as you are willing and able to go. And sometimes euthanasia is the only option. Be honest with yourself, your veterinarian, and your dog. Do what you can for your pet as the best caretaker you can possibly be, and don't allow guilt to influence you. There's no room for it when you are faced with the tough decisions.

10 Questions to Ask Every Provider

Before choosing a pet insurance or membership plan, be sure to get straightforward answers to all your questions. If it makes you more comfortable, get the answers in writing.

1. Does your policy follow fee/benefits schedules? If so, please send me your detailed coverage limits. In the meantime, please give me examples of coverage limits for three common canine procedures so I can compare them to my current veterinary charges.

2. Does your policy cover basic wellness care, or does it cover only accidents and illnesses? Do you offer a wellness care endorsement that I can purchase on top of my basic plan for an additional fee? What other endorsements do you offer, and how much do they cost?

3. Under your policy's rules, can I continue taking my dog to his current veterinarian, or do I need to switch to another veterinarian?

4. Does your policy cover hereditary conditions, congenital conditions or pre-existing conditions? Please explain each coverage or exclusion as it pertains specifically to my dog. Is there a feature where pre-existing conditions will be covered if my dog's pre-existing condition requires no treatment after a specified period? What is that period?

5. What happens to my premium and to my dog's policy if your company goes out of business? What guarantees do I have that I won't be throwing my money away?

6. How quickly do you pay claims?

7. What is your policy's deductible? Does the deductible apply per incident or annually? How does the deductible differ per plan?

8. Does the policy have payment limits over a year's period or during my pet's lifetime? How do the payment limits differ per plan?

9. What is the A.M. Best Co. rating of your insurance underwriter, and what does that rating mean?

10. Is there a cancellation period after I receive my policy or membership? How long do I have to review all my materials once I receive them, and what is the cancellation procedure?

Savings Plans and Insurance Plans—How They Can Help

In this era of HMOs and managed care in human medicine, there are plans offering similar options for the care of animals. In a variation of the traditional human health insurance concept, participating pet owners pay a set annual fee (which tends to increase as the dog ages), and receive certain veterinary services at either no charge or at a discount. The services vary by plan, but most do make provisions for specified serious illnesses. The problem is that the companies tend to come and go, so it's difficult to determine which will be in business next year. Nevertheless, they do help to offer a sense of security to those who are nervous about providing for their pet's future medical care, and they have been helpful to many owners faced with hefty vet bills.

If you're uncomfortable with canine health insurance, yet worry about future veterinary expenses, put some money away on a regular basis for "a rainy day" so you'll be prepared should your dog require costly veterinary treatment someday. Even the healthiest dogs eventually face challenges to their health that can require effective and expensive treatment. Start saving early for that eventuality, and you'll be more comfortable making the tough decisions later. It's for a good cause: your dog's health, comfort, and continued presence within your family.

5

Common
Health Concerns

In This Chapter

o Health Concerns Specific to Golden Retrievers
o Illnesses and Emergencies
o Is Your Golden Overweight?

N o matter how well-bred a dog may be, there comes a time when every dog becomes ill or injured. The savvy owner acknowledges this fact of life with dogs and prepares for the inevitable.

As we saw in Chapter 4, Goldens who have been initiated to the veterinary experience properly tend to enjoy their veterinary visits just as much as they do visits to the park. But sometimes the visit is more than fun and games. You make the appointment because you're worried. Your companion is ailing. Maybe it's just a slight limp. Perhaps it's a loss of appetite or a subtle change in attitude. Or it could be something more serious—something that involves

blood. Either way, you have to resist the temptation to panic. Remain calm, and get the dog to the doctor.

Educate yourself about what can go wrong with a dog's health and what you can do both to prevent and respond to such conditions, and you can reduce that inevitable worry considerably. You may not be able to protect your pup from all the bugs and dangers in the world, but you can ensure that he goes through life with an owner who is educated—an owner who cares.

Health Concerns Specific to Golden Retrievers

Before we get into the discussion of the conditions common to every dog, we'll first take a look at the problems, most of them passed on through the generations, about which those who live with Goldens need to be particularly aware. Every breed is prone to some type of condition—some breeds, and even some individual dogs, are prone to more conditions than others. As we have seen, you need to think about this before you even choose the dog who comes to live with you. No matter how well you have chosen and how diligently you have educated yourself, however, there is no guarantee that your Golden will escape every health problem out there. Read on and learn, just in case.

Hip Dysplasia

Probably the most common, and often the most serious, problem to affect the Golden Retriever is the malformation of the hips known as hip dysplasia. Because this condition is presumed to be passed on from parent to puppy, responsible Golden owners—especially responsible Golden *breeders*—have their dogs tested according to the protocols set by the Orthopedic Foundation for Animals (OFA). This involves x-raying a dog's hips at age two to determine how and if she is affected by hip dysplasia (the dog can, of course, be x-rayed at an earlier age, but only dogs of at least two years of age can be OFA certified). The x-ray results are subsequently evaluated by the OFA, which then certifies the dog with a rating ranging from "poor" to "excellent." In an ideal world, only those dogs who boast an OFA "Excellent" or "Good" rating would be bred. Because ours is not an ideal world, however—and because countless Goldens are bred that are never even x-rayed— this breed is one whose name commonly appears near the top of the list of dysplastic breeds.

If you find that your dog is dysplastic, don't panic. There are varying degrees of the condition's expression. I have known dysplastic dogs who, with proper diet and exercise, thrived and lived actively well into their teens with relatively little pain. Yet I have also known dogs who were diagnosed before their first birthday with severe hip dysplasia that required a series of surgeries just to enable the poor pups to walk. Witnessing dogs endure such ongoing procedures and pain truly drives home the critical importance of selective breeding.

Did You Know?

Dogs have extremely sensitive hearing and a sense of smell up to 1,000 times better than humans to compensate for their relatively poor eyesight.

While some cases of hip dysplasia can be managed with anti-inflammatory medications, moderate exercise, weight control, and proper feeding during puppyhood to promote slow growth and proper development, surgical correction is sometimes the only remedy for a seriously affected animal. Surgeries themselves range from the minor to the extreme. Though vast improvements are being made every day in the correction and replacement of dysplastic canine hips, surgery of this type can, of course, be emotionally and physically traumatic to both dog and owner. It can also be quite costly. Dysplasia treatment must thus be approached wisely and with common sense. Not every owner can afford to devote the kids' college fund to the surgical correction of the family pet's hip joints. And not every owner wishes to subject a pet to extreme and/or multiple surgeries. Either way, the decision must be guided by love and compassion, not by guilt.

Consider a poor four-year-old pup we'll call Arthur, a big sweet thing who could barely walk because of the pain in his hips. It was a difficult decision for his owners to give him up to a Golden Retriever rescue group when they were informed of his severe hip dysplasia, but they simply could not afford the surgical procedures required to correct his condition. Now, several surgeries and almost $10,000 in veterinary bills later—and months of pain for the dog—it looks like Arthur has made it through his ordeal. But was it worth it?

I have to admit that opting for the surgery would not have been my choice—but neither would sending a severely dysplastic dog to a rescue group. If all alternative therapies—such as nutrition and weight control, pain and anti-inflammatory drug therapies, and even acupuncture—had failed, I probably would have chosen euthanasia as the kindest choice for a case such as Arthur's. I personally have a hard time imagining subjecting a dog to multiple surgeries and all the attendant trauma, but the key word here is "personally." This is a most personal decision, and in most cases, there are no right or wrong answers.

The bottom line is that a dog with hip dysplasia needs an owner who is attuned to his needs and his condition, and who is willing to work closely with the veterinarian in determining the therapy route for that dog. Sometimes this condition can be controlled well through diet, exercise, drug therapy, and massage. If, however, surgery is the only option, and a course that you wish to follow, pursue this aim with a skilled, board-certified, veterinary orthopedic surgeon and feel free to obtain second opinions. Regardless of your decision, make sure you have a veterinarian you can trust, who is up-front and honest with you, and who is sensitive to the difficult decisions that can accompany the treatment of hip dysplasia.

Epilepsy

That first seizure can be frightening. It was for Golden Retriever rescuer Cheryl Minnier of Stonecroft Goldens in Dushore, Pennsylvania. Cheryl had spent months nursing an abused and abandoned Golden named Moses back to health, when, suddenly, he had his first seizure. Today, several seizures, medical tests, and veterinary consultations later, the Minnier family has learned to deal with Moses' seizures, to remain calm when they occur, to make sure someone is near Moses when a seizure begins, and to expect him to be up and around, his old cheerful self again, in a few minutes.

Because epilepsy is not uncommon in Golden Retrievers (and its causes are typically elusive though presumed to be hereditary), owners are wise to get over that first seizure quickly and remind themselves that while some cases can be quite severe and even life-threatening, in most cases epilepsy is nothing to fear. Nevertheless, the seizure should not be ignored. The first seizure means a veterinary visit is in order to rule out other non-epilepsy causes, such as a brain tumor, injury-related brain damage, or poisoning, and to get advice on how seizures can be controlled.

Once you receive a confirmed diagnosis of epilepsy, your dog may be one whose seizures can be controlled by anti-convulsant drugs similar to those that control seizures in humans. Whether or not your dog is a candidate for drug therapy, try to keep his stress to a minimum, feed him a proper diet, and make sure he receives regular exercise. Epilepsy need not spell a premature end to your relationship.

Skin Problems

It's not unusual to find bald patches, rashes, or hot spots on the coat and skin of a Golden Retriever. Stories abound of Goldens who suffer from skin problems. Those stories have, in fact, become so commonplace that you might start to think that these problems are official characteristics hailing from the breed's standard (they're not).

As we discovered in Chapter 3, Goldens are prone to food allergies, which can manifest in skin rashes and coat problems. Also common are various lumps and bumps, which are typically discovered during grooming sessions. Though most of these are benign in nature, they should all be called to the attention of the veterinarian as many warrant biopsy and surgical removal. The doctor will determine what, if any, course of action might be necessary.

Hot spots are another Golden problem. This is a specific type of dermatitis that results in patches of swollen, eventually bald, skin that is warm to the touch, quite painful, and may even emit pus and an unpleasant odor. Hot spots are best addressed as the wounds that they are. Begin with a veterinary examination. The doctor will probably prescribe a low-dose steroid or antibiotics and advise you to keep the area clean and hair-free. He may also have you apply some type of topical medication or household solution (such as diluted hydrogen peroxide) to the site. The greatest challenge may be to keep your pet from disturbing the healing area, from biting it or licking at it. This then becomes your grand opportunity to practice your skills of canine distraction.

Eye Problems

Canine eye problems, especially those transmitted genetically, are tracked by the Canine Eye Registration Foundation (CERF). To earn healthy-eye status from CERF, a dog must be examined each year by a qualified veterinary ophthalmologist, and, as with hip dysplasia, those dogs who don't pass the test should not be bred. CERF certification should be another documented element you ask for when looking for a dog or puppy from a breeder. Conscientious breeders take eye problems seriously and have their breeding animals examined and certified each year.

The primary conditions of which you should be aware are progressive retinal atrophy and central progressive retinal atrophy, the latter of which is becoming more common in Goldens. Both of these conditions cause progressive deterioration of the retina and destroy the overall quality of the dog's vision. This in turn can lead to behavioral changes in the affected dog, who may be confused by the fact that she once could see at night but now can't, or that she can see objects that are moving but not those that are standing still. We would no doubt find this rather disconcerting, as well. Goldens tend to be quite adaptable animals, and many have adjusted handsomely to limited vision or an entire loss of vision—I have actually known blind dogs who would run and play and defy all suspicion that they could not see. Despite this adaptability, however, it is to the dog's and the breed's benefit to help prevent such problems from ever becoming an issue in the first place through careful selective breeding and breed-stock screening.

Another eye problem common to Goldens is cataracts, a condition in which the lens of the eye grows hazy and opaque, often with a bluish or grayish caste to it. A cataract may affect only a small spot on, or the entire surface of, the lens, and, depending on the severity of a particular case, can ultimately lead to blindness. While the development of cataracts is common in the eyes of older dogs, and in many cases can be surgically corrected as in humans, there are specific hereditary cataracts characterized by early onset that affect several breeds, including the Golden Retriever. Hence, we find more evidence in support of genetic screening of breeding stock—and of the spaying and neutering of dogs affected by hereditary conditions.

Hypothyroidism

One condition the veterinarian should explore when presented with a Golden Retriever with skin problems and an unexplained weight gain is hypothyroidism, a condition where the thyroid gland is not performing as it should. Presumed to be somewhat hereditary, the sluggish thyroid that is caused by hypothyroidism results in skin and coat problems, obesity, and lethargy, the latter of which should be pretty evident in a dog who is customarily active and playful.

A dog with hypothyroidism, just like a person with the condition, does not naturally receive adequate thyroid hormones to fuel his many activities. This hormonal deficiency, coupled with a related slowed metabolism, can result in an all-around less-than-ideal quality of life for a Golden Retriever. The good news is that hypothyroidism is relatively simple to diagnose and control. Successful management does, however, require an owner who is observant enough to recognize what can be gradual symptoms and report them to the veterinarian, and dedicated enough to administer the necessary medication to the dog every day.

The veterinarian can diagnose this condition with blood tests and can then determine a proper dosage of an oral thyroid supplement to compensate for what is lacking in the dog's system. Of the many illnesses and conditions with which dogs can struggle, this is one of the easier to manage—assuming of course the affected dog lives with someone who is dedicated to taking on this rather simple management responsibility for the remainder of the dog's life.

> Recent progress in canine health care has resulted in a vast body of ever-increasing knowledge concerning the many ailments that can affect our canine companions.

The Sick Pup

Modern-day dogs are more fortunate in the area of health than any dogs in history. Recent progress in canine health care has resulted in a vast body of ever-increasing knowledge concerning the many ailments that can affect our canine companions. As your dog's owner, you are responsible for seeing that your pet receives the help she requires—preferably as soon as possible in the course of the illness. In most cases, the sooner treatment begins, the better the chance of recovery.

You will be better equipped to carry out this important duty if you know what to look for. This means getting to know your dog well—her habits, the contour of her skin and structure, her typical behavior, her daily rhythms—so that you'll be able to recognize right away when something diverges from the norm.

Signs of Illness

First, let's clear up one bit of confusion that typically emerges when the subject is illness. When we discuss such unpleasantries as severe diarrhea, excess salivation, seizures, loss of bowel control, and vomiting, these are not in themselves illnesses. They are *symptoms* of illnesses, vivid signs that all is not right within a dog's internal systems. When you notice your dog suffering from one of these signs, it's time to get him to the veterinarian.

Sometimes the signs are unmistakable: vomiting that won't stop and the dog's complete inability to keep anything in her stomach; diarrhea that lasts for more than one trip to the bathroom—especially when the diarrhea is tinged with blood or mucus; an abdomen that swells shortly after the dog eats; or a sudden inability to move or walk. It would be both dangerous and cruel to convince yourself that such symptoms will just disappear on their own.

But sometimes, the signs are more subtle. They develop gradually and are just as gradually recognized by the person with whom the dog lives. These can range from a change in energy levels, to periodic anxious behavior accompanied by heavy panting, to a disinterest in a game or activity that used to inspire tailspins, to a gradual loss of appetite. Illness can also make itself known in the dog's bathroom habits, as well as in the consistency and color of urine and feces. An increase or decrease in urination, or straining behavior that produces little urine, for example, are pretty clear signs that something has changed. An-

> You are wise to pay close attention to all aspects of your pet's day-to-day life, and remind yourself that you must not be embarrassed or afraid to consult your veterinarian about even your smallest suspicions.

other clear sign of a problem is a reduction in the number of a dog's daily bowel movements, from three to one, for example, over the course of several days.

You are wise to pay close attention to all aspects of your pet's day-to-day life, and remind yourself that you must not be embarrassed or afraid to consult your veterinarian about even your smallest suspicions. Sure, it might be frightening to acknowledge that something could be wrong with your pup, but ignoring the situation and deciding not to call the veterinarian will not make the problem magically vanish. It will only give the condition more time to take hold. When it comes to members of your family, wouldn't you rather be safe than sorry?

Illnesses and Emergencies

Now that you know to be ever vigilant to both subtle and sudden signs of illness that can afflict the unsuspecting dog—and now that you know what to look for—let's take a look at some of the illnesses that might cause those symptoms. Never underestimate your role in the protection of your pet's health. With your keen eye and instinct, and some rudimentary knowledge on your part of the illnesses that threaten the canine species, the veterinarian will be better able to make the proper diagnosis and begin treatment during that crucial early stage.

Canine Bloat

Though canine bloat, or gastric dilatation volvulus, can affect any dog, it is a great fear of those who live with larger dogs, who tend to

be the most prone to the condition. This fear became a reality for trainer Janet L. Boss of Ellicott City, Maryland, when her Golden, Teddy, began to exhibit the classic signs of this condition one day about an hour after he had enjoyed a leisurely meal. "He was moaning, salivating, and trying to figure out whether he wanted to lie down or stand up," remembers Janet. In response, Janet did exactly what one should do when faced with this situation: She rushed her pet to the veterinarian. Because she acted quickly, the gas trapped in Teddy's stomach was relieved without surgery. But had the condition been allowed to linger and the stomach had twisted, an event known as torsion, he would have died without surgical intervention.

Bloat is just what its name implies: Gas and fluids build up in the dog's stomach, typically after mealtime. The stomach bloats, and, if not relieved, eventually twists, trapping the gases permanently. The condition is uncomfortable, excruciatingly painful, and, without professional veterinary treatment, deadly.

The veterinarian may be able to release the gas by inserting a tube into the stomach, but once torsion occurs, the stomach must be readjusted and anchored surgically. You can help prevent bloat by feeding your dog several small meals throughout the day rather than one large meal, by feeding dogs within a multi-dog household separately so they will be less inclined to gobble their food, and by not feeding a dog immediately before or after a vigorous exercise session. Beyond that, get accustomed to watching your pup carefully, especially after meal times, for the tell-tale signs of this deadly condition which warrants an immediate trip to the animal hospital.

Gastrointestinal Disease

Various illnesses can attack the canine digestive tract and some of these are quite deadly. While we won't be discussing the symptoms

and treatments of most of the illnesses for which dogs are vaccinated, we will discuss those that fall into these particular categories: canine parvovirus and coronavirus.

You may recall from the vaccination discussion in Chapter 4, that sometimes even a dog who has been fully vaccinated against parvovirus can contract the disease. Having been through it myself with one of my dogs, this is a heartbreaking experience. The virus attacks the dog's intestinal tract, causing fever, lethargy, vomiting, loss of appetite, life-threatening dehydration, and bloody diarrhea. Coronavirus is marked by the same basic signs, but the virus is not quite as vicious.

In either case, the virus itself cannot be treated. Treatment is supportive in nature, meaning that the veterinarian does all he or she can to strengthen and comfort the patient in hopes that the dog's own immune system can successfully fight off the invading organisms. Depending on the health of the dog and how quickly treatment is sought, you may not know for several days whether the dog will survive. How joyous it is when you realize that he's going to make it. How well I remember finally seeing the spark return to my own dog's eyes. He could barely stand, but I knew he had won. Not all dogs are so fortunate.

A less dramatic gastrointestinal condition is gastritis. The causes of this inflammation of the stomach lining vary dramatically, from a poor diet, to poisoning, to the ingestion of a foreign object, to malformation and uncoordinated activity of various stomach muscles. Treatment is thus equally varied, ranging from a change of diet to surgical intervention. Regardless of cause, the signs of gastritis typically include: loss of appetite, lethargy, weight loss, vomiting, and, when poor diet is the culprit, a poor-

quality haircoat. The veterinarian is the one most qualified to determine the cause of a particular case and to prescribe appropriate treatment.

Respiratory Illness

Dogs are prone to many of the same types of respiratory illnesses that we are, but this does not mean you should offer them a tablet or two of the same over-the-counter remedy you take when your nose stuffs up. Rather, look for symptoms that indicate that all may not be right within the dog's nose and lungs and consult the veterinarian for proper diagnosis and treatment.

And just what might those symptoms be? Any type of coughing, for one, especially coughing that seems to go on for days (and nights), and coughing that seems to cause the dog pain. Wheezing is not uncommon in the ailing dog either. The veterinarian may determine that the dog is suffering from bronchitis, asthma, or canine cough (also known as kennel cough, which typically causes a cough that resembles a honk). Most of these ailments can be managed successfully with medications and a reduction of stress and exposure to air pollutants. Sometimes, however, the condition requires more serious treatment, as is the case when the dog's condition progresses into pneumonia, or is caused by a collapsed trachea (often a chronic condition caused by a malformed trachea that may require surgical correction), or a blockage caused by a foreign object. The lesson to be learned here is that we must never ignore a cough.

Urinary Tract Disorders

Unfortunately, dogs are quite prone to disorders of the urinary tract, ranging from bladder infections and bladder stones to the more deadly kidney failure. Again, I have some experience myself with these conditions, including kidney failure, which claimed the life of one of my dogs without warning. I have witnessed firsthand how painful these conditions can be for their victims.

There is little you can do to prevent the onset of urinary tract disorders, but there is much you can do to help ensure they don't run amok. First and foremost, observe your dog each and every day and get acquainted with his bathroom habits. You'll notice instantly, as I have, when your pet suddenly begins to lap up great amounts of water but cannot excrete it through urination (a sign of kidney problems), or when, on your daily walk, he strains and strains to urinate on all his familiar territorial markers yet produces little or no urine (a typical sign of a bladder infection, especially if you notice blood in the urine, as well). As soon as you notice such signs, get him to the veterinarian immediately.

Treatment varies with condition. First the veterinarian will diagnose the problem, which today, thanks to veterinary medical advancements, may be done relatively easily with a urine test (urinalysis) and blood tests. Once diagnosed, treatments can include medication (antibiotics, for instance, can usually clear up a bladder infection), surgery, and/or dietary management with special or prescription diets. Regardless of the condition, success typically rests with the immediacy of the treatment. The sooner you act, the better chance your pet has, and the less suffering he'll likely have to endure.

Parasites Inside and Out

No one enjoys pondering the idea of tiny organisms that feed on our dogs. But parasites are a fact of life, and one that we had better acknowledge if we are to protect our pets from their invasions. What follows are descriptions of the major parasites that lay in wait to hop aboard an available canine host.

Fleas and Ticks   The most common, most infuriating canine parasites are the bloodsucker twins: fleas and ticks. These tiny vampires can wreak unspeakable havoc for their victims and the people with whom their victims live. Fleas actually take the ultimate "bloodsucker" title, but fleas and ticks are usually mentioned together in the same breath because by launching a three-pronged attack on fleas on the dog, in the house, and in the yard, you usually fight ticks as well. (The control of fleas and ticks is discussed in greater detail in Chapter 7, Grooming).

Fleas, which are evident either by the presence of fleas themselves on the dog's skin or by the dark flea excrement known as "flea dirt" that they leave behind, cause untold misery with their itchy bites. And they're not discriminatory. They'll bite everyone in the household—both canine and human. The misery they cause is most profound when a flea infestation leads to flea-bite dermatitis, an endless skin irritation that affects the many dogs who are allergic to flea saliva. Flea-bite dermatitis continues to irritate long after the fleas are gone, potentially leading to secondary skin infections and compulsive scratching, self-licking, and self-biting. As if that weren't enough, fleas are also carriers of the relatively benign tapeworm (which we'll discuss in a moment). The effects of this worm, coupled with blood lost to fleas, can leave a puppy unkempt and anemic (deficient in iron).

Recently several new medications have been introduced to help in the battle against fleas. Talk to your vet to determine which one is right for your dog. Always consult with a vet before combining flea treatments, whether prescription or over-the-counter, to avoid harming your dog.

Imidocloprid comes packaged in individually dosed vials based on the weight of your dog. It can be used on puppies eight weeks or older. It is in a liquid form, and when placed on the fur over the shoulders of your dog, provides flea protection for at least a month.

Fipronil kills both fleas and ticks. For fleas, it can be used every three months, but to kill ticks, it should be used once a month. The sprayable form can be difficult to use on a big dog since dosage is extremely important and you should use one to two sprays per pound of dog. The liquid version is much easier. You apply one vial to the fur on the shoulders of your dog. You should use gloves when applying to your pet and, since fipronil is flammable, keep your freshly dosed dog away from fire until the drug has dried.

> Tick-borne illnesses can be quite serious, so it is important always to examine your dog carefully from head to toe after any excursion into tick-infested areas.

Lufenuron is sold as a tablet or combined with heartworm, hookworm, roundworm, and whipworm control in Sentinel. The drug stops the creation of chitin, which makes up the exoskeleton of a flea. The drug is very safe, and while it does not kill adult fleas, it prevents the next generation (the larvae) from growing into adults. Lufenuron can be used on puppies as young as six weeks old.

Ticks can also cause itching, but they are most notorious as carriers of disease, such as Lyme disease and Rocky Mountain spotted fever. Tick-borne illnesses can be quite serious, so it is important to examine your dog carefully from head to toe after any excursion into tick-infested areas. Should you find a small, dark, round, engorged tick on your pet's skin, it will need to be removed to prevent it from injecting disease-causing agents into the dog's body. If the dog is riddled with ticks, veterinary assistance may be in order.

To remove a tick, grasp it firmly yet gently as close to your dog's skin as possible using tweezers or a special tick remover. Do not use your fingers unless absolutely necessary (for example, if you are hiking in a remote area and have left tweezers out of your first aid kit) because the tick could spread disease to you. Pull back with a steady motion until the critter disengages. Never try to harm the tick while it is still attached, such as by placing a hot match on its rear end, as this will only anger it and could cause it to spew disease-laden saliva into your dog. Once the tick is free, flush it down the toilet or drop it in alcohol to kill it. Apply rubbing alcohol to the site of the tick bite and an ice pack if the area swells. Watch for signs of illness that could emerge in the days and weeks to follow, particularly a stiff walk and lethargy, which could indicate Lyme disease. Report such symptons to the vet right away.

Heartworm Disease   The heartworm is a potentially fatal parasite. This long, skinny worm that veterinarians often display in jars in their offices to drive the prevention point home, migrates to the dog's heart through the bloodstream via entrance gained by way of a mosquito bite. The worm settles in the dog's heart and pulmonary arteries, ultimately choking off the organ's activity and killing the canine host.

An added heartworm threat is the fact that the long and arduous treatment for ridding the body of this parasite is almost as dangerous as the infestation itself. It is thus worth our while to test our dogs' blood annually for the presence of the worms in the bloodstream, and to offer our dogs a heartworm preventive, which is usually administered once a month. This active (and very effective) prevention program should take place seasonally where mosquitoes appear only during the warmer months of the year, and annually in areas where they are a year-round scourge. That's not much effort to protect your dog from the unspeakable horrors of a heartworm infestation.

Tapeworms   Less of a horror is the tapeworm, although seeing small rice-like segments of this worm squirming around your pet's rear end may summon images of the cinema's more disgusting scream fests. More repulsive than dangerous (unless their victims are young puppies or frail adults who can't afford even a small amount of blood loss), tapeworms find their way into the dog's body by way of an intermediary: a carrier flea that a dog inadvertently ingests. Having gained access, the tapeworm embeds its head into the wall of the dog's small intestine and proceeds to grow strings of egg packets that break off and are eliminated from the body in the dog's feces. The packets are in turn ingested by a hungry flea, who then infests another unsuspecting host and carries on the tapeworm life cycle. Several prescription medications are available should you notice the tell-tale, unmistakable signs of tapeworm infestation, so a visit to the veterinarian can help ease the disgust you experience when you make your unfortunate discovery.

Roundworms and Hookworms   Two other intestinal worms are the roundworm and the hookworm. A dog can contract hookworms when he is exposed to hookworm larvae in feces from an infected dog. Roundworms are transmitted when a dog comes into contact with roundworm eggs in the soil. Puppies, who are more severely affected than are adult dogs, can actually contract them in utero or from their mother's milk.

You may be able to spot the worms in your pet's feces, although often only a veterinarian can detect their presence. It's wise, then, to have the feces of an active, outdoorsy Golden examined each year by the veterinarian to detect and stop any infestation (this involves simply taking a fresh fecal sample to the office for examination). Though you will see "over-the-counter" deworming medications available at pet supply stores, it's best to consult the veterinarian for treatment, as he can determine precisely which worm you need to attack, and the best, and safest, medication for the job. In the meantime, you can try to prevent infestation by restricting your dog's exploration of feces from other dogs and soil in public areas frequented by a large canine population.

Coccidia   Coccidia are one-celled protozoa that cause a disease called coccidiosis, a common problem in overcrowded, unsanitary kennels. It is also a serious problem for puppies—and yet another reason why you should steer clear of puppies from unsanitary, overcrowded breeding situations (like commercial puppy mills).

A dog can be a host to this potentially dangerous intestinal organism and appear healthy enough himself. But then, in a moment of physical weakness, the coccidia can blossom, causing a full-blown infection that results in all the classic signs of illness: bloody diarrhea, general weakness, anemia, loss of appetite, and dehydration

(all of which can be potentially deadly to young puppies). Only the veterinarian is qualified to make the proper diagnosis of this disease and to prescribe the specific medications designed to treat the infection. If the infection has been allowed to progress unchecked, the treatment regimen may include supportive fluid therapy to reverse the effects of anemia and dehydration.

Collecting a Fecal Sample

When you take your dog out to eliminate, bring along a plastic sandwich bag and a container in which to store the sample. A clean plastic dish with a lid, such as an empty margarine tub, is ideal.

Place the plastic bag over your hand, pick up the sample, and place it in the container. It should be collected no more than 12 hours before your dog is examined by the veterinarian. Refrigerate it until you can get to the veterinary clinic.

Giardia   Giardia is another protozoal threat to the canine family, one typically contracted when a dog is exposed to feces from an infected dog, or when he laps up giardia-infested water from an infected water source (a common threat to dogs out hiking with their owners). The giardia organism is equally transmittable to humans, causing blood- and mucous-tinged diarrhea in both its canine and human victims. Prevention for both parties includes staying away from feces and water that might be contaminated, and keeping your home clean and disinfected. Treatment for both species should be sought only from professional practitioners.

Ringworm   Contrary to its name, ringworm is not a worm at all, but a fungus. The condition takes its name from the fungus' habit of forming a red, hairless, ring-like shape at the infection site on its victim's skin. It hops from victim to victim (who may be human as well as canine), either through direct animal-to-animal contact, or through soil that harbors ringworm spores. Left unchecked, the itchy rings will become increasingly irritated, scaly, and sore. It's rare that an owner won't notice the tell-tale ring on her pet's skin, so consult the veterinarian for both diagnosis and treatment, the latter of which may include a combination of topical and oral medications.

Demodectic Mange (Demodicosis) Caused by a tiny mite known as *Demodex canis,* demodectic mange, or demodicosis, can affect dogs to varying degrees, from a mild irritation to a life-threatening infestation. Virtually every dog plays host to a population of these mites, which reside in the hair follicles. Most inherit these mites from their mothers during the first days of puppyhood and remain unaffected by their presence. But if a dog is either born with a weak immune system or develops one later in life, these opportunistic mites can take advantage of the situation and begin to multiply their numbers, resulting in a case of demodicosis. The dogs at greatest risk are those who have suffered severe health problems, abandonment, and neglect (just ask those who have devoted their lives to Golden Retriever rescue). Researchers believe that dogs born to parents who themselves had problems with this disease may also be at risk.

Treatment, which must be carried out by a veterinarian (who is also the one best equipped to diagnose the condition), depends on the severity of the case. The most common signs of what is known as localized demodicosis (which is most common in young dogs) are hair loss and scaly, red skin, usually on and around the head, face, and forelegs. This may be treated by a veterinarian-prescribed topical medication formulated to kill mites, or the condition may just correct itself on its own. A more severe case known as generalized demodicosis, on the other hand, will involve more widespread hair loss, scaling, irritation, and inflammation, as well as secondary infections. Such a case must be treated aggressively by a veterinarian with mite medications and dips to eradicate the mites, and antibiotics for the secondary infections. Such treatment can take weeks, and the prognosis is never guaranteed positive.

Sarcoptic Mange (Scabies)   A potentially more irritating mite-caused condition is sarcoptic mange, or scabies. This is caused by mites who reside on a dog's skin—usually the skin on the dog's belly, ear flaps, and front legs. Once they have gained access to such a site, the mites reproduce rapidly and are highly contagious from one dog to the other, causing incessant scratching and biting, hair loss, and skin damage.

Unlike certain cases of demodicosis, scabies will not go away on its own. Diagnosis and treatment can, however, be quite frustrating, and should be pursued in partnership with the dog's veterinarian. Once the doctor confirms a sarcoptic mange diagnosis, treatment involves weeks of bathing and dipping the dog (and any other dogs and cats in the household) with special shampoos and dips, antibiotics for any secondary infections that may have cropped up, and corticosteroids to help relieve the itching that invariably accompanies this condition. As for prevention, keep your home clean and restrict your dog's exposure to strays and similarly unknown dogs who may be carriers of these devastating parasites.

> As for prevention (of mites), keep your home clean and restrict your dog's exposure to strays and similarly unknown dogs who may be carriers of these devastating parasites.

What to Do in Case of an Emergency

Some illnesses and health conditions take their time to develop, affording you the luxury of seeking veterinary treatment at your convenience. But when you are faced with an emergency, you may need to act fast. And if you happen to be in a remote location at the time, perhaps on a mountain hike far from the nearest animal hospital, you may need to play paramedic yourself until you can get your dog to the veterinarian. Before we address just how you might someday have to go about this, we will take a look at the circumstances that can lead to the need for emergency medical care.

Dogs can suffer a wide variety of injuries in the course of their daily activities, resulting in a wide variety of emergency situations. These can involve profuse bleeding, shock, broken bones, a foreign object lodged in the windpipe, and the ingestion of a poisonous plant or substance. These situations can arise from an equally wide variety of circumstances, from an unprovoked attack by a neighborhood canine bully, to the unfortunate meeting with the tires of a moving automobile, to the chewing of a live electrical cord, to the intentional swallowing of a tack or other foreign object.

You can't go through life protecting your pet by locking him into a gilded cage, but there are steps you can take to increase the odds that he will remain safe as he goes through his day. When you consider the potential for accidents that lurks in your dog's everyday life, you can see why it's important to keep him on leash and to get him obedience trained. Both contribute to the ultimate safety of your dog.

Even a beautifully trained and flawlessly obedient Golden can be tempted at times by either a rousing game of catch or another dog's invitation to play. If a busy street stands between the dog and that irresistible temptation, you'll be thankful that your pup is on a leash. If he's not, let's hope you boned up on your first-aid skills.

Someday, when you least expect it, you may be called to save your dog's life. If at that fateful moment you are not prepared with both know-how and equipment, your dog could suffer severe consequences—and you could be sentenced to a lifetime of guilt. Read on and regard the following not as an end-all reference on canine first aid, but as an introduction to the kinds of emergencies you might expect when living with a dog, and how you might go about helping a dog in need.

As you read, remember that even a mild-mannered Golden who is hurting from a sudden and serious injury may be frightened and thus uncharacteristically aggressive toward those who try to help her. Don't take this personally (and make sure you include a muzzle in your canine first-aid kit, just in case). Put yourself in your pup's situation. You probably wouldn't be the most tolerant patient either, if you were hit by a car when you were running out to catch a Frisbee.

Shock

A dog who experiences an unfortunate meeting with a live electrical cord, an oncoming car, or some other major trauma, is a prime candidate for the condition known as shock. You'll know a dog is in shock if he is lying very quietly and refusing to stand; he has a weak, though rapid, pulse; his breathing is shallow; his body temperature has plummeted well below the canine norm of 100 to 102 degrees Fahrenheit; and his gums are pale.

With the onset of shock, heroic veterinary treatment is usually the dog's only chance of survival. Without treatment to stabilize the animal, the next stage is coma, followed by death. To prevent this, get your dog to the vet immediately. Try to keep the animal warm with a blanket or a heating pad wrapped

Did You Know?

The tallest dog on record was 42 inches tall at the shoulders and weighed 238 pounds.

inside a towel, and do your best to keep him relaxed. You must also get any bleeding under control (see the following section for advice on how to control bleeding).

This can be quite a challenge: You struggle to maintain your own calm as well as your dog's, while simultaneously controlling blood flow, stabilizing broken bones, and keeping the dog still so as not to cause further injury, all with the ultimate goal of getting your patient to the veterinarian as quickly as possible. A makeshift stretcher made out of a large blanket can help, as can your own steely demeanor. Keep a cool head. Your dog depends on you. There will be ample time for tears later, after your pet is safely in the hands of the veterinarian.

Bone Fractures

Broken bones can be the result of a variety of circumstances: a fight with another dog, a fall while hiking, an encounter with a moving car, or even, as was the case with a Golden Retriever I once met, an encounter with a moving train (this latter fellow, by the way, survived the event with the help of a devoted rescuer and lived happily for many years thereafter, albeit with three legs). Regardless of cause, broken bones must never be viewed as conditions that you can or should treat on your own.

> Broken bones must never be viewed as conditions that you can or should treat on your own.

Given the active nature of the species, the most common site of broken bones in dogs is the leg. You should suspect a broken bone if, of course, you see it protruding from the leg or other part of the body. But you should also suspect a break if the dog cannot stand or walk, if he limps, if you notice a sudden swelling, or if your pet exhibits uncharacteristic aggression—the latter of which can be a natural response to the intense pain caused by a fracture. An immediate trip to the veterinarian is in order to confirm your suspicions and have the bone tended to properly. The treatment regimen will closely follow that for human bone breaks: x-rays, resetting of the bone, pain medication, casting, and perhaps even surgery.

Regardless of where the fracture might be, you can employ the same basic techniques to get the dog to the veterinarian as you do for shock (which the dog may also be experiencing). And as with shock, you don't want to injure him further in the process. First, evaluate your pet's demeanor. If your dog is blinded by the pain, you may first need to muzzle him so you can help him. Use either a commercially available leather muzzle, or a strip of soft cotton bandage, or nylon stockings (be careful not to restrict the dog's breathing by applying the muzzle too tightly, and remove it as soon as it is no longer necessary). A large blanket or flat board can act as a stretcher. If you are fairly certain of a leg break, and your patient is amenable, you can immobilize the leg further by wrapping a thick towel around it. Remember to keep calm. Your dog is relying on you for strength and relief from his own fear.

> Remember to keep calm. Your dog is relying on you for strength and relief from his own fear.

Bleeding

Those who cannot stand the sight of blood had better cast that aversion aside right away if faced with a dog with a bleeding wound. The

same accidents that cause broken bones can also cause bleeding wounds—a car accident, a hiking mishap, or a dog fight. And again, the bleeding may be accompanied by other emergency conditions, such as broken bones and shock. But if you fail to get the bleeding under control, the dog could die before you ever make it to the veterinarian.

Some bleeding is the body's way of cleansing a wound, and some wounds are so minor that they may not even require a follow-up veterinary visit. In such minor cases, you can often just clean the site with soap and water, apply antiseptic, and dress the wound (remember that some dogs will not tolerate dressing so you'll just have to make sure that you continue to keep the wound as clean as possible). To be on the safe side, you may want to have minor cuts checked out anyway, just in case there is an unseen glass shard or other foreign object embedded in the wound. If, however, the blood is flowing beyond the point of natural cleansing—in other words, bleeding that will not stop—engage your emergency action instincts. The bleeding must be stopped, and professional help is in order.

First, if necessary, muzzle the dog (again, without restricting his breathing), and if possible, restrain him by wrapping him in a towel. Then press a towel or gauze pad directly on the site of the bleeding (if no such material is available, use your bare hands; your dog's life depends on it), and apply direct pressure to the

site with your hands or fingers. After about 30 seconds, let up on the pressure and check the wound. If it's still bleeding, give it another 30 seconds, and continue this pattern for several minutes. If, however, the blood is pulsing, it is coming from an arterial wound, and you'll need to apply pressure for five minutes at a time rather than 30 seconds (even if you suspect that something might be embedded in the wound, controlling the blood flow comes first). Continue this pattern until you get the dog to the animal hospital. If you are alone and the blood is still flowing, wrap the wound in gauze (not too tight!) or whatever you have available. Use several layers if necessary, and get the dog to the doctor right away.

Choking

Dogs are curious animals, and it's not uncommon for them to ingest foreign objects they discover while investigating their world. Sometimes one of those objects lodges in the dog's throat and obstructs his breathing. The signs of canine choking are virtually identical to those that occur when a person is choking and can include an open mouth, salivation, unproductive attempts to vomit, gasping or struggling for air, and perhaps frantic pawing at the muzzle. The dog may or may not be able to breathe, making for an all-around terrifying scene.

If your dog is choking but can still breathe, get him to the animal hospital immediately. If he can't and is turning blue or losing consciousness, you must take immediate action. Cardiac arrest occurs within a minute or less from the time a dog loses consciousness from choking. Whether the dog is conscious or not, extend his head, open his mouth (and perhaps, if he is unconscious, prop it open with a horizontally positioned screwdriver handle or similarly shaped object), pull out his tongue (carefully so as not to lodge the offending object in deeper) and look for the culprit. If you can see it, try to pull it out with pliers or tweezers. Pliers or tweezers are superior to fingers, which can push an object in deeper. Fingers, however, may be all you have available, as was the case years ago for my dad when he extracted a small ball out of the throat of our family dog. This method can be dangerous with a conscious dog, even a typically sweet and gentle Golden who is frightened by a sudden inability to breathe and may be inclined to bite. Before you attempt to pull an obstruction from your dog's airway, be absolutely sure that it is actually a foreign object—the dog's larynx feels like a foreign object, but if you pull on it you will severely injure the dog.

Another, rather new, method for helping a choking dog is one we use on humans, too. You can try a Heimlich-like maneuver: Lift the dog up, wrap your arms around his waist (the region just below his rib cage), and then pull upward quickly, though not too forcefully. As is the case with humans, this should force a burst of air out of the lungs that in turn pushes the object out of the airway, freeing the dog to breathe once more. Try this several times if you must. Then get the dog to the veterinarian's office as soon as possible for follow-up care.

Heatstroke

I remember vividly that unexpectedly hot afternoon in California when a friend's dog began to exhibit the undeniable signs that her body was overheating: heavy panting, pale gums, vomiting, and panic. The dog was experiencing heatstroke and in the end, despite all efforts to save her, she didn't make it.

When faced with these tell-tale signs, you must act quickly to get her to the animal hospital. Quickly bathe the dog with cool, not cold, water using a tub or towel and offer her small sips of water to help cool her inside and out. Once you have dampened her skin and gotten some water into her, immediately get her into an air-conditioned car for a quick trip to the vet.

Heatstroke is one emergency condition that you have the power to prevent. For starters, don't take your dog out for vigorous exercise during the high heat of the day, and always bring a supply of water with you when you are out and about. Whenever your dog is outdoors, make sure she has access to shade and cool water (and make sure she drinks), no matter where the sun will be throughout the course of the day. And finally, even if the air is only moderately warm, leave the pup at home when you are running errands that require you to leave your dog in the car. Cracked windows cannot protect a dog from the intense heat that can build up inside a car in only a few minutes' time. Too many people—and too many dogs—learn this the hard way (or they learn it from me, as I routinely carry cards that tell an owner that the dog inside his car could die from the heat.)

Poisoning

The world is rife with poisons, and dogs tend to be expert at finding them. Your job is to prevent that curiosity from leading to a poisoning incident. Keep an eye on your pup (know where he is, what he's doing, and what he's getting into), and don't leave poisons such as antifreeze and cleaning chemicals out where he can get to them. The problem is, there is no single "poisoning" remedy. What works as an antidote for one type of poison, can spell doom for another.

Despite the variety of poisons that can injure and even kill your dog, the classic signs of poisoning are somewhat standard: restlessness, excessive salivation, seizures, depression or hyperactivity,

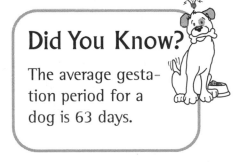

Did You Know?

The average gestation period for a dog is 63 days.

rapid breathing, loss of muscle control (and bowel and bladder control), and loss of consciousness. To respond to these signs, you will need expert advice from a veterinary poison control center and/or your veterinarian—and you'll need it fast.

In the event of poisoning, call your veterinarian or the National Animal Poison Control Center (888) 426-4435. Keep both numbers posted by your telephone. Try to identify quickly what your pet has ingested and listen carefully as the person on the other end of the telephone tells you whether to induce vomiting, to offer water or whatever is required to neutralize the poison. This may be your pet's only chance of survival. And of course, follow this up with a trip to the veterinarian for continued or follow-up treatment.

> In the event of poisoning, call your veterinarian or the National Animal Poison Control Center at (888) 426-4435.

Burns

As with most injuries that befall active dogs like the Golden Retriever, burns can result from a variety of situations and a variety of sources from live electrical cords, to the heat of an iron that falls from an ironing board, to the flame of a campfire.

A minor burn, which results in a slight reddening of the dog's skin, can be cooled with an ice pack, treated with a dab of antibiotic ointment, and left to heal in the fresh air on its own. More serious burns that result in severely damaged layers of skin (and perhaps damaged lungs if the dog breathes in fumes and smoke) must also be cooled down. This is done with cold water and/or ice packs. Then, if possible, cover the site with a clean piece of gauze, cloth, or bandaging material, and get the dog to the veterinarian for treatment designed both to heal the burn and prevent serious secondary infection. Burns caused by chemicals or electricity should be left to the veterinarian to handle; in the case of chemicals, identify the agent and inform the doctor of the details.

The message here is simple: Protect your pet from fire, electricity, and burn-producing chemicals, and in doing so, you protect your pet from the excruciating brand of pain for which burns are legendary.

Bites and Stings

Both dogs and people require similar treatment when stung or bitten by a bee, spider, fly, or other critter of the insect or arachnid kind. You may not see the culprit who makes your dog yelp, but examine your pet carefully post-yelp, and you're likely to find a lump, a bump, redness, and, if a bee is the culprit, the stinger the bee inevitably leaves behind. A bee sting can be treated by removing the stinger, applying an ice pack to the site to relieve the swelling, and following up with a dab of antibiotic ointment to prevent infection. Most other bites and stings, especially those of unknown origin that appear suspiciously red and inflamed, should be directed to the attention of a veterinarian, just in case they require special treatment.

If you do find the perpetrator, and the dog seems to be having an adverse reaction to the attack, try to collect it and transport it in a jar or bag to the veterinarian. Though most bites and stings are more irritating and uncomfortable than they are dangerous, in the event that the dog has an allergic reaction to the wound, or if the perp happened to be of a poisonous variety (certain spiders or a scorpion perhaps), effective treatment (and perhaps the dog's life) could hinge on

an accurate identification of the creature that did the biting or stinging.

Animal Bites

Dog fights are, unfortunately, not all that uncommon, often re-sulting in bites that need tending. In the wake of such an event, it's wise to get the dog to the veterinarian, even if the wounds seem minor. Dog bites tend to be puncture wounds, often deeper than they appear on the surface. Without proper treatment, which may include the administration of antibiotics, they can ab-scess or become infected.

Of course there is also the rabies question to ponder. In the event that your dog is attacked by a free-roaming, vicious dog, we assume that your dog has been vaccinated, and we hope that the perpetrator has been, as well. If you know who the biter's owner is, call animal control and demand that the owner provide proof of vaccination. Let the other dog's owner know that you expect reim-bursement of your dog's veterinary treatment, too (unless, of course, your dog started the fight by invading the other dog's territory). Of course if the dog was a stray or otherwise unknown to you, you must also call animal control to track down the dog, investigate his rabies status, and remove a vicious, free-roaming dog from the streets.

In a perfect world, this incident would be a clear message to the owner of a dog prone to fighting with other dogs that his dog should be securely confined from now on—but in our imperfect world, don't count on this happening. While accidents and inadvertent incidents do occur, even between otherwise friendly dogs, responsible owners rarely allow vicious dogs to run loose in the first place.

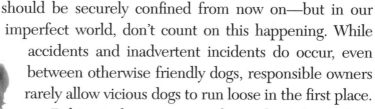

Rabies is also a concern when a dog is bitten by a wild, obviously unvaccinated animal, such as a skunk, a raccoon, or a coyote. Of course, if your dog is on a leash and safely confined, he is less likely to meet up with one of these wild critters than if he is running loose. If such an event does occur—say when a skunk waddles into your backyard some evening—you needn't worry much if your pup is current on his rabies vaccines. A visit to the veterinarian is still wise because you'll want the wound cleaned and examined thoroughly, and stitched and medicated, if necessary.

A curious Golden Retriever who enjoys hiking or camping with her family may also eventually come into contact with a snake. Should your dog sustain a snake bite, your primary goal is to restrain the dog and keep her relaxed and calm. Most snakes in the United States are not poisonous. But if your pup is bitten by a rattlesnake—immediately evident by fang marks in the wound and a dazed demeanor in the dog—you want to slow blood flow that will carry toxins more quickly throughout the body by keeping the dog still.

> Rabies is also a concern when a dog is bitten by a wild, obviously unvaccinated animal, such as a skunk, a raccoon, or a coyote.

If the bite is on the leg, you can wrap it in a bandage or cloth and apply pressure. If the bite is elsewhere, such as on the face (another common site), apply ice. If you have a snakebite kit handy, which you should if you are in a remote area, follow the instructions and get the dog out of the area and to the veterinarian as soon as possible. Indeed the veterinarian should be your first destination after any snake bite episode. He may have access to toxin antidotes designed specifically for the snake that bit your dog. A bite from a non-venomous snake should be examined, as well, for it may be prone to infection. Hope that it takes only one such episode to satisfy your dog's curiosity about those long, slithery things, inspiring your pet to turn her attentions toward safer "toys" such as tennis balls and teddy bears (but don't count on it).

Eye Injuries

Eye injuries can be caused by anything from a bite from another dog to a foreign object embedded in the eyeball. Any type of injury to the eye, whether minor or severe, must be labeled "serious" and a condition requiring immediate veterinary attention. After all, only the veterinarian is qualified to evaluate the severity of the injury, especially if the dog has clamped her eye shut and refuses to open it. Depending on the nature of the injury, you may not even be able to tell if it's an injury to the eyeball or simply the eyelid. If you wait around in hopes that it will clear up on its own, your dog could end up with severely impaired vision or outright blindness.

Eye injuries can be frightening, especially if accompanied by bleeding, which can be profuse with any injury to the head region. Your dog relies on you, however, to ignore the fear, and to think of his well-being. In the event of an eye injury, there is nothing you can do other than prepare your pet for an emergency visit to the animal hospital and get her there as soon as possible. Prevent the dog from scratching at the eye, and, if you can, saturate a piece of cotton, gauze or a washcloth with water and hold the material over the eye until you reach the veterinarian's office. If you have someone handy to assist you, he can drive while you tend to the dog.

Fishhooks and Porcupine Quills

We would all agree that it would be less-than-pleasant to have a fishhook stuck through our skin, but this can happen to a curious

Golden who accompanies his owner on a fishing or camping trip. If it does occur, you can't just back the hook out the way it went in. Attempt to slide it out in this way, and that tiny barb can and will do great, bloody, and painful damage, so don't succumb to that tug-and-pull impulse. A better remedy is to hold the dog still and cut the hook in half with metal cutters, which should be carried in the tackle box. Another option is to push the hook all the way through, which will also help prevent the tearing effects of the barb at the end of the hook.

Barbed porcupine quills can also be extremely painful. You should thus do your best to keep your dog away from the owner of those quills by keeping your dog on a leash while hiking in porcupine country. I remember reading about a dog who emerged from an unfortunate porcupine encounter with a muzzle riddled with quills. I was horrified to read that instead of transporting the dog to the nearest veterinarian for a mass removal that would surely require general anesthesia, his owner opted to perform his own version of what amounted to full-blown surgery—without the anesthetics, of course.

If your own dog emerges from such an encounter with only a quill or two as a souvenir and you are in a remote area nowhere near an animal hospital, you might be able to remove them by grasping the quill with a strong pair of pliers and twisting as you pull. But if the quill breaks, you could end up leaving a piece inside the skin, ripe for infection. My point is that in the event of embedded porcupine quills, get help from a veterinarian and, if possible, resist the do-it-yourself mentality that can result in excruciating canine pain and infection.

Did You Know?

Dogs see color less vividly than humans but are not actually color-blind.

The Canine First-Aid Kit

You shouldn't leave home without a first-aid kit for your pooch, especially if you are the active type who enjoys being out and about with your Golden. What follows are items that you should always have on hand should the unexpected occur. The kit will be valuable for you, too, since many of the items are useful for human emergency care, as well.

○ Your vet's phone number

○ The National Poison Control Center's hotline number: (888) 426-4435

○ Muzzle

○ Canine first-aid book

○ Sterile gauze bandaging, rolls and pads of various sizes and lengths

○ Non-stick would pads, gauze squares, and roll cotton

○ Adhesive bandaging tape

○ Cotton balls and swabs

○ Antiseptic ointment

○ Antibiotic cream or ointment

○ Hydrogen peroxide

○ Rubbing alcohol (handy, too, for removing tree sap from the coat)

○ Penlight flashlight

○ Styptic powder (in case nails are cut too short)

○ Eye dropper

○ Saline eye drops

○ Tweezers

○ Needlenose pliers

○ Snakebite kit

○ Clean towels

○ Clean socks (for foot injuries)

○ Scissors

○ Large blanket (for stretcher)

○ Tincture of iodine

○ Rectal thermometer

Is Your Golden Overweight?

To determine if your dog is carrying a little excess weight, which, sadly, many Golden Retrievers are, a squeeze will tell you all you need to know. Place one hand on each side of your dog's rib cage.

Do you feel ribs? If not, your dog needs to loose a few pounds. If you do feel a healthy contour of rib and muscle, then your dog is probably fine. If, however, those ribs feel a bit too sharp along your fingertips and you detect not a hint of meat, then you may have that unusual pup who could afford to gain a few pounds (with veterinary advice on how this should be done safely and healthfully, of course).

Either way, weight is an issue. Excess weight has become a national epidemic for America's canine population. Here we are in an age where dogs can and should live longer than ever before, thanks in part to revolutionary advancements in canine nutrition, yet we are sabotaging our pets' potential by overfeeding them or feeding them incorrectly. But all is not lost. You have the power to protect your dog from this epidemic.

> Excess weight has become a national epidemic for America's canine population.

Maintaining a Healthy Weight

And just what's the big deal about weight, you ask? Even an overweight dog seems happy and smiley, so why worry? The primary concern stems from the fact that almost every health malady we have discussed in this chapter is amplified when the patient is overweight. Excess poundage places extra stress and strain on an animal's heart, lungs, muscles, joints, and virtually every organ system in her body. That leaves little energy when the body is called to fight off disease or engage in serious healing. Add to this the fact that a slim and trim dog will probably outlive her overweight counterparts (and thus enjoy more time with her loving family), and you have all the evidence you need for the importance of maintaining a dog's healthy weight. This should also be ample motivation for you to stick to your dog's weight reduction program if she is currently over that ideal weight.

Maintaining your dog's weight can be more of a challenge for the owner than it is for the dog. We explored this in Chapter 3. We humans just love to feed dogs. We love to see those eyes light up and that tail wag when they know we intend to share with them our four-cheese pizza or our chicken enchiladas. We just can't bear the thought of depriving them.

But we must bear it, and we must stick to the recipe. That means offering the dog only her daily ration of high-quality dog food each day, the ideal amount of which will vary from Golden to Golden because of the vast range of sizes found in this breed. This ration should be divided up in two or three feedings a day, supplemented occasionally by healthy treats such as dog biscuits or sliced carrots or zucchini. It's so simple, yet so challenging for far too many owners. Be strong. The rewards are immeasurable in terms of your pet's health and the many years you will be able to spend together.

Trimming Down a Chubby Dog

Once you discover—or confess—that you are living with a chubby dog, take heart. You're not alone.

It took Maryland dog trainer Janet Boss almost two years to admit that her Golden Retriever, Teddy, had a weight problem. Fortunately, Janet had three dear friends who came right out and told her that her almost two-year-old pup, sweet as he was, was fat. Janet had no choice but to look honestly at her beloved companion and admit it was true. She analyzed carefully how and when Teddy was eating, and she switched him from a free-feeding regimen to a carefully scheduled and measured feeding schedule with few treats. For the last nine years, now 11-year-old Teddy has maintained his ideal weight in the low 70s. Had he continued as he was, one wonders if he would have made it to his tenth birthday, let alone his eleventh and beyond.

So let Janet be an inspiration to you. She did what she had to do, and her dog benefited from her commitment. Indeed her prescription is solid: A carefully chosen, carefully fed diet, coupled with moderately offered treats and daily exercise. To make matters even more positive, we now have access to a wide variety of low-calorie, low-fat, high-quality commercial dog foods designed to make the weight loss program even more comfortable for the overweight pup—and for the doting owner of that pup.

Exercise is another important element in this program, but do take it easy with this. This is a breed who needs and craves exercise (those working retriever roots, remember), and the lack thereof probably accounts for the obesity problems in the breed today. You cannot, however, take a dog who was the quintessential couch potato one day and expect him to be a world-class athlete the next. You must approach the process gradually, just as you would for yourself. Prevent sore muscles and a strained cardiovascular system by building up gradually on the length and time of your daily walks, hikes, jogs, and such. You'll both find it much more enjoyable this way—something to look forward to rather than dread. And that's why you live with a dog like this in the first place, isn't it?

6

Basic Training for Goldens

By Liz Palika

In This Chapter

○ When to Begin Training
○ The Teaching Process
○ What Every Good Dog Needs to Know

All dogs need training to learn how to behave around people. When your dog learns to walk nicely on a leash, he won't drag you down the street choking himself and pulling your arm out of the socket. When your dog learns to sit, he can sit when he greets people instead of jumping on them.

Basic obedience training gives your dog some necessary rules to govern his behavior. Does your Golden insist on carrying something of yours in his mouth? Does he chew on your slippers or shoes? Does he raid the trash can? Does he jump on your guests, scratching them and threatening to knock them down? These are all very normal behaviors for a healthy, active young Golden Retriever, but they are also unnecessary, potentially dangerous, and annoying behaviors that can be changed (or at least controlled) with training.

Your Golden carries things in his mouth because he is a retriever and that's what retrievers do. He wants to carry something of yours because you're important to him; he doesn't understand that you would prefer your things dry instead of covered in dog saliva! Your Golden chews on things for a variety of reasons. If he's young, he may still be teething. Or he may be bored, alone too much, or not getting enough exercise.

However, just because these are natural behaviors doesn't mean they should continue. Raiding the trash can be very dangerous—your dog could swallow any number of potentially dangerous or poisonous things. Jumping on people is a very bad habit and could result in dirty or ripped clothing, scratched skin, or more serious injuries should your Golden knock someone down.

With training, your Golden Retriever can learn to control himself so that he's not reacting to every impulse. He can learn social rules such as sitting (not jumping) when greeting people and walking nicely on the leash. When your Golden behaves himself at home, you're more likely to let him spend time in the house with you instead of exiling him to the backyard. When your Golden learns to behave himself in public, he is a joy to take for a walk rather than a monster and, as a result, you'll be more likely to take him places because you'll enjoy it more.

A well-trained dog will accept your guidance even when he would rather be doing something else.

Basic Commands Every Dog Should Know

Sit: Your dog's hips should move to the ground while his shoulders stay upright.

Down: Your dog should lie down on the ground or floor and be still.

Stay: Your dog should remain in position (sit or down) when you walk away from him. He should hold the stay until you give him permission to move.

Come: Your dog should come to you on the first call despite any distractions.

Walk on the Leash: Your dog can walk ahead of you on the leash but should not pull the leash tight.

Heel: Your dog should walk by your left side with his shoulders by your left leg.

Bella is a 14-month-old Golden Retriever who is owned by a service dog organization. Service dogs work as guide or assistance dogs. She is being fostered by a family in San Diego, whose job it is to raise this energetic puppy, socialize her, introduce her to basic obedience training, and get her ready for her training as a future service dog. Bella's foster owner, Kelley, said, "Bella is my third Golden Retriever service-dog puppy. She is a happy puppy but is so full of energy, she just bounces everywhere! Sometimes I've wondered if she'd ever learn to control herself." She added, "But my previous foster puppies finally learned and Bella will, too. It just takes training, consistency of training, and lots of patience!"

Training is an ongoing process. It teaches the dog to behave himself at home, to ignore the trash cans, and to chew on his own toys. It also applies out in public, teaching him to greet people by sitting instead of jumping on them. Training applies to every aspect of the dog's life.

What a Trained Dog Knows

A trained dog knows:

❍ The appropriate behaviors allowed with people (no biting, no rough play, and no mounting)

❍ Where to relieve himself and how to ask to go outside

❍ How to greet people properly without jumping on them

❍ To wait for your permission to greet people, other dogs, and other pets

❍ How to walk on a leash nicely so that walks are enjoyable

❍ To leave the trash cans alone

❍ To leave food that is not his alone (on the counters or coffee table)

❍ Not to beg

❍ To chew on his toys and not your personal things

❍ To play with his toys and not the kids' toys

❍ That destructive behavior is not acceptable

❍ To wait for permission before going through doorways

A trained dog is a happy dog; secure in his place in the family.

When to Begin Training

Ideally, training should begin as soon as you bring your Golden Retriever home. If you have a new eight- or nine-week-old puppy, that's okay. Your new puppy can begin learning the very basic rules. He can learn that biting isn't allowed, that he should sit for every meal, and where he should go to relieve himself. By 10 weeks of age, you can start attaching a

Start training early so that your puppy learns good behavior instead of bad habits.

Kindergarten Puppy Classes

The ideal time to start group class training is as soon as your Golden puppy has had at least two sets of vaccinations. Many veterinarians may recommend that you wait even longer, so ask your vet what he thinks. Most puppy classes recommend that puppies start any time between 10 and 12 weeks of age. Kindergarten puppy classes teach you how to teach your puppy and include the basic commands: sit, down, stay, and come—all geared for the baby puppy's short attention span. Puppy classes also spend time socializing the puppies to other people and other puppies.

leash to his collar and letting him drag it around for a few minutes at a time under supervision so that he gets used to the feel of it. Puppies have a very short attention span, but they are willing and eager students—especially when you make training fun.

Keep in mind as you start teaching your puppy that this adorable Golden pup will grow up to be a big, strong dog. Don't let the puppy do anything now that you will regret later. For example, don't teach your puppy to cuddle up on your lap now if you won't want him on your lap when he weighs 65 pounds!

If you adopt a Golden who is an older puppy or an adult, you can still start training right away. Your Golden will need time to get used to your household, especially if he was a stray, in a shelter, or at a breeder's kennel. However, the training will help your new dog learn what you expect of him and, as a result, make that adjustment easier.

Start teaching your new Golden the rules you expect of him right away. For example, if you don't want him to get up on the furniture, never allow him to do so. Don't make excuses, "Oh, this is a new house to him and he's upset. We can teach him to

Basic Obedience Training Class

Most dog obedience instructors invite puppies to begin the basic class after they have graduated from a puppy class or after the puppy reaches four months of age. Even if your Golden is older than four months and has never attended a puppy class, he would still go to the basic class. This class teaches the traditional beginners' commands: sit, down, stay, come, and heel. In addition, most instructors spend time discussing problem behaviors such as jumping on people, barking, digging, and chewing. A group class such as this helps your Golden learn to control himself around other dogs and people, which can be serious distractions!

stay off the furniture later." If you don't want him on the furniture, teach him right away what your rules are. Breaking bad habits later is much more difficult!

Is It Ever Too Late?

Do you have a three-year-old Golden Retriever who is not as well behaved as you would like? It's not too late; you can still train him. The downfall to starting training later is that you then have to break bad habits as well as teach new behaviors. With a young puppy, you're starting with a clean slate, and you can teach the proper behavior before he learns any bad habits. If you've ever tried to stop a bad habit (smoking, for example) you know that it can be very difficult. However, with most Golden Retrievers up to about seven years of age, you can, with consistent training and lots of patience, control most bad habits.

If your dog is older than eight or nine years of age, your success at changing bad habits will be much more limited. You can

Private Training

Private training is usually recommended for Goldens with one or more serious behavior problems, such as biting, growling, or uncontrolled behavior. Private training is done one-on-one either at your home or at the trainer's facility. It gives you the ability to tailor the training to your needs and to your dog's specific problems.

teach new commands—heel, sit, down, stay, or come—and your dog will be able to learn those without too much trouble. If your dog has been jumping on people for eight years, you can probably teach him to sit instead. As an older, heavier, and possibly arthritic dog, he's going to become less apt to jump anyway, and the praise he gets for sitting will make it more worthwhile.

Sometimes, though, there are behavior problems that are just impossible to solve. A habit may be too deeply ingrained, or the behavior causing the actions too strong. If your dog has been raiding the trash cans, for example, and has learned that there is food and other treasures in the trash cans, you will have a hard time changing that behavior. Each time the dog raids the trash, he gets rewarded for doing it (i.e. the food in the trash). With a problem like this, training will not help as much as prevention will. Make the trash cans unavailable to the dog.

Basic Dog Psychology

People and dogs have a long shared history. Archaeologists have found evidence of this history in archaeological sites dating back thousands of years. Why did early man want to cooperate with the wolf? Researchers don't know for sure, but they guess that the wolf, as an efficient predator, had hunting skills early man could use or perhaps people learned to watch the wolves, using them as early warning systems against other predators or trespassers. Why did the wolf decide to cooperate with man? Again, we don't know. Maybe some wolves learned to follow people, scavenging the scraps of hunts or the garbage people left behind. All of this is speculation, though, as we have no written history telling us exactly what happened. We do have the end result, however—domesticated dogs who have been protectors, helpers, and companions of man for thousands of years.

Families and Packs

In the wild, wolves live in packs. The pack is made up of a dominant male, a dominant female, several subordinate adults, a juvenile or two, and the latest pups. Only the two dominant adults breed, and the others help hunt for and protect the resulting puppies. This pack has some important social rules—including no breeding except between the two dominant adults—and these rules are rarely broken. The leaders usually initiate the hunt, and then direct where and when the hunt will take place. They eat first, with the subordinate animals grabbing what they can until the leaders back off. The leaders decide where the pack's den will be, and the rest of the pack follows. These and other rules help keep the order among the pack members, and there is usually little disruption in the pack unless one of the wolves decides to move up in the pack order. If an older wolf is disabled, dies, or leaves the pack, or if a younger wolf gets ambitious, then there may be some posturing or fighting until the new pack order is established.

Dogs today fit into our family life because they have this pack history. Our family is a social organization similar to a pack, although our families have significant differences from a traditional wolf pack. We do often have an adult male and adult female, although today there may be just one adult. There are rarely any other adults in the pack, as a wolf pack might have, and there may or may not be juveniles (teenagers) and children. In addition, the rules of our family are rarely adhered to as strongly as the social rules in a wolf pack are. For example, in a wolf pack, as we mentioned, the leaders eat first. In our families, people eat any time and the order of eating has no specific rhyme or reason. These family rules, or lack of rules, can be very confusing to our dogs.

What Does It Mean to Be Top Dog?

Top dog is a slang term for the pack leader. In the wolf pack we discussed, the top dogs are the dominant male and dominant female; often called the alpha male or alpha female. In your family pack, there should be no confusion; the top dog should be *you*, the dog's owner, and your dog should maintain a subordinate position to any additional human members of the family.

Often during adolescence, a Golden with a particularly bold personality may try to become leader of her family pack. Luckily, Goldens are not usually as dominant as some other breeds so this is not as common as it could be, but it does happen. Adolescence

Don't let your dog use his body language to show dominance. Your dog should recognize you (and your children) as above him in the family pack.

You Are the Top Dog!

○ Always eat first.

○ Go through doors and doorways first; block your dog from charging through ahead of you.

○ Go upstairs ahead of your dog; don't let her charge ahead and then look down at you.

○ Give her permission to do things even if it's after the fact. For example, if she picks up her ball, tell her, "Get your ball! Good girl!"

even though she wasn't waiting for your command.

○ Practice your training regularly.

○ Have your dog roll over for a tummy rub daily.

○ Do not play rough games with your Golden—no wrestling on the floor or tug-of-war.

○ Never let your dog stand above you or put her paws on your shoulders. These are dominant postures.

usually strikes at sexual maturity, usually between eight and 12 months of age, and may last for a few months.

If the dog's owner is less dominant than the dog, or if the owner is unaware of the signals that the dog relates to dominance, the dog may actually think she is in charge. For example, as we mentioned, eating first is one signal dominant dogs use. When do you feed your Golden? Many dog owners feed the dog first to get her out from under foot while cooking. If your Golden eats first and you eat later, she could interpret this as a weakness on your part—even though it means nothing to you! What else signals dominance? The order in which you walk through doorways. Consider who goes through first when you open the door. It should always be you; have your dog wait for you to go first.

A dog who takes over can make life miserable around the house. This is when we see mounting (sexual) behavior toward the owner. The dog may growl whenever you try to do something—such as make her move off the furniture—and the growl may escalate to a snap or bite. Your dog should not view herself as the top dog in your household; after all, it is your house!

Although it is very important that your dog regard you as the leader or top dog, don't look at every action your dog makes as a dominance challenge. Most of the time your Golden won't care about her position in the pack; she knows you're in charge. After all, you supply the food! However, for those dogs who do have a dominant personality, training during adolescence is very important.

The Teaching Process

Training your dog is not a mysterious process, although sometimes it may seem to be. Teaching your dog is primarily communication: rewarding the behaviors you want so they continue and interrupting the behaviors you do not want so they stop. Let's use the kitchen trash can as our example. If you are in the kitchen fixing lunch and your dog follows you into the kitchen, watch her out of the corner of your eye. When her sniffing nose moves toward the trash can, use a deep, growling tone of voice and tell her, "Leave it alone!" When she reacts to your voice by stopping the sniffing and backing away, tell her in a higher pitched tone of voice, "That's good to leave it alone!"

Did you notice I specified different tones of voice? Dogs are verbal animals just as we are, and tone of voice is very important to their communication. When your dog wants to play, her barks or yelps are much higher in tone than when she is warning you of someone coming up the walk to the front door. You can aid the training process by copying some of these tones. When you give your dog a command, such as sit, use your voice at a normal speaking strength. When you praise your dog to let her know that she has done something right, use a higher pitched tone of voice, such as when you say, "Ice cream!" When your dog makes a mistake, use a deeper tone of voice—a "Grrr!" type of voice.

Don't confuse high and low tones of voice with high and low *volume*. In fact, when using these different tones, concentrate on not raising your volume. Your dog hears very well—in fact, much better than we do. Volume isn't important. Instead, when you give your dog a command, praise her, or correct her, sound like you mean what you're saying. If you tell your dog something and then giggle, she's not going to take you seriously. For example, if she tears something up and you catch her in the act and tell her, "No," you cannot laugh at her, no matter how cute she may look with sofa cushion stuffing hanging out of her mouth.

> Dogs are verbal animals just as we are, and tone of voice is very important to their communication.

Your dog wasn't born understanding English, French, German, or any other human language, so you need to teach her that your spoken words have meanings. The tone of your voice and any gestures you make can teach her a lot. She learns that "Good dog" is a positive thing because you say it in a high pitched tone of voice and you usually pet her when you say it. She learns that "No!" means something bad because you say it in a deeper, growly tone of voice and you look unhappy when you say it.

A treat can be a wonderful training tool to help teach your dog to pay attention to you. When he looks at you, praise him, give him the treat, and then follow through with other training.

Corrections should be given as the dog is making the mistake, not after the fact.

But how does your Golden learn what the word *sit* means? Or *down*? Or any other spoken command? You need to teach her. When teaching her, say the word as you help her follow through with what you ask her to do. Tell her "Lucky, sit!" as you take a treat and hold it above her nose, moving it slowly back over her head towards her tail. As her head goes up, her hips will go down. When her hips touch the ground, praise her "Good to sit!" and give her the treat. The treat is called a lure. It helps your dog to do something by causing her to move or assume a position. In addition, when she does what you ask, the lure becomes part of your positive reinforcement, letting the dog know she has done something right.

Your timing is very important when teaching your dog. Praise her as she does something right, and let her know she's making a mistake *as she makes it.* Let's continue with the kitchen trash can example. You need to let her know she's making a mistake *as she sniffs the kitchen trash can;* not when you walk into the kitchen to find the trash all over the floor and your dog is gone. Let her know as she does something right that it's right or as she does something wrong that it's wrong.

During the training process, don't hesitate to set up your dog for success. Both dogs and people learn more from successes than from failures. Your Golden will be more willing to try again (whatever it is you are teaching her) each time she succeeds and is rewarded. When setting up your dog for success, think about what you are teaching her. If you want to keep your Golden off

Training Vocabulary

You should know the meaning of the following terms as they refer to your Golden's training:

Positive reinforcement: Anything that your dog likes that you can use to reward good behavior. This could be verbal praise, food treats, toys, tennis balls, or petting.

Praise: Words spoken in a higher-than-normal tone of voice to reward your dog for something he did right; part of positive reinforcement.

Lure: This can be food treats or a toy. You use this to help position the dog as you want him, or to gain his cooperation as you teach him something.

Interruption: The moment when you catch your dog in the act of doing something and you stop him. This could be a deeper-toned verbal sound, "Leave it alone!" or it could be a sharp sound like dropping your book to the floor. An interruption stops the behavior as it happens.

Correction: Usually a deep, growly verbal sound or words used to let your dog know that he has made a mistake; preferably as he is doing it. The correction can serve as an interruption, but can also let your dog know you dislike what he's doing. This can also be a snap and release of the leash. A correction should be enough to get your dog's attention and stop the behavior at that moment and that's all.

the furniture, ask her to lie down at your feet *before* she has the opportunity to jump up on the sofa. If you want her to stop jumping on people, ask her to sit *before* she jumps on your neighbor. When you learn to think ahead, you can prevent a lot of problem behavior from happening, and at the same time, you can teach your dog the right way to do things.

Also during the training process, do not rely too heavily on corrections to teach your dog. You can let your dog know that she's made a mistake when you catch her in the act—with her

The Training Process at a Glance

When teaching a new command:

○ Show the dog what to do with a lure, your hands, or your voice.

○ Praise him for doing it and reward him with the lure if you used one.

With problem behavior:

○ Interrupt the behavior when you catch the dog in the act. Let him know he made a mistake.

○ Show him what to do instead.

○ Correct him for mistakes only when he knows and understands the command and chooses not to do it.

○ Set up the dog for success by teaching him to do something else and then rewarding that behavior.

nose in the trash can—but do not correct her after the fact. She may associate the correction with many things—the trash on the floor, you catching her in the kitchen, or even the trash itself. But she may not actually associate an after-the-fact correction with the act of dumping over the trash can. A correction or interruption is effective only when you catch her making the mistake.

A properly timed correction can let your dog know when she's making a mistake but it doesn't tell her what to do instead. For example, if you try to teach your Golden not to jump on people, you can try to correct her, "No jump!" and she may learn what that means, but you aren't teaching her how to greet people. After all, she's jumping on people to greet them. So your training needs to address that problem, too. Teach her to sit to greet people, then after she knows how to do that, you can let her know when she does make a mistake and jumps up.

Turning a Negative into a Positive

Amber, a dark red Golden Retriever from Huntington Beach, California, disliked grooming. When her owner tried to comb or brush her, Amber would fight him. When her owner asked me for help, I watched one of their horrible sessions. Amber obviously hated this handling and fought with every ounce of her being even though it didn't appear to be painful; she wasn't matted and there were no tangles in her coat. She was just used to fighting, so she did. I went in the house and came out with a jar of peanut butter and a big spoon. I had Amber sit and offered her a glob of peanut butter. When she licked it, I asked her to lie down. She did and her owner rolled her over onto her side. I continued to give her some peanut butter as her owner began brushing her. She wiggled, but she was so focused on the peanut butter that she put up with the grooming. I had her owner stop after a few minutes and praise her as she was licking the last of the peanut butter off her lips. I told him to continue to give her the peanut butter and to break the grooming sessions into small increments so that it wouldn't escalate into a horrible fight again.

Teaching Your Dog to Be Handled

Your Golden Retriever cannot care for himself; that's your job. You need to be able to comb and brush him; check for fleas and ticks; and look for cuts, scrapes, bumps, and bruises. When he has a problem, you need to be able to take care of it, whether it's cleaning and medicating his ears when he has an ear infection, caring for his stitches after neutering, or washing out his eyes if dirt gets in them.

Before you need to do so, teach your dog that he can trust you when you touch his body. When you bring your Golden home—either as a puppy or an adopted adult—one thing you can do every evening is to teach your Golden to accept social handling. Sit on the floor and invite your Golden to lay down between your legs or in front of you. Start giving him a tummy rub to help him relax. When he's relaxed, then start giving him a massage. Begin massaging at his muzzle, rubbing your fingers gently over the skin, and at the same time, check his teeth.

A tummy rub can help relax your dog if he's over-stimulated. You can also follow through with any needed grooming. In addition, this is a wonderful time for bonding with your dog.

Then move up his head, touching the skin around his eyes, looking for discharge or a problem in his eyes. Move up to his ears, stroking the ear flaps, massaging around the base of each ear and while you're there, looking inside the ear for potential problems. Continue in the same manner all over your dog's body, from his nose to the tip of his tail. If at any time, your Golden protests, go back to a tummy rub for a moment, or offer him some peanut butter.

Do this exercise daily and incorporate your grooming into the process. Comb and brush one side, then roll him over and do the other side. Trim his nails after you've massaged his feet and checked them for cuts and scratches.

If your dog needs medication or first aid treatments, you can do that while massaging, too, so that the treatment doesn't turn into a big fight. It simply becomes matter of fact and a part of the daily massage.

There is a welcome side benefit to this daily massage. When you are through massaging your Golden Retriever, he is going to be totally relaxed, like a limp noodle. So plan ahead and do it when you want your dog to be quiet and relaxed. If he's hyper and overactive in the evening when you would like to unwind and watch television, turn on the TV while you're massaging your dog. Then when you're done massaging him, he'll fall asleep and you can watch the rest of your show!

The Importance of Good Socialization

Socialization is a vital part of raising a mentally healthy, well-adjusted Golden Retriever. A young Golden who has been introduced to a variety of people of different ages and ethnic backgrounds will be a social dog; one who is happy to meet people on a walk and who will not be afraid. Dogs who are not properly socialized may grow up afraid of children, senior citizens, or people of a different ethnic background than their owners. These dogs often become "fear biters," and they may eventually have to be destroyed because they're dangerous.

Socialization also refers to meeting other dogs and pets. A well-socialized dog will get a chance to meet dogs of a variety of sizes, shapes, colors, and breeds and will

Introduce your dog to other friendly, well-behaved, healthy dogs. Avoid rowdy, poorly behaved, aggressive dogs; they could scare your dog and ruin the socialization you've done so far.

learn how to behave around these dogs. Ideally, you should also introduce your dog to dog-friendly cats, pet rabbits, ferrets, a horse, or a llama. Why socialize a city dog to horses? San Diego is a good-sized city, and not many horses reside within the city limits anymore. However, the city police has a horse patrol for certain areas of the city, including the beautiful Balboa Park. Many city dogs meet a horse for the first time when they are walking in the park with their owners. Some dogs react with panic when they see a horse for the first time and try to pull away not only from the horse, but from their owner. Other dogs try to attack the horse. However, a well-socialized dog will sniff toward the horse to identify it and then relax. After all, it's just a horse! The important lesson is, whether it is horses, llamas, or trash trucks, the more your Golden is exposed to, the better.

Socialization also includes introducing your Golden to the world around him—the sights and sounds of the world he will experience during his life. He should see and hear a motorcycle going down the street, kids on skateboards and inline skates, the garbage truck, and birthday party balloons. Walk him past the construction crew working on the house down the street, and let him stop and watch the road crew working on the intersection. The more he sees and hears, the better his coping skills.

Don't, however, introduce your Golden to everything all at once or you may overload him! You can start socialization when your puppy is about 9 to 10 weeks old. Start by introducing him to friendly neighbors. Let them play with him, pet, and cuddle him. Don't allow rough play or handling, however—keep the experience positive. As your puppy grows up, continue introducing him to different people, sights, and sounds. Take him to the local pet supply store and let people pet him. While there, he can see a shopping cart and follow it with you as you shop. Socialization is an ongoing, gradual process.

Should your puppy be frightened by something, do not hug him, pet him, and try to reassure him. Your puppy will assume those soft words are praise for being afraid. Instead, use a happy, joking tone of voice, "What was that?" and walk up to whatever scared him. Don't force him to walk up to it—just let him see you walk up to it. For example, if your puppy sees a trash can rolling in the street after the wind has blown it over, and he appears afraid of it, hold onto your puppy's leash (to keep him from running away) and walk up to the trash can. Ask your puppy in an upbeat tone of voice, "What's this? Fido, look!" Touch the trash can. Pat it several times so that your puppy can see you touch it. If he walks up to it, praise him for his bravery.

Luckily Goldens are by nature very social dogs, however, that doesn't change the need for actively socializing your dog. Kindergarten puppy class is a wonderful way for Golden puppies to meet other people and other puppies. In addition, most instructors have playground equipment and toys that the puppies can play on to increase their socialization skills and confidence. Adult Goldens can still be socialized although the best time to do this is during puppyhood.

How a Crate Can Help

Originally built as travel cages, crates have become very popular training tools for a variety of reasons. A crate can help you house-train your Golden puppy by confining her to a small place during the night and for small periods of time during the day. Because your puppy doesn't want to soil her bed, she will develop better bowel and bladder control.

A crate helps your puppy develop bowel and bladder control, prevents accidents from happening, and becomes your puppy's special place.

The crate is also a good training tool to prevent other problems from occurring. If your Golden sleeps in her crate during the night, she can't sneak away to chew things up or raid the trash cans. If she's confined when you go to the store, she isn't shredding the sofa cushions. When your dog is prevented from getting into trouble, she is also prevented from learning bad habits. As she grows up, she can gradually be given more freedom; but not until she is mature mentally and emotionally—about three years old for most Goldens!

As you use the crate, it becomes your dog's special place. She can retreat to her crate for a nap when the household is quiet, or she can go to her crate when she's overwhelmed or doesn't feel good. She can hide her favorite toys in her crate or chew on a special rawhide there. It is her place, her refuge.

Many first-time dog owners initially have a problem with the idea of confining their dog to a crate; some even compare it to a jail cell. But dogs are den animals. In the wild, wolves and coyotes give birth in a den or cave and the puppies are restricted to that den until the mother feels they are old enough to venture out. Most mother dogs are the same way and prefer to give birth in a quiet, secure spot. This is why most breeders give their pregnant bitches a whelping box designed to provide the mother and puppies with a secure, quiet place.

Introduce your Golden to the crate by propping the door open and tossing a treat or toy inside. Let her reach in to grab the treat and then back out. Praise her for her bravery! Repeat this several times. Then offer her a meal in the crate. Keep the door propped open, but set her dinner bowl inside the crate so she needs to step inside to get it.

As you are introducing her to the crate, start teaching her a command. As you toss the treat in, wait for her to move toward the crate. When she steps inside, tell her, "Fido, crate!" or "Fido, go to bed!" Use a command that will be comfortable to you. In the early training steps, give her a treat incentive each time she goes inside the crate. Not only will this make her go inside faster and with more enthusiasm, but it will make her think of the crate as something positive instead of something confining.

The best place for the crate is in your bedroom. I moved my nightstand into the garage, put the dog crate right next to the bed, and now use that as the nightstand. This way I can hear the dog and know when she needs to go outside. In addition, she gets to spend eight uninterrupted hours with me. In our busy society, that's important time! She can hear me, smell me, and be with me even though we aren't really doing anything together. It's still time for her to be with me—a member of her family pack.

If you don't want the dog crate in your bedroom, you could put it in one of the kids' rooms. Or perhaps you could put it in the hallway outside your room. Whatever you decide to do, do not isolate your Golden. Do not put her in the backyard, garage, or laundry room alone. Remember, dogs are social animals; isolation causes many behavior problems including self-mutilation and destructiveness.

Your Golden can spend the night in her crate and a few hours here and there during the day. Other than at night, she should preferably not be in the crate for more than three or four hours at a time. She needs time out of the crate to play, exercise, follow you around, and learn the rules of the house.

What Every Good Dog Needs to Know

Life with your Golden Retriever will be less than fun—as well as embarrassing—if he doesn't have good social skills. Dogs were domesticated to be friends, companions, and helpers—not pains in the neck! However, social skills are not difficult to teach.

Choosing the Right Crate

Crates come in two basic styles. There are solid-sided plastic crates that are used for airline travel and wire crates that look like cages. Each style has pros and cons. The wire-sided crates provide more air ventilation and are good if you live in a very warm climate. However, because they are more open, some dogs feel very vulnerable in these crates; they don't provide as much security for the dog. These crates are usually collapsible, but even when collapsed, they are very heavy. The plastic crates do not collapse and take up more room to store, but they are lighter weight. They do not allow as much air circulation as the wire crates, but they do provide more security for the dog. Look at your needs and your dog's personality to choose the right crate style.

The crate should be big enough so your dog can stand up and turn around in it as an adult. You will use the crate for many years, so get one that will be big enough for your dog as an adult (or get one for him as a puppy, then replace it later). As we mentioned in Chapter 2, if you use a large one for your puppy, pad the sides with towels and blankets to reduce the interior space, as excess space could make the puppy nervous. If you aren't sure what size to get, ask for help at the pet supply store.

No Jumping

Your Golden Retriever is (or will be) much too big and strong to jump on people, so that should be the first social skill you teach him. Teach your Golden to sit every time he greets people—you, your spouse, your kids, guests, and people on the street. We'll talk about how to teach him to sit later in this chapter. Once he knows how to sit, you should enforce it every time he greets someone.

There are several ways you can do this. First, if your dog doesn't have his leash on—like when you come home from work—

make sure you greet him with empty hands. As your dog dashes up to you and begins to jump, grab his buckle collar (which should be on him with his ID tags) and tell him, "Fido, no jump! Sit!" and with your hand on his collar, help him sit. Keep your hands on him as he sits so that you can help him maintain that position. Praise him for sitting, "Good boy to sit! Yes, you are!"

The leash is also a good training tool to help the dog sit. When guests come to your house, ask them to wait outside for a moment as you leash your dog. Once your dog is leashed, let your guests in. Have your dog sit before the guests pet him. If he bounces up, have your guests back off, and don't let them pet him again until he sits. This, of course, requires training your guests, too, to make sure they cooperate. If your dog learns that he can jump on *some* people, he'll be confused when *other* people get upset with him for jumping up.

You can do the same thing while out on walks. Have your dog sit prior to allowing people to pet him. If he gets too wiggly and bounces up, have the people step back for a minute until he sits again.

When training a young dog of my own, I found that some people protest when I'm doing this training, "Oh, I don't mind," they say, usually as they brush paw prints off their clothes. But I consider this important training. I don't want my dogs ruining people's clothes, scratching people, or knocking them down. So if people take offense, I just try to explain why it's important to me, and I find that most will then cooperate with my training efforts.

To Bark or Not to Bark

All dogs bark; it is their way of communicating. And while some barking is acceptable—say when someone comes to the front door or a trespasser is climbing over the back fence—too much barking is annoying. In addition, neighbors are quick to complain when a loud barker disturbs the peace of the neighborhood. Luckily, Golden Retrievers are not normally problem barkers although when Goldens do bark, their bark can be very loud!

The easiest way to stop problem barking is to first control it when you're at home. Invite a neighbor over and ask her to ring your doorbell. When she does and your dog charges the door, barking loudly, step up to your dog, grab his collar, and tell him, "Fido, quiet!" If he stops barking, praise him! If he doesn't stop, close his mouth with your hand, wrapping your fingers around his muzzle as you tell him again to be quiet. When he stops, praise him.

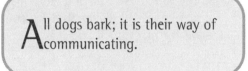

All dogs bark; it is their way of communicating.

Many dogs will learn the quiet command with repeated training like this. However, some dogs are a little more persistent, more protective, or just like to bark. With these dogs, the correction needs to be a little stronger. Take a squirt bottle and put about 1 part vinegar to 8 parts water in it. Squirt the mixture on the palm of your hand and smell it. There should be just a whiff of vinegar smell—not too strong—just enough so you know some vinegar is there. If it's stronger, dilute it with more water.

This time, when the dog charges to the door barking when the doorbell rings, you will follow him and very quietly say, "Fido, quiet!" If he stops barking, praise him. If he doesn't, squirt a mist of the vinegar water toward his nose (and away from his eyes). He will smell the vinegar, and because he has such a finely tuned nose, he will not like it. He will stop barking, back off, and lick the water off his nose. Praise him for being quiet! The squirt bottle works as an interruption because it can stop the behavior (the barking) without giving him a harsh correction.

Bark Collars

Several different types of bark control collars are available on the market. Some give the dog an electric shock or jolt when he barks, some make a high-pitched sound, and one gives a squirt of citronella when the dog barks. The citronella collar works with the same concept as the vinegar/water squirt bottle; the smell is annoying enough to the dog to make him stop what he's doing. This is the collar that I recommend for most dog owners; it is very effective for most dogs and it is a very humane training tool.

Use the same training techniques (verbal correction, collar, closing the muzzle, or the squirt bottle) to teach your dog to listen to your quiet command around the house. When he's reliable there, then move the training outside. If he barks at the gate when kids are playing out front, go out front (out of your dog's sight) and be prepared to correct him as soon as he barks with a verbal command and a spray from the squirt bottle. Always, of course, praise him when he's quiet.

No Begging

There is no reason for any dog to beg while you're eating. Most of our dogs have never known what real hunger is; their food comes regularly! Begging is a terrible habit. The dog may start hiding under the table waiting for a tidbit to fall. If he's not corrected for this behavior, he might start laying his head in your lap while you're eating, hoping to catch the tidbit before it even hits the floor. Again, if the problem is not addressed, it can escalate to the point where your dog begins stealing food from children's hands, and sneaking food off the table or counters.

Fortunately, begging is a problem that is relatively easy to solve. Later in this chapter we'll teach the down-stay command. Once your Golden has mastered the down-stay command, use this to make him hold his position while people are eating. I don't like to exile the dog to the backyard—that just creates more frustration. Instead, by having the dog lie down in a corner of the room, out from under foot and away from the

Teach your dog to hold a down-stay while you're eating. He will learn that he gets to eat when you are finished so he must be patient.

table, the dog can learn to be still, control himself, and wait. When everyone has finished eating, the dog can then be given a treat *in his bowl* away from the table.

If one member of the family has trouble resisting your dog's pleading eyes, make sure that the dog does his down-stay away from that person's line of vision. That way those pleading eyes won't cause that person to feel guilty about not dropping a treat.

When you first begin this training, make sure you use the leash and collar on the dog, because if the dog has been doing some begging, he is not going to want to give it up. You will need to have him do a down-stay, drop his leash next to him, and sit at the table. When the dog gets up from the down (which he probably will) tell him "No!" and put him back in the down-stay at the same place where you originally left him. (Don't let him crawl across the dining room floor!) Your first meal under this new regime will probably require several corrections, but be persistent. Remember that you're teaching a new behavior and breaking a very bad habit.

No Biting!

All it takes is one bite, and your dog could be taken from you and euthanized. All dog owners need to take this issue seriously. Most people don't realize that a dog bite is legally defined as an incident where the dog's teeth touch skin. Breaking the skin is not necessary nor are puncture wounds. If the dog touches skin with an open mouth, that is a dog bite. Vicious intent is not required, either. If your dog is in the backyard with the kids and grabs the neighbor's son with his teeth, it's a dog bite, even if the dog just wanted to be a part of the game.

It's important to teach all dogs that teeth are not allowed to touch skin—ever! That means the dog is not to grab at your hand when he wants you to do something nor is he to protest (with his teeth) when you take something away from him. He should not use his mouth when you play with him—no grabbing your arm or pantleg. To keep your dog safe, simply do not ever allow him to touch teeth to skin no matter what the circumstances.

This can be very difficult for some Goldens. Some seem to need to have something of yours in their mouth—either your hand, your pant leg, or the leash—and to these dogs, an empty mouth is horrible! If you have such a dog, teach him to carry a tennis ball or a toy instead. When your Golden reaches out to grab you or your clothes, hand him a ball, and praise him when he takes it. When you find him carrying the ball (or toy) on his own, praise him enthusiastically!

It's easy for young puppies to learn to not use their mouth. Every time the puppy grabs skin or clothes, tell him, "No bite!" in a deep tone of voice and take your hand away. If he does it during games, simply stand up and end the game. If he does bite hard, say "Ouch!" in a high pitched, hurt tone of voice, being very dramatic. Then tell the puppy, "No bite!"

No Rough Stuff

To many boys and young men, one of the favorite games to play with the family dog is wrestling. The owner and dog get down on the floor and roll around, pinning each other and having a great time. Most dogs enjoy the game, too.

Another game that most dogs love is tug-of-war. Your dog has one end of a toy (or something of yours, like a shoe) and you have the other end. Your dog may think it's a game, but depending on the situation, you may not—especially if you're trying to get your shoe back!

Unfortunately, although these are often your dog's favorite games, they are not always safe games for dogs. If your dog has a tendency to use his mouth in these games—to grab and hold on—wrestling and tug-of-war reinforce that tendency. In other words, these games teach the dog that he can use his mouth on people. This is a bad lesson for the dog to learn. So resist the urge to play these games and have a nice game of fetch instead.

If the puppy is persistent and keeps trying to use his mouth, take hold of him by his buckle collar with one hand and close his mouth with the other hand as you give him a verbal correction. Do not let go until he accepts the correction. If he struggles and fights you, sit down on the floor and hold him on your lap or between your legs until he relaxes. If you let go too soon, he will simply turn and try to get you again.

Older puppies or adult Goldens who have been allowed to use their mouth will have a little harder time changing their bad habit. Again, you must let the dog know each and every time he does it that it is no longer accepted. Tell him, "No bite!" and take your hand away. If he does it during play, end whatever game you're playing. Don't let him mouth you while you're grooming him, petting him, or trimming his toenails. Be consistent and make sure other family members are, too.

Time Out!

If your puppy throws a temper tantrum when you correct him—he throws himself around and acts like a wild animal—simply take him to his crate and put him inside, closing the door behind him. Don't yell at him; don't scold him. Just put him away and give him a 15 or 20 minute time-out. This gives him a chance to relax and you a chance to take a deep breath. Most puppies will throw a temper tantrum at some point during puppyhood, but you don't want to give in to that kind of behavior. Set the kitchen timer and let him out in 15 or 20 minutes.

If your dog seems intent on mouthing you, or if you have a bad feeling that your Golden may actually bite you one day, call a professional trainer or behaviorist for help. Don't wait until a bite has already happened. Get help if you feel that you simply cannot control the situations where your dog may want to use his mouth (or teeth).

Dogs have received a lot of bad press lately, especially in dog bite situations. Every time a dog bite story ends up on the evening news, more and more anti-dog legislation is introduced. It is now illegal to own certain breeds of dogs in some parts of the United States. England and other countries have outlawed some breeds of dogs. For dog owners, this should be very frightening—our ability to actually own a specific breed of dog is being threatened. So, please do your part and be sure to train your dog to not bite!

Digging

Dogs dig for a number of reasons, all of which are very natural and normal to the dog. Your Golden may think the dirt smells good after a rain or after the sprinklers have been on. Perhaps you have a gopher or mole, and she wants to investigate this intruder. If the weather is hot, she may want to dig down to some cool earth to lay on. Your dog has no idea why you are so upset about digging; a smooth, green lawn with no holes in it is not one of your dog's priorities!

Because digging is so natural, it's a good idea to give your dog someplace where she can dig. If there is a particular spot she really likes—perhaps in a corner behind the garage or next to the back porch—let her have that spot. Frame it off with wood if you want, or with bricks. Dig it up even more so it's nice and soft and then bury and partially bury some dog toys and treats. Invite her to dig here and then praise her when she does.

In the rest of your yard, fill in her holes and sprinkle some grass seed over them. If there are a couple of holes that she has dug up repeatedly, after you fill the holes in spread some hardware cloth (wire mesh) over it and anchor it down. Let the grass grow up through this mesh; you can leave it permanently if it's anchored well enough. If your dog tries to re-dig her hole, she will hit the wire mesh, won't be able to dig, and will quit because the wire mesh won't feel good on her paw pads.

If you catch the dog in the act of digging, you can correct her as you would for any other misbehavior, but don't count on catching her. Most dogs seem to dig when they are alone, usually in the morning just after their owner leaves for work. A strenuous morning run or a good game of catch might alleviate the digging problem—it's worth a try!

Destructive Chewing

As with many other undesirable activities, chewing on things is a natural behavior for puppies. Your Golden puppy started chewing to relieve the discomfort of teething, but he probably quickly

Too Many Toys?

If your dog is a chewer, don't try to change his behavior by giving him lots of toys. Too many toys may give him the idea that everything is his and that he can chew on everything because he has all these toys! Instead, just give him two or three toys at a time. If you like getting him toys, that's fine, just rotate them. On Monday, give him a rawhide and a squeaky toy. On Tuesday, you can give him a new rawhide, a rope tug toy, and a tennis ball. By rotating the toys, you can keep him interested in them, at the same time, you won't give him the message that it's okay to chew on anything and everything.

discovered that chewing was fun. It gave him something to do when he was bored.

Unfortunately for you and your dog, chewing can be very destructive and costly so it is a behavior that needs to be controlled. Notice I didn't say "stopped"—I said "controlled." Your puppy needs to be able to chew, so you will need to teach him what to chew on first, then prevent destructive chewing.

As with the other problems we've discussed, prevention is important. Close closet doors, make sure shoes and dirty clothes are put away, and have the kids put away their toys. Don't let your Golden have free run of the house until he is grown up and totally reliable. Keep him close to you and prevent him from wandering away. When he picks up something he shouldn't have, take it away from him as you let him know that was wrong, "No! That's mine!" Then hand him one of his toys, "Here, this is yours!"

When your dog picks up one of his toys on his own, praise him! Tell him what a smart dog he is and how proud you are of him! Really go overboard. When he learns that this is a good choice, he will be more likely to repeat it later.

If you find that he has chewed something up when you weren't around, don't scold him. Remember, after-the-fact corrections don't work.

Other Undesirable Behaviors

Golden Retrievers are usually pretty good dogs. Unlike some other breeds, their owners don't have to deal with too many problem behaviors. The common problems faced by most Golden owners (especially the owners of young Goldens) include rowdy behavior, lack of self-control, and jumping on people. Training can help all three of these problems, and maturity (combined with training) will help the first two.

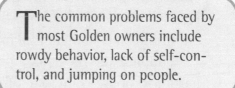

The common problems faced by most Golden owners include rowdy behavior, lack of self-control, and jumping on people.

If your Golden has any other behavior problems, you can approach them using the same methods we've discussed. What is your dog doing? When does he do it? Why does he do it? Does he need more training? More exercise? Can you catch him in the act so that you can teach him? Can you set him up so that you can catch him in the act? If you can't catch him in the act, can you prevent it from happening?

If you are unable to solve this or other behavior problems, don't hesitate to call a reputable trainer or behaviorist for some help. Ask your veterinarian whom he recommends.

House-Training

House-training is primarily a matter of taking your dog outside when he needs to go, making sure he relieves himself, and restricting his freedom in the house until he is reliably trained.

Using a Crate to House-Train

When we introduced crates a few pages ago, I said that a crate is a wonderful training tool to help you house-train your puppy or adult Goldens (even if the adult was never in a crate as a puppy). Because puppies are born with an instinct to keep their bed clean and will toddle away from their bed as soon as they are able, a crate builds on that instinct. When the puppy is confined to the crate during the night, the puppy can develop greater bowel and bladder control. Of course, that means you must let the puppy out of the crate and get him outside when he cries to be let out.

Puppies who have been purchased from a pet store are often harder to house-train than other puppies, because the puppy has had to learn to relieve himself in his cage at the pet store. His instinct to get away from his bed was lost because he had no alternative; he had to relieve himself in his cage.

House-Training Guidelines

Using a crate is not all that needs to be done to house-train a baby puppy, older puppy, or adult Golden. He also needs to be taught to ask to go outside and to relieve himself when he is outside.

Sending the dog outside alone won't work. If you just open the door and shove the dog outside, how do you know that he has relieved himself when you let him in a half an hour later? He may have spent that half hour chasing butterflies! You need to go outside with your dog. When you take him out and he sniffs the ground, tell him "Go potty!" (or whatever command you wish to use). When he does what he needs to do, praise him, "Good boy to go potty!"

Once he's done what he needs to do, bring him back inside, but don't let him have free run of the house. Put up baby gates or

House-Training Timetable

Your dog will need to relieve himself after:

○ Each meal
○ Drinking water
○ Playtime

○ Waking up from a nap
○ Every two to three hours in between

Be alert; when you see the puppy sniffing the floor and circling, grab him quickly and get him outside!

close doors so that you can restrict his activities. Do not consider him house-trained for at least six to eight months. If he has no accidents, it just means you're doing everything right!

One of the most common mistakes dog owners make in regards to house-training is that they give the puppy (or dog) too much freedom too soon. Many dogs don't want to take the time to go outside to relieve themselves, especially if their family is inside. Instead, the puppy will hide behind a sofa, or wander off to a back bedroom and relieve himself there. You may not find the "accident" for hours, and then it's much too late to do anything about it. By restricting the puppy's freedom to the room you are in, you can keep an eye on the puppy, and the puppy will be less likely to have an accident.

When Accidents Happen

If you catch the puppy in the act, you can let him know he made a mistake, "Oh no! Bad boy!" and take him outside. However, if you find a puddle, don't scold him at that point. It's too late.

When you're teaching the puppy, keep in mind that he has to relieve himself, and having a bowel movement or emptying his bladder is not wrong. If he does it in the house, the place is wrong—not the actual act of relieving himself. If the puppy misunderstands you or if you convey the wrong message and the puppy believes that relieving himself is wrong, he will stop doing it in front of you and will become sneaky about it. He will sneak to a back bedroom, or will go behind the sofa. He may hold it for hours when you're nearby, then when his bladder is ready to burst, he will go somewhere inappropriate.

You can make sure you convey the correct message if you go outside with him and praise him when he relieves himself outside, restrict his freedom inside, and correct only those accidents that you catch happening

Asking to Go Outside

Barking dogs cause many neighborhood complaints, so teaching a dog to bark when he needs to go outside can be counterproductive. Your dog does need some way to tell you he wants to go outside, however, so teach him to ring some bells instead.

Go to a craft store and get two or three bells (each about two inches across). Hang them from the door knob or handle where you want the dog to ask to go outside. Make sure they hang at your dog's nose level. Cut up some hot dogs in tiny pieces. Rub one bell with the hot dog, then invite your dog to lick it. When he licks the bell and it rings, open the door quickly, invite your dog outside, then give him a piece of hot dog as you praise him, "Good boy to ask to go outside!"

Repeat this training three or four times per session for a few days. When he starts ringing the bell on his own, praise him enthusiastically, and let him outside!

Five Basic Obedience Commands

Every dog should learn a few basic commands. You will enjoy your outings with your Golden when you know you can depend on him to be well-behaved.

Sit

When your Golden learns to sit, he also learns to control himself and his actions. When he learns to sit, you can prevent him from jumping on people; you can feed him without him knocking the bowl out of your hands; and you can get his attention to have him do other things. This is an important lesson for bouncy young Goldens.

Hold a treat in your hand and let your dog sniff it. Then take the treat up and back over his head. As his head comes up, his hips will go down.

There are several ways to teach any dog to sit, and any method is right if it works. One of the easiest methods was mentioned earlier in the chapter. Tell your dog "Lucky, sit!" as you take a treat and hold it above his nose, moving it slowly back over his head toward his tail. As his head goes up, his hips will go down. When his hips touch the ground, praise him "Good to sit!" and give him the treat.

When your dog sits and his hips are on the ground, praise him.

Another easy way is to shape the dog into the position you want as you

tell him to sit. Place your right hand on the front of your Golden's neck, under his chin. Your left hand will slide down his back as your right hand pushes up and back. (Think of a teeter-totter—up and back at the front and down in the rear.) At the same time, tell your dog, "Fido, sit!" When he sits, praise him.

With one hand on the front of the dog's chest under his neck, push gently up and back as you slide the other hand down his hips and tuck under. At the same time, tell your dog to sit. Praise him when he does.

Down

When combined with the stay command, the down command teaches your Golden to be still for gradually increased lengths of time. You can have him do a down-stay at your feet in the evening when you would like some peace and quiet. You can have him down-stay when guests come over so he isn't pestering them. He can also do a down-stay in a corner of the dining room so he isn't begging under the table. If you drop a glass to the kitchen floor and it shatters, you can tell your dog to down-stay right where he is so he doesn't walk in it and cut his feet. The down-stay is a very useful command.

Start by having your dog sit. Once he's sitting, show him a treat in your hand. As you tell him, "Fido, down!" take the treat from his nose to the ground right in front of his toes. As he moves down, you may need to rest a hand on his

Have your dog sit and then show him a treat. Tell him to lie down as you take the treat from his nose down to the ground in front of his paws.

When your dog lies down, praise him.

shoulder to keep him from popping back up. Once he's down, praise him, and give him the treat.

If he doesn't follow the treat down, gently pull his front legs forward and shape him into position. Try to help him perform the command himself, rather than physically positioning him, so he learns that the command means for him to do it, not for you to do it to him. However, if he refuses or fights you, then go ahead and shape him into the position.

If your dog doesn't lie down for the treat, just scoop his front legs out from under him and gently lay him down. Praise him even though you're helping him do it.

Stay

You want your dog to understand that stay means hold still. You will use this command when your dog is sitting or when he's lying down. In either case, it tells your dog to remain in that position until you tell him he can move.

Start by having your dog sit. Use one hand to make the stay signal, an open palm in front of your dog's nose, as you tell him, "Fido, stay!" When you're certain your dog isn't going to move, take a step or two away. If he tries to follow you, use a deep verbal correction and repeat the process. After he stays still for a few seconds, go back to your dog, pet him, and praise him.

As he learns the command, you can *gradually* increase the time and distance for the stay. For example, for the first few days, take one step away and have him hold it for 10 seconds. Later that week, take two to three steps away, and have him hold it 20 seconds. Increase it very gradually; if your dog makes quite a few mistakes, that's a sign you are moving ahead too fast. Make your increments smaller.

The signal for stay is an open-palmed gesture right in front of the dog's face.

Once you have trained him to stay and sit, introduce him to staying and down. Since he is more comfortable lying down and you've already taught the stay, he should be able to hold the down-stay for longer periods of time. Again, if your dog is making a lot of mistakes, don't increase the time and distance quite so rapidly—slow down.

Walking Nicely on the Leash

Taking your Golden for a walk should be a pleasurable experience. I enjoy walking my dogs; we visit with neighbors, watch the herons down in the riverbed, and stop to sniff the spring flowers. Our walks are enjoyable because my dogs are well behaved in public. They have learned their social manners. They don't pull on the leash, jump on people or bark at other dogs.

It's no fun to walk your dog when he pulls the leash so tight your arm hurts and he's choking himself. Your dog needs to learn

instead that the leash should be treated as something fragile and that he needs to pay attention to you.

Start by hooking the leash to your dog. Have some dog treats in one hand and hold the end of the leash in the other hand. Show your dog the treats and back away from him, encouraging him to follow you. When he does, praise him. If he doesn't follow you or doesn't pay attention, show him the treat again and back away. If he is distracted and doesn't seem motivated by the treats, try using a squeaky toy or different treats.

If your dog still wants to fight the leash or ignore you, con-

Use a treat and your happy verbal praise to encourage the dog to follow you on the leash as you back away from him. Praise him when he follows you.

tinue with the treats and backing away, but this time when he ignores you, use the leash to give a snap and release correction with the collar. A snap and release is like the bounce of a tennis ball: snap to pull the leash tight very quickly and release to let off the leash tension. The force of the snap should be only as much as necessary to get the dog's attention and *no more*. When he reacts to the snap by looking at you, praise him, show him the treat, and encourage him to follow you.

When you can back up and your Golden will follow you, turn so that you're walking forward with your dog walking close to your left side. If he pulls ahead, let him go as you hold onto the leash and back away. When he hits the end of the leash, act surprised, "Wow! How did that

When your dog is following you nicely, turn so that the both of you are walking forward together. Keep a treat handy to pop in front of his nose should he get distracted. Praise him.

When in Doubt, Sit!

If you are out in public with your Golden Retriever and he starts to get excited about something and you're afraid you might not be able to control him, have him sit. Training your Golden that sit means to sit, and sit still, teaches him self control. He can learn that when you have him sit, he had better sit still until you give him an additional command.

If, for example, another dog excites your dog, you should turn your Golden Retriever away from the other dog and make him sit. If he tries to turn around, correct him, "No! Sit, stay," and put him back in position. Repeat this routine as many times as it takes for him to calm down and listen to you. The first time you try it, you may have to repeat the sit several times. However, as your dog learns that he must control himself, the corrections will decrease.

When he does sit nicely, praise him enthusiastically!

happen?" and continue walking. Show him that when he walks with you and pays attention to you, good things happen (he gets praise and treats), but when he pulls ahead, he may get a leash correction.

Come

Life is much easier when your dog comes when you call him. Daily life is much calmer when you don't have to chase your dog all over the house to put him outside and when you don't have to worry about the dog dashing through the open door to play keep-away with the neighborhood kids.

To teach the dog to come, put your dog on leash, and have his box of dog treats in one hand. Shake the box of dog treats, tell your dog "Fido, come!" and back away from him. When he follows you, praise him, and give him a treat. You are using a sound stimulus (the box of dog treats) to make him pay more attention to your verbal command. Continue using the box of treats for as long as you need them to create a good response to the come command. With some dogs, that might even be months.

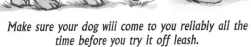

Make sure your dog will come to you reliably all the time before you try it off leash.

When your dog is responding well to your verbal command, make a long leash—20 to 30 feet of clothesline rope works well—and practice the same thing with the long leash. Take your dog out to play while dragging the long leash, then call him to come using the treats. If he comes, praise him, and give him a treat. If he doesn't come, reel in the long line to make him come and praise him anyway, but don't give him a treat.

Train the dog to come on both the regular leash and the long leash for quite a while before trying it without a leash. Make sure your dog will come to you reliably all the time before you try it off leash.

Training Is an Ongoing Process

Training your Golden can be a lot of work. It requires that you pay attention to your dog and think about what your dog is doing. You may also need to make some changes around the house and in your daily routine. Other family members will have to cooperate and you may even need to ask some neighbors to help.

A well–behaved dog is a joy to own and a pleasure to spend time with.

The payoff, however, is well worth all the effort. A well-trained dog who will reliably behave himself both at home and out in public is a joy! When your dog behaves himself, he won't be exiled to the backyard and will, instead, be a part of the family. When your dog behaves himself, you will want to spend more time with him; he will become your best friend, companion, and confidant. A well-trained dog is a joy forever!

7

Grooming

In This Chapter

- ○ Home Grooming Versus Professional Grooming
- ○ Routine Grooming Every Golden Retriever Needs
- ○ Grooming to Fight Fleas and Ticks

T he Golden Retriever is one of those rare creatures who defies the notion that beauty is only skin deep. A born beauty, this dog possesses both a captivating inner glow and an awe-inspiring external beauty.

Indeed the Golden is one of the most beautiful dogs around. That 24-karat coat alone makes this dog legendary among a more earthly canine field of tans, beiges, blacks, and browns. It is puzzling to understand how a dog of such luster could emerge from the fields and marshes of the hunting life, but that is precisely the background that sculpted this animal's phoenix-like beauty. Unfortunately, it is possible to take that beauty for granted.

Although this dog is whelped with all the necessary ingredients for becoming a classically beautiful dog, she will only claim her birthright if her gifts are properly cared for and nurtured by a devoted human caretaker. Every day, Golden Retrievers come to the nation's animal shelters and Golden rescues, the victims of unworthy caretakers who failed to carry out their responsibility. An untended coat with mats, mites, and hot spots is a nightmare to look at, and a nightmare for a dog to endure. On the other hand, a dog who is well groomed and well cared for will shimmer and shine as she prances down the street with the one she loves most.

> A dog's external appearance provides countless clues about her internal health.

Many people don't realize that a dog's external appearance provides countless clues about her internal health. Skin and coat condition are indicators of the quality of the dog's nutrition and the overall health of her internal organs, as well as indicators of how committed the owner is to the dog's basic needs. The owner who allows that golden coat to grow dingy and dull with bald patches here and there, who ignores crusty skin, incessant scratching, and the tiny critters that have taken up residence on the dog, is broadcasting to the world that he has no business living with a dog.

The responsible owner would never dream of broadcasting such messages. He understands the importance of grooming to overall health and the need to address it as a serious and permanent element in the pet-care routine. The responsible owner also knows how to read the signs of health problems often made evident by changes in his dog's appearance. The Golden Retriever is not particularly challenging in her grooming requirements, but she does require—as every dog does—a commitment to grooming from head to toe, from teeth to nails, from brush time to bath time—for as long as the dog shall live.

Home Grooming Versus Professional Grooming

Before we discuss the requirements and methods of Golden grooming, let's spend some time exploring how you might fit your dog's grooming needs into your household routine. In this area, you may face the question of home grooming versus professional grooming. And you must decide whether to do the grooming yourself, or hire someone to do it for you.

This has never been an issue for me, as I have been comfortable doing both. I have washed many a dog, many a time myself, but, when my schedule is too hectic, I also have not hesitated to call upon a good professional groomer to do the job. The latter option usually ends up as much a treat for the dog as for me. You can certainly spot the marks of a professional groomer on a dog who prances out after a day at the spa or salon. Additionally, most Golden Retrievers revel in the attention they receive at the hands of a skilled groomer.

> If you keep up with the demands of your dog's grooming, the Golden Retriever should be a relatively easy-care breed in this area. She requires no special haircuts or trims.

If you keep up with the demands of your dog's grooming, the Golden Retriever should be a relatively easy-care breed in this area. She requires no special haircuts or trims. The major grooming procedures facing those who live with this breed include routine brushing, tooth brushing, bathing, and nail clipping.

Entrusting your dog's grooming to the pros is convenient (how lovely it is to relegate that post-bath cleanup to someone else), and results in a beautiful dog who will probably come home to you with a little ribbon in her hair. But professional grooming can be too costly for some people. In addition, many owners prefer to tend to their dog's grooming themselves, which is indeed a lovely way to build and maintain the bond between a dog and her family. You'll come to know your dog so well that you'll know instantly when her coat suddenly begins to feel a bit dry to the touch or appears a little dull to the eye, or you'll recognize the first bulge of a mysterious bump on her ear flap or neck that is easily treated in its early stages.

So, I have no preference toward either home grooming or seeking out the services of a professional. It's a matter of personal preference, finances, and even housing situation. I also have no problem in combining both professional and personal services. You may decide that the warm, cozy, well-equipped grooming shop is the ideal venue for your dog's mid-winter bath, while you would like to take on the task come mid-July when the warm weather is conducive to a bath with a hose in the backyard. You don't need to choose one or the other. You can do both. Help your dog get acquainted with grooming and make positive associations with the procedures dispensed by both her owner and her groomer and enjoy the flexibility.

A clever variation on this theme was practiced by a Southern California grooming shop that I used to frequent. On certain days each month, they would welcome owners to bring their pups in to use the bathing facilities for a nominal fee.

What to Look for in a Groomer

On the whole, the Golden Retriever is one of the most amenable breeds when it comes to tolerating and even enjoying professional grooming, but it's your job to nurture that characteristic by ensuring that your dog's initial experiences with the groomer are positive ones. The first step is to choose a groomer whose personality meshes with this goal.

When seeking out the individual to whom you will entrust the care of your dog's coat and skin, do your homework. First, it helps to get some good recommendations from other dog owners. Then visit a shop or two and—as you do when searching for a veterinarian—look around and ask some questions. Is the facility clean? How does the groomer handle the dogs? Why did she become a groomer? Does the groomer ask you about your dog's likes, dislikes, and past grooming experiences? Does she ask for details about what you would like done for your dog and offer details on how these tasks are typically handled in this shop?

As with any animal-related career, some people get into grooming because they genuinely love animals and have an interest in making them beautiful and some don't. I have known both. The former were easy to spot: by the great rapport shared with their four-footed clients; by the contented attitude that stayed with those clients when they left the shop; and by the groomers' willingness to work with dogs who needed rehabilitation from past negative grooming experiences.

Sometimes this was offered only for particular breeds—Golden and Labrador Retrievers being the prime candidates, perhaps because these large active dogs tend to get into messy situations that require they be bathed more than once every month or two. It was a great idea and a surefire way to win loyalty from customers who live with some of the most popular breeds in the country. Today, many facilities provide such services, so pick up a copy of the Yellow Pages and look for a facility advertising fees for the use of their sinks, shampoos, and blow dryers.

Why Groom?

The Golden Retriever is a relatively easy-care breed, but like all dogs, she does require routine care. Because of her long hair, she isn't quite as low-maintenance as her fellow Retriever, the Labrador. In addition, like her hunting brethren, she is graced with special oils in her coat that protect her from cold water and weather. The downside is that these oils can leave a faint scent within the household that indicates to visitors that a dog lives there. Routine care of the coat and skin will help ensure that the scent doesn't get out of control.

Unless you want to be running to the groomer every couple of days, you better get acquainted with the necessary routine grooming procedures—and commit to their routine practice. Even if you have little or no experience with grooming, don't underestimate the potential of your own abilities. Bathing, brushing, tooth care, and other tasks are all skills that you can learn only by doing. You can work in partnership with your dog to master them and find a rhythm that works well for you both. The result will be a stunning 24-karat Golden and hours of pleasurable time spent deepening the bond you share.

> Unless you want to be running to the groomer every couple of days, you better get acquainted with the necessary routine grooming procedures—and commit to their routine practice.

Keeping It Positive

Success in the Golden grooming arena rests in the roots of experience. A dog who is taught from the earliest age to tolerate—and even enjoy—grooming will certainly be a superior grooming subject to an animal who wiggles and fights and makes the experience unpleasant for both of you. Fortunately, because of the Golden's natural affinity for anything that even hints of human attention, it doesn't take much effort to help a Golden Retriever become a great lover of the grooming session.

Let positive reinforcement be your guide. As soon as your Golden comes to live with you—whether as a puppy or an adult—begin to design your grooming routine. If yours is a well-adjusted adult, this should be no problem. She already knows the ropes and will help you figure out what's best for your particular partnership. But if you have a squirmy puppy on your hands, it could take a bit more work, especially because puppies tend to view the grooming tools as just a new collection of toys. By the same token, an adult with little or negative grooming experience, will require some rehabilitation in patient, gentle hands.

> For both the ornery adult and the squirmy puppy, you should keep the introductory grooming sessions short and sweet.

For both the ornery adult and the squirmy puppy, you should keep the introductory grooming sessions short and sweet. Schedule them in a quiet part of the house during quiet times of the day and keep plenty of treats, kind words, and gentle tickles handy as rewards. Make the sessions as positive as possible, and work with your pet to help her accept your attentions. You want to teach your dog to accept your touching her feet, her ears, and her tail, and to allow you to open her mouth for toothbrushing. A dog who will cooperate with these strange requests will be a far better grooming subject and a better patient for the veterinarian, as well.

If yours is a particularly resistant pooch, relax. If you feel the impulse to manhandle the dog to get the job done, and start to lose your temper, it's time to call an end to that particular session and start again when you're both fresh. The process can take time—weeks or even months with a dog who has been groomed little or not at all—but the success you reap with your calm demeanor and patience is well worth the effort.

Routine Grooming Every Golden Retriever Needs

Now that we have explored the importance of grooming and how to make it work, let's look at the procedures themselves: what you need to do for your Golden to keep her both beautiful and healthy.

Brushing

Lest you believe that brushing is performed solely for the sake of creating a beautiful dog, think again—and don't dare utter such ideas to those who rescue Golden Retrievers from abandonment and neglect. These individuals have seen far too many Goldens whose coats have rarely, if ever, felt the bristles of a brush or the bubbles of a bath. There should be a law against allowing a lovely dog like this to deteriorate so that her coat becomes dull, drab, matted, crusted with filth and parasites, and painful.

The Golden's coat is surprisingly resilient, and truly severe cases among rescued Goldens typically involve skin rather than coat problems (usually the result of neglect as well as hypothyroid conditions and food allergies). Most rescuers have stories to tell. Robin Adams, cofounder of Delaware Valley Golden Retriever Rescue in Pennsylvania, and writer and producer of the video *Grooming Your Golden,* remembers one female Golden found wandering a New Jersey street. "She was so badly matted," remembers Robin, "that the ladies who found her thought she was a goat." Like most rescued Goldens, this girl cleaned up beautifully and was very cooperative—grateful for the attention and affection.

Think, then, of the power you possess when you hold your dog's brush in your hand. Use the power wisely, and use it regularly.

The whole idea of brushing can sound easier than it really is. Not that it's some mammoth task, but it can be a bit more involved than what appears on the surface—and the surface is where too many people confine their efforts. Your goal is to brush those shining strands from skin to tip and everywhere in between. Performing this task correctly—brushing from root to tip and from head to tail—will take far longer than simply running the brush lightly over the coat and going on your way. Doing it right means setting aside an ample amount of time and practicing effective brushing techniques.

The tools you employ for this grand mission can be a pin brush (a metal-bristle brush with ball-tipped bristles that protect the skin and prevent tearing of the hair) or a slicker brush (a fine metal-bristle, rectangular-shaped brush with delicate bristles that are especially handy when your dog is shedding).

To begin, choose a section—say the right side of your dog's back—and concentrate on that section, taking great care to brush down to the skin to help distribute the oils evenly from the skin to the tip of each strand of hair. Brushing against the lay of the hair growth is one way to make sure you get down to the skin. Then

Did You Know?

Human bites are usually more dangerous than dog bites because a dog's mouth has fewer germs and bacteria.

brush with the grain to finish it off with a clean look, and move on to the next section. If along the way, you come across a mat, my suggestion is to cut it out rather than use a mat comb, which can be painful to the dog. Either way, mats must be removed as they inhibit air flow to the skin and tighten up when saturated with water from swimming or bathing. Keep those mats under control! A severely matted Golden will require whole-body shaving by a professional, and the result is rarely a pretty sight.

If you can't complete the entire dog in one sitting, don't fret. You can come back to the job later. Over time, you may even develop a weekly pattern you follow that ensures you address the entire pup at least twice a week—and preferably more. You should also brush your dog after outdoor activity to prevent mats and to remove twigs, foxtails, or other items these active dogs often pick up in their coats. Pay attention to what you find during these post-activity grooming sessions. Remember that the better you know your dog's coat, skin, and overall structure, the quicker you'll notice just the slightest change—a lump, a bump, a bald patch, a tick, or other parasite—that could indicate problems that might now be easily nipped in the bud.

Bathing

Bathing can be fun, but not if you insist on getting through it without getting wet. We're talking about a big, water-loving dog here. At some time during the bath, he will decide to shake all that water off his coat, and you will find yourself right in the line of fire. So accept the inevitable and enjoy yourself!

> Bathing can be fun, but not if you insist on getting through it without getting wet. We're talking about a big, water-loving dog here.

First, choose the bath site. This can be in your own bathtub, or if the weather is warm, outdoors in a makeshift tub or simply on a concrete surface with a hose (a lawn invites and inspires rolling behavior, which results in a dirty, possibly flea-infested dog). Next, assemble your supplies: several clean towels, a washcloth, shampoo, and, if you will be using them, conditioner or flea dip. Then retrieve your Retriever. Goldens are water dogs, so you would think they would naturally enjoy bath time, but even the dog who takes a dip in your pool whenever possible may run and hide when he realizes that this particular dip involves shampoo. So track him down, bring him to the bath, give him a quick brushing to rid the coat of tangles that will mat with water, and get him wet.

Because of that somewhat water-resistant coat, this could take a while. One effective outdoor method I recommend, for those willing and able to engage in heavy lifting, involves filling a large, clean garbage can with lukewarm water and placing the dog inside the can (with his head above the water, of course). Take him out and you will have a saturated dog.

The next step is shampooing. A variety of shampoos are available on the grooming shelves at pet supply stores. Choose one that is best suited to your dog's needs: a flea shampoo, one for sensitive skin, one for puppies, or one for dogs prone to hot spots. Apply the shampoo, and as you do with brushing, try to scrub down to the skin for thorough cleaning. While you're at it, be cautious with the head area. Some people place cotton balls in the dog's ears to prevent water from infiltrating the ear canal, but I personally have never needed to do this even with dogs with erect ears. I find it easiest to wash the rest of the dog's body first. Then, at the end I wash the head with the washcloth without allowing water and soap to get into the eyes or ears.

Did You Know?

Nose prints can be used to identify dogs just as fingerprints are used to identify humans.

Now on to the step that typically takes the longest: the rinsing. Again this thick coat can prove a challenge to your efforts to remove every last sud from its golden strands. You must rinse, rinse, rinse, and when you can't see anymore evidence of soap, rinse again. And again, for good measure. Residual soap can dry the skin and coat, something the skin-problem–prone Golden Retriever can't afford to risk.

Once you have completed the rinsing—and if applicable, the flea dipping and conditioning that occur after rinsing—look out! Your dog will want to assist you in the drying process by shaking all that excess water off of his newly cleaned coat, and that can provide quite a shower for you. If you're not outside already, you may want to get the dog outside before the shaking begins (good luck!), then let him do his stuff to his heart's content. One word of advice though: Make sure he's on a leash, because as soon as he's outdoors he may run to the nearest dirt pile or mud puddle, plunge in, and start to roll. Then it's back to square one.

Water dogs that they are, Goldens dry fairly quickly, but you should still try to keep your dog in a relatively warm place to dry. As the coat dries, brush or comb it lightly to prevent tangles in the coat.

Ears

The after-bath brushing session is also a good time to clean your pet's ears. Do this using mineral oil on a cotton ball and rubbing it on the inside of the ear flap only. Nothing should go inside the ear. You should, however, smell your dog's ears occasionally to detect any change in the normal scent that could indicate infection or parasites, and thus, veterinary attention. And finally, reward your pup for tolerating your ministrations.

Anal Glands

Some suggest that bath time is the time to express the anal glands, but I will not suggest this as I am not a fan of this routine procedure. (Expressing the anal glands means squeezing fluid from the glands at the opening of the anus.) I have always made sure that any groomers to whom I took my dogs did not do this as a routine part of the bath, because performing this rather gruesome task can result in a dog's requiring it from then on. The anal glands of a healthy dog should be expressed naturally when the dog defecates. If your dog has a problem in this area, it might be more pleasant for you and your dog to get veterinary help and instruction for the procedure.

Nail Clipping

This is one task that causes much grief to dog owners who live with all breeds, all sizes, and all mixes of dogs. Most Golden Retriever rescuers will tell you their unfortunate charges rebel against this one grooming act most vehemently. This is usually because the rescue dog has had little or no experience with the procedure, and consequently, his feet are sensitive and may be aching from sore, overgrown, and neglected nails.

Early positive training will help prevent the stress and strain that so often accompany this task, which somehow or another must be addressed for the health of the dog. Overgrown nails can result in deformed feet, intense pain, and crippled movement. If you absolutely don't think you're up to nail

Did You Know?

Dalmatian puppies are born pure white; they don't start getting spots until they are three or four days old.

clipping, ask the veterinarian or groomer to do it for you, but make sure it is done regularly.

Of course it really isn't as bad as it looks. First, purchase a sturdy set of nail clippers made for large dogs and, just in case, a container of styptic (blood-stopping) powder from the pet supply store or through mail order. Now look at your dog's nails and note the light-colored tips and the darker base, the latter of which is the blood-rich quick. You will want to clip only that light colored tip; if you cut into the quick, profuse bleeding and some pain will occur, thus the need for the styptic powder. If your dog's nails are naturally black in color (where you can't tell where the quick begins), then clip only the very tips and clip them more frequently (say, every week).

If your dog has his dewclaws (the nails that grow from the ankle and don't touch the ground when the dog walks), don't forget to trim them. Left unattended, these nails can curve around and ultimately pierce the dog's leg, causing great pain and potential infection.

> If your dog isn't a big fan of nail clipping, don't force the issue. Keep the treats handy, and don't insist that the dog tolerate getting of all his nails clipped in a single session.

Needless to say, overgrown nails and their attendant pain are common problems for dogs who have not received the adequate care that all dogs require. After being through such foot-related pain, you'll understand why it may take some time and gentle rehabilitation to convince such dogs that they can allow humans to touch their feet and pull on them with these noisy clippers.

If your dog isn't a big fan of nail clipping, don't force the issue. Keep the treats handy (and perhaps reserve a special treat that is offered only for nail clipping), and don't insist that the dog tolerate getting of all his nails clipped in a single session. You may need to divide the feet up over the course of a few days, doing a few nails (or even only one nail), at a time. Do whatever you need to do to get the nails trimmed. Contact the groomer or vet for help if you need to. Your pup's foot health and overall comfort depend on it. Remain calm, cool, and consistent, and don't be surprised if in time your dog learns to tolerate the procedure gracefully—and maybe even starts to enjoy it!

Tooth Care

Dogs are prone to most of the same dental problems that we humans are—problems that can be averted through solid preventive tooth care. Proper care of the teeth involves a partnership between the dog's owner and his veterinarian. Your job as Golden caretaker is to brush your pup's teeth on a regular basis (every day if you can). This is supplemented by professional cleanings from the veterinarian twice a year (ideally), or as needed—a process you cannot do at home because the dog must be anesthetized to ensure thorough and proper cleaning. Such sessions also permit the veterinarian to examine the mouth for signs of potential gum infections or the need for tooth extractions. As an added word of warning, steer clear of groomers who claim they can clean a dog's teeth as effectively as a veterinarian. They may charge less, but without anesthesia (which only veterinarians can legally administer), groomers can't possibly do as thorough a job. They are also not equipped to prevent, diagnose, or treat the problems that so often develop in the mouth, a region ripe for infection.

Dogs today are living longer than ever before, so their teeth need to last longer than ever before, too. To ensure our dogs enjoy their senior years

with their teeth and gums intact and their mouths free from pain, we cannot afford to ignore the teeth or to underestimate the importance of our role in their care and preservation.

To live up to this responsibility, you will need the proper tools: a toothbrush and toothpaste made specifically for dogs. Leave products made for humans to the humans—such toothbrushes do not properly accommodate the unique contours of the canine mouth, and human toothpaste will upset the canine stomach. Toothpastes made for dogs will also make your job easier, because they are flavored to appeal to the unique tastes of the canine palate. You would probably refuse to brush with a meat-flavored toothpaste, but your dog will love it.

> Toothpastes made for dogs will also make your job easier, because they are flavored to appeal to the unique tastes of the canine palate. You would probably refuse to brush with a meat-flavored toothpaste, but your dog will love it.

As you do with most of the more challenging grooming activities, choose a quiet time of day for toothbrushing, and, just like all interactions with your dog, keep the toothbrushing experience as positive as possible. I like to rest the dog's head, shoulders, and front legs on my lap—a position that proves comfortable for brusher and brushee alike. I then place a dab of paste on the brush and hold it in one hand, while I pull the lips apart and expose the back molars by pulling back with my finger in the corner of the dog's lips. If your dog is accustomed to the practice, he'll know what to expect and should anxiously anticipate this unique "treat." I then brush the teeth in a circular motion from the molars in back to the front teeth on one side of the jaw. After that, I place another dab of toothpaste on the brush and repeat the process on the same side. I then

Grooming Tools

Even the amateur Golden Retriever groomer should assemble a complete grooming kit and keep it handy for those times each week when you are called to do your part. The following are some suggestions for what kind of items you might include in your kit. Assemble these items, and keep them all together in a roomy, covered plastic box or crate.

- ○ Pin brush and/or slicker brush
- ○ Wide-tooth comb
- ○ Flea comb
- ○ Shampoo (shampoo for fighting fleas, sensitive skin, etc.)
- ○ Conditioner (optional)
- ○ Flea dip (optional)
- ○ Several old bath towels (wash after each use)
- ○ Sturdy nail clippers for large dogs
- ○ Container of styptic powder
- ○ Mineral oil
- ○ Cotton balls
- ○ Blunt-nosed scissors (for quick, painless mat removal)
- ○ Rubbing alcohol (for removing tree sap from the coat)
- ○ Special treats (for bribes)

switch sides and repeat the process twice on the other side of the jaw.

Grooming to Fight Fleas and Ticks

Of course we cannot discuss grooming without also discussing one of the most frustrating problems associated with that topic: the war against fleas and ticks. Although both blood-sucking parasites are capable of causing a great deal of discomfort, fleas are far more prevalent and pervasive than ticks. In most cases, by fighting the flea, you also fight the tick. In a sense, you kill two parasites with one spray, pill, or whatever magic bullet you choose for this battle. And, indeed, a battle it can be.

For most Americans, fleas are a seasonal problem, and flea control is an activity owners need pursue only during the warmer months of the year. But in more temperate regions—Florida for instance—fleas are a year-round scourge. Either way, you'll need to get a handle on the problem—preferably before it grows to epidemic proportions within your household. Prevention will not only protect your dog, but also the human members of your family as well.

Secret to Success

The secret to a successful flea-control program is the three-pronged attack. Find a flea or the telltale black specks of flea excrement on the dog's skin (called "flea dirt"), and you have a problem. Fleas are not only on the dog, but also in the dog's environment—your environment. You'll need to attack them on every front simultaneously, or you will never succeed in controlling their phenomenal reproduction and infiltration rates.

The products you use in this fight can be highly toxic, especially if combined with other products with which they are incompatible, so choose carefully. This is best done with some advice from your Golden's veterinarian, especially if your dog suffers from skin prob-

lems caused by hypothyroidism and food allergies, or has flea-bite dermatitis or other skin sensitivities and allergies. Whether you obtain your flea-control arsenal from the veterinarian's office or the pet supply store, you will need to make sure that whatever you choose is safe for your pet and your family, and that it meshes safely with the other products you choose for the attacks within the house and in the yard.

The Art of War

The first theater of war in the fight against fleas is, of course, the dog. A variety of methods exist to kill fleas and flea eggs living on your dog. Contrary to what many advertisements may tell you, a flea collar snapped around the dog's neck won't do the job. It may kill the fleas on the neck right where the collar lays (and may simultaneously cause an annoying rash in the region, too), but it won't do anything for the groin area, a favored flea hang-out, nor will it be able to keep up with the constant threats that await in the outdoors.

A better route is a more topical, systemic plan that involves flea shampoos to destroy an existing flea population on the dog's body. This should be followed by compatible dips and/or sprays with residual punch that will help keep new populations from taking hold. Another new-and-improved, not to mention exciting method of prevention is oral and topical (applied directly to the skin) medications obtained only by prescription from a veterinarian. These medications keep fleas at bay internally, often by making the dog's skin unappetizing to fleas and/or preventing pre-adult fleas from maturing (see Chapter 5). Consult your dog's veterinarian on how these promising products may benefit your pet.

> Whether you obtain your flea-control arsenal from the veterinarian's office or the pet supply store, you will need to make sure that whatever you choose is safe for your pet and your family.

Though researchers are constantly discovering new and effective methods for killing fleas, Golden owners are just as constantly reporting negative reactions in their pups to both high-tech medications and topical sprays and dips. Golden Retrievers are dogs who can be highly susceptible to skin problems. So, treat the dog only as directed and as needed, and get veterinary advice on what might be best for your particular pet as well as on any potential adverse reactions he may experience.

Your second front in this battle is your home. You may not see the fleas, but if they have taken up residence on your dog, you can rest assured that they have done the same in your home. For this attack, you will find sprays and bombs designed to destroy these unwanted guests who have staked claims in your carpets, your furniture, even your beds. Because these products are essentially poisons, respect them as such. Read the packaging carefully and use them only as directed. Also be sure to choose products that are designed to kill both adult and pre-adult (larvae) fleas.

And finally, don't forget the great outdoors—the third front. You can make heroic efforts to rid your pet and your home of fleas. But the moment your dog walks into the backyard, where he spends a good deal of time, a whole new population hops aboard before he has even had a chance to find his tennis ball. These will soon find their way into your home, too. Of course you can't rid the fleas from your local park, lakefront, or all the other places you frequent with your dog, but you can keep your yard— the outdoor area closest to your own front door—under control. Here, too, only safe, compatible, and properly administered products should be used.

So, good luck to you. When confronted seriously and with an unflappable commitment, a successful flea-control battle need not

be nearly as daunting as it may sound. It can also leave you with a sense of satisfaction when you realize that your efforts are resulting in a healthier, happier, more comfortable existence for the Golden Retriever with whom you share your life.

8

Family Life

In This Chapter

o Play Time
o Playing Nicely with Children
o Making Your Golden Retriever a Good Neighbor
o Traveling with and Boarding Your Dog

Discuss family around a Golden Retriever and you are speaking this dog's true native language—one that transcends the barks, whines, and tail wags that comprise the traditional canine "tongue." Although almost every dog is whelped with a natural affinity for kinship with both humans and canines, for the Golden Retriever, such kinship is a vocation, a higher calling, and the reason for this dog's existence.

And what an honor it is to be deemed family by this golden dog. Life is never dull with a Golden Retriever around the house, and the people who live with this dog are never lonely. Whether you want company or not, you'll have it, as this dog cannot allow any family project or get-together to pass by without her participation. So, if you are looking for a devoutly independent pet, this is not the breed for you.

If, however, you are looking for the kind of human-canine relationship of which legends are made, this is the dog. Commit to this animal, and you also commit to providing her with regular (every day) activities, exercise, and companionship that will stimulate both her mind and body. And, as you'll quickly discover, what's good for the Golden is equally good for the Golden's person, so dive in and enjoy the delightful turn your life can take once this golden dog crosses your threshold.

Play Time

If we were to attempt to list all the games that Golden Retrievers and their people play, and all the activities in which they participate together, that would fill an entire encyclopedia. From basic fetch-and-retrieve games, to competitive obedience and agility, to search-and-rescue, to therapy work, to football in the backyard— nothing is too complex or mundane for the playful Golden Retriever.

The variety of games Goldens play is testament to this breed's love of fun, and its creativity in concocting new games and activities with those who regard their Goldens as family. Once a Golden Retriever enters your household, together you will immediately begin to design your play and exercise routine.

Exercise

We have said it over and over, but here it is again: Golden Retrievers need lots of exercise. And they need that exercise every day. This dog was made for a life of work and hunting. As we have seen, when a dog with such vigorous working class roots is plopped down in a modern-day "family dog" situation, those ingrained working energies must be channeled in some other direction. If that direction is not positive and one of your own choosing, the dog will create his own outlets, and in 90 percent of such cases, the results won't be pretty.

You must thus ensure that your Golden receives the exercise he requires every day. Now don't worry. This doesn't mean that you need to run marathons and climb Mount Everest together. No, you can satisfy your pet's exercise needs through far more simple, accessible pursuits, using activities that will benefit you as well as your pooch.

> Golden Retrievers need lots of exercise. And they need that exercise every day. This dog was made for a life of work and hunting.

Just taking your dog out on a daily walk is a great way to start. I'm not talking about forcing the dog to walk by your side for a mile in a perfect heel. That's no fun for anyone. Go ahead and practice some of your obedience commands, but the bulk of the walk should be for enjoyment purposes. You shouldn't allow the dog to pull you down the sidewalk, but he should be allowed some freedom to explore. The walk (with the dog on a leash, of course) provides the perfect opportunity for enjoying the fresh air, stretching the muscles, lubricating the joints, conditioning the cardiovascular system, stimulating the digestive tract (don't forget the cleanup bags), and arousing the dog's natural curiosity and exploration instincts. A basic dog walk can work wonders for body and soul.

Once inspired by the joy of walking, you may want to take this a step further by trying jogging, cycling, or even in-line skating with your dog. Keep in mind, though, that obedience training (and appropriate safety gear) lies at the heart of success in these areas. You must be able to trust that this big athletic dog will obey you when you are in the vulnerable position of rolling alongside him on a set of wheels.

Swimming is another excellent exercise for those Goldens who embody their water-retriever roots—either laps with an owner in the swimming pool, or swimming out over and over again to fetch a stick thrown into a lake or ocean. An East Coast Golden owner I know reports that one of her dog's favorite games is to "rescue" swimmers who venture into the deep end of the family's swimming pool. So diligent is he in his mission, that he won't stop until he is assured everyone is "safe." Once he realizes that they are all safe, he emerges satisfied that he has accomplished a great task, and fully exercised in mind and body.

> You can take the dog walk one step further by introducing your Golden to the joys of hiking.

Be warned, however, that exercise of any kind must be pursued carefully. This means working up to athletic prowess and meeting exercise demands gradually, exercising your pup during the cooler times of the day (to prevent heatstroke), and bringing water along to keep your pup properly hydrated.

Careful exercise also means working within the parameters of your dog's age and capabilities. Though puppies are bundles of energy, demanding the same from them as you would a dog of four or five can hinder proper growth and development and basically amounts to cruelty. A safer, kinder exercise program for a puppy would be game-oriented activities, such as short fetch and chase games coupled with short walks, short swims—everything short, sweet, and stress free. The same can be

Hiking with Goldens

You can take the dog walk one step further by introducing your Golden to the joys of hiking. The same rules apply: Condition your dog properly for the demands of hiking, build up gradually in the distance of hikes you pursue, beware of the dangers of extreme temperatures (anything hotter than 80 degrees can safely be considered "extreme"), keep your dog on a leash (be considerate of the wild animals who may be frightened by the presence of a big domestic dog in their midst), and bring along ample supplies of water for you both. In addition, follow the rules of the trail, and clean up after yourself and your dog. Once you return home, check your pup carefully for ticks, embedded foxtails, and foot injuries.

If you decide you would like to remain in the great outdoors for longer than a day, you can outfit your pup with a backpack made especially for dogs (available by mail order and from camping stores). Train your dog to wear the backpack at home, then on walks. She'll soon be ready to tackle the trail carrying her own food, water, and cleanup supplies on her back (which she can do on a day hike, too). I told you life would never be lonely with a Golden Retriever by your side.

said of overworking an older dog. Use your common sense and listen to your dog.

If, for instance, recruiting your Golden as a jogging partner is your goal, once your pup is at least two years old, begin with walking ever-increasing distances, then gradually segue into jogging ever-increasing distances. Consult your veterinarian first, especially if your Golden is dysplastic, even mildly so. Goldens are some of the most eager-to-please pups on the planet, and they will do anything to please those they love, even if that means pushing themselves through debilitating pain. Don't put your dog in that position. Ask only what he is capable of doing, and make sure that he enjoys doing it. You'll both end up winners in the long run—and you'll both probably live longer too.

Fun and Games

To most Goldens, any type of exercise is itself fun and games. They adore the activity, the opportunity to get out, to seek new scents and visit with all the other dogs and people they encounter along the way, and to spend time with the people they love. But there are some activities rooted purely in fun.

You usually come up with these games together. If, for example, you are a swimmer and your Golden is one who loves water (not all do, so never assume), you will probably devise a variety of water games. You might enjoy swimming together in a local lake or even bodysurfing when the waves aren't too high at the beach. Even if your dog doesn't enjoy ocean swimming (or you are leery of the danger), you can take advantage of the waves—the ultimate retrieval toy. During a walk along the beach, your dog can run after the waves as they retreat back into the ocean, then run back to the sand when the waves turn around and "chase" the dog.

Land-based games usually begin with the Golden's natural love of retrieving everything—tennis balls, Frisbees, squeaky toys, and even water bottles. This blossoms into the retrieval of a humorous collection of items, which in one case I know of involves a Golden with a shoe fetish. This dog retrieves one shoe, then searches the house for its mate; his owner plays along by hiding shoes in different rooms to make the game more challenging and more fun.

Dog trainer Janet Boss of Ellicott City, Maryland, is amazed by her Golden Teddy's delight in retrieving virtually anything that is thrown into the swimming pool—including swimmers. Teddy has also been known to retrieve live seagulls, pigeons, quail, and even a rabbit.

You might also tailor traditional games to your dog's abilities. I devised a canine football game with one of my dogs years ago. My husband and I would form the defensive line. One of us would throw a small football, and the dog would run and fetch it. Then, with the ball held protectively in his mouth, our canine receiver would attempt to run through our defensive line. Once successfully through, he would stop and dance around like an NFL pro, essentially knowing that he had scored. All that was missing was the spiked ball!

> Games usually begin with the Golden's natural love of retrieving everything—tennis balls, Frisbees, squeaky toys, and even water bottles.

Just use your imagination. The sky's the limit in the number and nature of games you can create with your pet, so don't underestimate your dog. Dogs are intelligent animals by nature, and in the Golden, this is compounded by an intense desire to please. Play on these natural instincts and delight in the brilliance of this fun-loving creature with whom you have the honor of living and playing.

Formal Activities

Take full advantage of life with a Golden Retriever, and your days will be filled with laughter and new adventures. You may also choose to participate in the many formal activities available in this golden age of dog ownership. These, too, may be pursued as family activities, as the entire family realizes that there is no finer partner than the Golden Retriever—the veritable king (and usually the champion) of all manner of canine activity.

In the Ring   Conformation dog showing—referred to by some as the beauty pageants of the dog world—is an activity in which dogs are judged on how well they meet the ideal standard for their breed. The theory behind it is that only those dogs who closely meet the ideal should be bred (although there is some controversy over where the various, often invisible, genetic maladies, fall into this equation).

In the American Kennel Club (AKC) show ring, Goldens show as part of the Sporting Group. They first compete against each other according to their age and gender, after which one is deemed "Best of Breed." That dog then competes with the other breed winners in his group. The various "Best of Group" winners then compete for "Best in Show" honors. Shows are held throughout the year all over the country and can be located by calling the AKC, reviewing the schedules published in national dog magazines, or by contacting local kennel clubs in your area.

Conformation showing isn't for everyone, and newcomers to the ring might have a tough time winning with a breed as immensely popular as the Golden Retriever. But don't let that dissuade you. Everyone has to start somewhere. If this is an activity in which you think you'd like to participate, start by attending dog shows to get acquainted with the ins and outs—and the politics—of dog showing. Then you'll need to get yourself a show-quality dog, best obtained from a serious, ethical show breeder with whom you are compatible, who understands your desires, and who is willing to help you out as a mentor. This is the best route to take into the complex and even frustrating dog show world.

Regardless of your aspirations, your dog must be a pet first, a show dog second. That means choosing a dog or puppy according to the same health and behavior factors you would if seeking a family pet. Show the dog only if he enjoys it (not all dogs do), and never take showing too seriously. Keep a sense of humor, and you'll all have more fun.

Beyond Beauty Pageants—Obedience, Agility, and Field Trials
If conformation showing isn't your thing, there are other show-ring pursuits you might find more enjoyable—pursuits that call upon the Golden Retriever's natural instincts, wit, and inclinations. These include obedience competitions, agility, and field trials.

As the annals of canine obedience competition demonstrate, there is no greater competitor in canine obedience than the Golden Retriever. Additionally, it is not unusual to see a long list of letters following a Golden's official name. Those letters boast to the world that this dog has earned virtually every obedience title on the planet. It's also a strong possibility that the dog adored every minute of earning those letters.

The road toward those titles begins in basic obedience classes. Once a dog graduates from those, he can move on to more advanced classes designed to prepare him for competition.

> It is not unusual to see a long list of letters following a Golden's official name. Those letters boast that this dog has earned virtually every obedience title on the planet.

The beauty of obedience competition is that a dog is essentially competing against himself, flexing his own ever-increasing obedience muscles. The process, which involves ongoing obedience classes and practice at home—all pursued with a sense of humor—can be fun and challenging for the whole family. It can also be an excellent bonding experience. Obedience work itself builds closeness and confidence for dogs and their owners, especially when part of the daily routine.

Another wonderful, and rather new, activity for Golden Retrievers is agility. Here the competition level is low, the fun level sky high. That fun revolves around a course of obstacles, tunnels, bridges, and such that the participating dogs are asked to traverse as quickly and gracefully as possible. The dog's handler (his owner) is intimately involved every step of the way, from the training to the actual competition. During the latter, the owner plays cheerleader and coach as the dog goes through his paces. The dog is never alone, and neither is his human partner. It's no wonder that agility is one of the fastest growing, and most popular, entries to the canine sports scene.

> Obedience work itself builds closeness and confidence for dogs and their owners, especially when part of the daily routine.

Finally, if pursuing the vocation for which your Golden Retriever was originally bred is your goal—the vocation of retrieving felled birds—you can even do this in a formal setting. Known as field trials, these are get-togethers in which hunting dogs go out into the field and are tested on their retrieving abilities. If this interests you, attend some trials (the AKC can be your guide to locating field trials in your area), get to know the people, and perhaps find a mentor. As with conformation showing, don't ask your pet to participate unless he demonstrates a genuine interest and talent for this calling. With their contemporary role as companions, not all Goldens are natural retrievers, so respect your pet and his skills.

Working with People

Most dogs are happiest when employed, and for Goldens, working side-by-side with those they love makes them euphoric. In a more formal sense, this can be seen in the dogs who have been trained as guide dogs or service dogs, but even "plain old" pet Goldens revel in the responsibility.

Take search-and-rescue, for example. While the dogs you usually see searching for victims of earthquakes, avalanches, and such are paired with professional emergency rescue personnel, civilians, too, can get involved. If you're lucky, there's a club in your area—a group of people who get together with their dogs for training. This begins with playful games of hide-and-seek, ultimately leading to a point where the "item" being sought is a human being. How delighted the dogs are when they find that particular quarry. But there is more to this, of course, than fun and games. When disaster strikes, civilian teams may be called in to help if they are qualified to do so.

Another people-oriented vocation custom-made for the Golden Retriever is therapy work. Therapy dogs are those special animals who accompany their owners on visits to hospitals, convalescent homes, abused children's centers—anyplace where broken bodies and broken souls are in need of the mystical magic of the human/animal bond. There is no dog better equipped to offer that healing touch than the Golden Retriever. Sure, this dog's size may be intimidating to those meeting her for the first time, but within seconds, the dog's sweet smile and loving aura win over even the most fearful patients.

> Most dogs are happiest when employed, and for Goldens, working side-by-side with those they love makes them euphoric.

Before you run out to visit your local children's hospital with pup in hand, however, be warned that not every dog—not even every Golden Retriever—is cut out for therapy work. And even those who are can't just walk into venues in need of therapy dogs with no questions asked. Therapy dogs must be trained, evaluated, tested, and certified for the job by various organizations throughout the nation that are qualified to determine whether a dog is a safe and effective therapeutic addition to a medical staff.

Playing Nicely with Children

Kids are masters of negotiation when they get it into their sweet little heads that they absolutely must have a puppy. Their expertise in pursuing this aim is rather amazing to witness—the soulful look in the eyes, the comparisons to what other kids' parents let them have, and oh, the promises!

Indeed, kids go with Goldens as naturally as ice cream and apple pie or meatballs and spaghetti. Yet universal assumptions can get us in trouble. Just as some people prefer their pie not be served a la mode and some prefer their pasta without meat, it's not at all fair to expect every Golden to take to children. We must respect each dog's personality, both for the contentment of the animal and the safety of the children with whom he comes into contact.

A Tale of Two Goldens

First let's meet Cassie, golden companion to the Witt family of Orchard Park, New York.

Cassie's greatest desire is to demonstrate for all the people of the world just how wonderful the human species is—especially the smaller, younger members of that species. And the feeling is mutual. The children in her neighborhood regard her as some

Ten Great Games Kids Can Play with a Golden Retriever

What follows are 10 games kids and Goldens can play—only a sampling of what they will invariably come up with on their own. When encouraging such interactions, remember to teach the kids not to demand too much of the dog; to maintain their sense of humor; and to play games in enclosed, confined spaces and, when necessary, on a leash. Make sure, too, that an adult is on hand to prevent "arguments," mistreatment, or exhaustion.

1. Fetch Anything

2. Frisbee Catch

3. Backyard Football (as described earlier in this chapter, see "Fun and Games")

4. Hide-and-Seek (Ask the dog to "stay," then you go hide and call the dog to you; a great indoor game.)

5. Basic Obedience Class (at-home practice of the commands)

6. Playing House (You'd be surprised to see how well a Golden can co-operate with "pretend" games.)

7. Dress Up (Though I'm not a fan of animals in clothes, most Goldens will gladly cooperate with such shenanigans, even when it's not Halloween.)

8. Swim Team (water fun and swimming)

9. Golf (The child drives the ball, the dog retrieves it; no doubt adult golfers in the family will take to this game, too.)

10. Beauty Parlor (grooming practice, from brushing to bathing)

sort of canine pied piper. They run to Cassie the moment they emerge from the school bus each afternoon, or as soon as they return home from a trip to the grocery store with Mom. They pet her, lie on her, roll around on the grass with her, and tell her all about their day—and Cassie listens intently. She comforts them with her interest, her silence, the curled smile of her mouth, and the affectionate glow in her eyes. Cassie is the quintessential Golden Retriever.

Now we turn our attentions to Cricket, a Golden residing in Kansas City, Missouri. When Cricket's "parents" welcomed a new "sibling"—a darling, dark-haired baby who would soon answer to the name of Alison—Cricket was less than impressed. He'd hide whenever she cried. As Alison grew, a sibling rivalry developed, culminating in a few episodes of jealous growling and all-around unrequited affection between family dog and child. In time, however, Cricket came around, thanks to her parents' efforts to shower Cricket with love, attention, and rewards for his good behavior. Eventually Cricket appeared to realize that Alison was not a threat. The point is that Cricket, too, is the quintessential Golden Retriever.

How could that be? Remember the assumptions? Were you to poll the nation's Golden Retriever rescuers about common misconceptions about their breed, many would point to the assumption that all Goldens simply adore all children. Sadly, that's not exactly true. But there are steps you can take to bring out the best child-loving instincts in your pup. Read on and find out how.

Playing Matchmaker to Kids and Goldens

How irritating it is to be out walking your dog, enjoying the fresh air and sunshine, and suddenly find that you are about to be attacked by a young child. Like a torpedo, the youngster bee-lines straight toward you, an earsplitting shriek emanating from his small throat, his hands outstretched and ready to pound clumsily upon the unsuspecting head of your dog. Meanwhile, his parents stand off to the side, nodding their heads in approval, silly smiles on their faces in response to the adorable spontaneity of their child. Little do they know, that youngster is just asking to be the next dog-bite victim among the thousands of children who meet that fate each year.

A child's natural love of dogs is enough to bring tears to the eyes, but children need to be taught how to approach dogs properly and how to respect the canine view of the world—for their own safety and that of the dog.

I was once in the grocery store when I came upon a blind woman, her Golden Retriever guide dog, and a gaggle of young boys standing off admiring the dog, but hesitant to approach. People partnered with guide dogs who are on the job typically prefer that those they encounter allow their dogs to carry out their responsibilities uninterrupted. But this woman, a natural educator, invited the hesitant crew to come forward and meet her dog. She proceeded to teach them how best to introduce themselves: You don't run up and pound her on the head. Instead, hold your hand out so she might catch your scent, then stroke her on the shoulder where your hands are in her plain view. It was a lovely scene. The dog reveled in the attention, and the boys learned a lesson in respect that I imagine has remained with them to this day.

> People partnered with guide dogs who are on the job typically prefer that those they encounter allow their dogs to carry out their responsibilities uninterrupted.

Once you teach a child to approach a dog properly, you help to ensure that that dog will in turn enjoy the presence of those of tender age. By the same token, dogs subjected to a host of negative experiences are likely to forge similarly—and permanently— negative associations with the presence of youngsters, even a dog as typically resilient and forgiving as the Golden Retriever. Your job, then, is to work with both parties to ensure that both are taught what they need to know to live happily ever after in each other's presence.

Initial Introductions, First Impressions

The first step in your mission to foster your Golden's natural affinity for children (and to get a child off on the right track toward safe interactions with dogs) is to teach both how to make the proper introductions. From those first impressions, lasting associations for both are born. Your job is to make sure that those associations are as positive as possible.

Meeting on the Street   The world is filled with children who love dogs, yet don't know how to approach them correctly and safely. This is not something we are born knowing. We must learn the protocols, and parents can do their children a great service by making this one of their offspring's earliest lessons.

Let's say your child spots a Golden Retriever being walked in the park. First ask the dog's owner if it is okay to pet the dog (if he says no, respect that). If the answer is yes, show your child how to approach the dog quietly; no screaming, yelling, or pounding. Hold the back of your hand out to the dog so he can sniff it and get acquainted with your scent. Then, just as we learned from the blind woman earlier, gently pet the dog on the  shoulder (not the head) so your hand is in full view of the dog. If you're lucky, this will be one of those endearing creatures who instantly rolls over on his back, begging for rubs and tickles on the tummy. It is impossible to resist such an invitation.

If you are the dog owner in this situation, you are also in the position to instruct approaching children in the protocols of canine introductions. In addition, it is also your job to prepare your pup for such inevitabilities. If your pet comes to live with you as a puppy, start introducing him to lots of children as soon as possible. Make sure, however, to monitor all such interactions carefully. You're trying to flood your pup with positive experiences, not negative ones.

You will want to keep piling on those positive experiences for as long as your dog lives. Bring treats along on your walks to reward your pup for his exemplary behavior in the presence of children (and for the children to offer to the pup as a bribe to ensure that behavior remains exemplary). Show the children how to greet and interact with your dog. And above all, keep your eyes open to see who might be approaching for a surprise "attack". Protect your dog from children who have not yet been instructed in the fine art of canine interactions. While the Golden is likely to be one of the most forgiving of dogs, it's not fair to force your dog, even the mildest-tempered of the bunch, to endure a negative, not to mention potentially painful, experience.

The New Baby and Beyond One of the saddest fates to befall a dog is the arrival of a new baby in her family. This is not because a household with a baby should be automatically off limits to a dog. It's because in far too many cases, the new parents don't know how to introduce the resident dog to the infant newcomer and manage the two from then on. And we all know who will emerge the loser in such a conflict. The dog is relegated to permanent residence in the backyard, jealousies fester, and before you know it, yet another dog has been dropped off at the local animal shelter. I've seen this happen more times than I even care to think about.

Did You Know?

Millie, President Bush's English Springer Spaniel, earned over four times as much as her owner in 1991.

Of course a new baby doesn't enter the relationship with any preconceived conceptions or experience in how to greet her new pet. The responsibility for establishing that relationship rests with you and how you prepare and manage the dog.

As an example of how the initial introduction should transpire, we will assume that you are the proud owner of a lovely, friendly Golden. Once you know a new baby is on the way, prepare your pup. Take her to the park or to the homes of friends and relatives to watch, listen to, and play with a variety of young children (always under your supervision, of course, to prevent pulled tails, tweaked ears, or other mishandling). Once the baby is born, send an emissary home with a blanket that carries the baby's scent, so the dog can start to get accustomed to this new perfume that will now be a permanent one in your household.

> Make time for the dog and allow her to hang around during baby and child care activities, so that she will continue to know that she is a special member of the family, too.

When the day of homecoming arrives, hold the baby in your lap and invite the dog to come forward and investigate. (Remember, this must be done only if you know your dog well and can trust her completely.) The friendly, loving dog will relish the moment, sniff the strange little creature, and probably offer a kiss or two. Allow the dog to do this, perhaps rewarding him with treats.

This is not to say that all will be ideal from that day forward. Even if you handle the situation as prescribed, there are no guarantees that your dog will bond with the baby and both will be inseparable from that day forward. Successful first introductions are a start, but from then on, you will have to institute some new house rules that will ensure that the relationship blossoms as the baby grows into a toddler and beyond. Abide by the following and you'll move in the right direction.

○ Do not regard your dog as in-home baby-sitter, and no matter how gentle and child-loving she is—for the safety of both dog and children—do not leave them alone unsupervised. Ever.

○ Make sure that your dog always has a way to escape quickly and easily from the child whenever she wishes. Also, keep child and dog separated when necessary. There may be times when a dog really is not all that crazy about the curious toddler and his tendency to pull on ears and tail.

○ Make time for the dog and allow her to hang around during baby and child care activities, so that she will continue to know that she is a special member of the family, too. That's the best way to prevent unnecessary jealousies.

○ Teach your children gentle handling techniques. Show them how and where to pet a dog and make sure this is how it's done each and every time.

○ Even if your dog allows it, you must not permit children to manhandle or to mistreat your dog in any way. It's cruel to subject your dog to such treatment, and it could end up in a biting incident. By law, the dog will automatically be named as the guilty party.

○ Remember that despite all the promises, dog care is an adult responsibility. Teach your children to feed, groom, water, and exercise the family pet, but make sure these duties are carried out properly every day and intervene when necessary.

Praise for the Puppy Raisers

One way for an older child to interact with a Golden Retriever is to accept the exalted role of puppy raiser. A puppy raiser takes in a puppy (often a Golden) who is destined for life as a guide dog or service dog, and sees that puppy through her earliest obedience training and socialization. Typically sponsored by such organizations as 4-H or scouting, puppy raisers can be seen anywhere and everywhere (by law, the dogs wearing those brightly colored training vests are allowed access into places other dogs are not).

Imagine taking your Golden puppy everywhere you go: to the bank, the grocery store, the library, even school. You attend regular obedience classes together, and the dog sleeps peacefully at the foot of your bed every night.

But there's a catch.

Once that puppy reaches about two years of age—a puppy who has undeniably become a member of the family in the most intimate, day-to-day sense—it is time for her to leave her puppy raising family behind and move on to seek her destiny. The relationship typically culminates in an emotionally charged graduation ceremony where the dogs are turned over to a service organization to begin their specialized training. The puppy raisers are thanked for their dedication and courage, and the tears flow. It's a sad moment, of course—the end of an incredible experience—but one that celebrates the greatness of these dogs and the people who sacrifice their time, energy, and emotions to make it possible for those dogs to go on to fulfill their noble mission.

Making Your Golden Retriever a Good Neighbor

Think about your neighborhood for a moment. Now think about what makes a good neighbor. You no doubt prefer to live next to people who aren't too noisy, who don't mess up your lawn, who treat others well, and who don't attack you or your family. You have just outlined what makes a dog a good neighbor, too.

A dog who makes a welcome addition to the neighborhood is one who doesn't bark incessantly, whose owners don't allow him to use everyone else's yards as his own private bathroom (and who clean up after him if he does), and who is friendly and non-aggressive to those he meets each day. All of these traits are the result of responsible dog ownership. In other words, it's your responsibility to make your Golden Retriever a good neighbor.

This process begins as soon as your dog comes to join your family, whether he is a puppy or an adult dog. You need to prevent problems, such as separation anxiety that results in the incessant barking that can drive even the most benevolent neighbor crazy. Design a household routine and a walking and exercising schedule that will help your dog expend all that excess Golden Retriever energy every day. Attend ongoing obedience classes together, as a well-trained dog is far more likely to be a good neighbor than one who runs uncontrolled through the neighborhood wreaking havoc wherever he goes.

Another important element in good neighborhood citizenship is proper socialization. Work on socializing your pet from the beginning so he learns to enjoy the company of children, adults, and other animals, and won't be inclined to behave aggressively toward those with whom you share your turf. I speak from experience about this subject. I make periodic trips to Lake Tahoe, where I enjoy walking my dog, always on leash. Unfortunately, many of the dog owners I encounter along the way don't share my belief in the neighborhood's posted leash laws. We have been repeatedly threatened by countless dogs, many of them Golden Retrievers, whose owners' neglect have convinced the dogs that this turf is theirs alone. Needless to say, neither these dogs, nor their owners, are good neighbors.

When you're out and about with your pooch, keep him on his leash, and bring plenty of cleanup bags along—enough for you to clean up after your pet, plus some extras to offer those who have conveniently "forgotten" to prepare for their own cleanup duties. It takes only one neglectful owner to cast a negative light on all dog owners, including those who are diligent in cleanup detail.

And finally, make your pet's fine behavior official by helping him earn his Canine Good Citizen title. This is a mission at which the Golden Retriever excels, for the Golden prides himself on his good citizenship. How delightful that the American Kennel Club now offers a program through which he can boast to the world—with the initials "CGC" after his name—that he is an extraordinary canine citizen.

> Work on socializing your pet from the beginning so he learns to enjoy the company of children, adults, and other animals.

To earn his CGC, a dog must pass several tests designed to test his socialization skills in a variety of circumstances. He must (among other tests) stand politely while he is brushed by a stranger, allow a stranger to approach and greet him and his owner, and demonstrate knowledge of the basic commands, all without evidence of shyness or aggression. Needless to say, this is all comes fairly easily to most Golden Retrievers. Nevertheless, you will need to prepare your pup for the testing event (these are held periodically throughout the country each year). Many obedience trainers offer courses specifically designed for CGC preparation, so if you're interested, get out there and get to work! Your dog, and the population of dogs as a whole, will be better for your effort.

Traveling with and Boarding Your Dog

As we have seen, the household is never dull with a Golden Retriever around. But there comes a time in each family's life when they want to go on a vacation, perhaps to visit relatives or do some sightseeing. So what should you do with the dog?

In some cases, you can bring the pup with you. In other cases, for example, a trip to Hawaii where dogs must endure several months of quarantine before they may officially set foot on the islands—this just isn't possible. You will do your dog a great service, then, by preparing her for both family travel and boarding. A dog who can tolerate both will make family life easier for everyone.

Taking the Dog Along Versus Boarding

When it's time to decide your dog's fate at travel time, your first mission is to be honest with yourself. Of course the preferred choice is to have your dog with you, but as we have seen, that's not always an option. Even if it is, you must be honest about how your dog's presence might undermine your own enjoyment during your trip. So let's move on and explore what you must consider when you are faced with this decision.

The Traveling Option The pros of bringing your pet along are obvious: You get to have your dog with you. If that dog is a well-trained, beautifully behaved Golden Retriever, all the better. This becomes yet another life experience you share, bonding even deeper in your identity as family members. In this day and age, this is made easier by the various books and guides now available that list lodgings that welcome pets.

On the "con" side, things become a bit more practical. First, your choice of

Did You Know?

Chinese royalty considered their Pekingese dogs to be sacred and provided them with human wet nurses, servants, and guards to protect them from other dogs.

vacation and where you stay will be determined by the fact that you are bringing a dog along with you. Disney World and Hawaii are probably out of the question. You must ensure that dogs are welcomed at the hotel, campground, or even relative's home that you will be visiting, and you must be sure that your pup is sufficiently trained and polite so that she won't be a nuisance to hosts and fellow travelers. You will need to take even greater care to ensure that your pet is always confined and on a leash. You will need to pack appropriately for your pet: supplies, bedding, exercise pen, and perhaps even a hefty supply of food. In other words, you must decide whether spending a big chunk of your trip tending to your dog's needs is honestly how you wish to spend your time off. Remember, be honest.

The Boarding Option   This brings us to the boarding option. As a strong proponent of this option, I believe that a good boarding kennel and a dog amenable to boarding are a dream come true to owners who need to get away for a little while. Knowing your dog is in safe, competent, and affectionate hands while you are away can make your trip all the more enjoyable, and boarding may even be a bit of a vacation for your dog, as well. If you'll be traveling during the summer months, your dog may also be safer staying home in a kennel

> Some kennels offer doggie day care, in which dogs are dropped off only for the day. This is an excellent way to help your pet get accustomed to both the kennel and the kennel staff.

because of summer's warm temperatures. So make your reservations and relax. Since Goldens tend to always be hungry for new experiences and acquaintances, with the proper training and socialization, they typically make ideal boarding candidates.

The negative side of this equation is really rather minimal. You will miss your dog, of course, but that you can overcome. A good kennel will invite you to call to see how he is doing. You also want to make sure that your dog is prepared emotionally for boarding—something that is best done by introducing him to boarding during puppyhood. Of course a dog with abandonment issues will not tolerate kenneling easily. If your dog is one of these, work with the kennel to overcome his fears. Some kennels offer doggie day care, in which dogs are dropped off only for the day. This is an excellent way to help your pet get accustomed to both the kennel and the kennel staff— so much so that he might soon willingly accept an overnight visit.

Boarding can also be costly, but in my opinion, the good ones are worth the expense if it means peace of mind. Boarding is also negative if we are speaking of a less-than-pristine kennel with an incompetent staff. But if you do your homework, you can ensure that that is not the type of establishment at which you leave your pet. Keep reading, and you'll find out just how you might choose a good one.

Traveling with Your Dog

Suppose you have decided to bring your pup along with you on a trip. This will best be accomplished by thinking everything through ahead of time to ensure that all goes as smoothly as possible. Whether you will be traveling by car or air, you will need to make arrangements ahead of time. Pack supplies for your dog's nutrition (food and bowls), bedding,

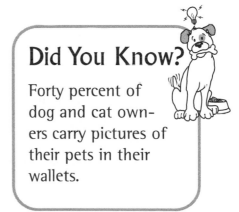

Did You Know?

Forty percent of dog and cat owners carry pictures of their pets in their wallets.

playtimes, bathroom cleanup, and grooming (brush, toothbrush, nail clippers). Here, too, you will discover the value of crate training. A crate is a must for air travel, a smart safety component for car travel, and it can make a great bed for your pet once you reach your destination.

You must also make sure that those waiting at your destination—your cousin, your mom, the hotel or campground staff—are all aware that you will be bringing a big golden dog with you. I cannot emphasize enough the need to prepare for your dog's security. Commit now, before you leave, that your dog will never be off the leash or unconfined en route to (or once you arrive at) your destination. Toward this end, never underestimate the power and convenience of the exercise pen. With this simple, collapsible contraption, you can confine your pup safely anywhere—indoors or out.

> Whether you will be traveling by car or air, you will need to make arrangements ahead of time. Pack supplies for your dog's nutrition, bedding, playtimes, bathroom cleanup, and grooming.

Now let's discuss the specifics about two modes of travel.

Traveling by Car   Of course only a dog who enjoys riding in a car (and who is preferably not prone to car sickness) should be invited to accompany you on a car trip. We will thus assume that your dog falls into this category. Ideally, you'll want to make sure that your dog is safely restrained, either in a crate (if your vehicle is large enough to allow for one) or with a seat-belt system designed specifically for dogs (available at pet supply stores or by mail order). Make sure he remains cool in the car, and stop periodically to offer him water and a snack. Remember, you must not leave him in a hot car, even if only for a brief stop along the way.

To avoid overfeeding him while you're on the road and to help prevent digestive upset, feed him small, healthy snacks throughout the day.

You will also need to stop periodically to allow your dog to stretch his legs, perhaps get a bit of exercise, and certainly to relieve himself. And again, I must remind you: Clean up after your pet and keep him on his leash! Imagine losing your dog on a remote country road in the middle of nowhere just because you didn't want to snap on the leash. Once you reach your destination, make sure your pup receives ample exercise, and lots of praise from you for being such a cooperative traveler.

Traveling by Air   I'll be honest: If I had the choice of flying a dog somewhere or leaving him home, I would choose the latter. But sometimes, as I have experienced myself, you have no choice. In such instances, you must first contact the airlines to find out which flights can accept pets. Unlike Toy Poodles or Pomeranians who can often ride in under-seat crates in the cabin, larger dogs such as Goldens must fly in the cargo area. Discuss with the airline their policies on cargo compression and temperature. During the summer, pets may typically fly only during the middle of the night because the heat is too intense during the day. I frankly prefer a red-eye flight anyway, since the dog is more likely to sleep in keeping with his daily rhythms.

If you have not already done so, you will need to purchase a properly sized FAA-sanctioned dog crate for your dog's flight. It is also wise to visit the veterinarian to make sure your dog is healthy enough to fly. There is some debate about whether dogs who travel by air should be tranquilized for the flight. If your veterinarian is of the very large anti-tranquilizer camp, he may okay a mild sedative instead, just to relax the passenger a bit (tranquilizer effects can frighten a dog or compromise or endanger his health).

When it's time for the trip, take the dog for a nice long walk before takeoff to expend all that Golden energy and offer him some water. Make sure he is securely confined in his crate and delivered properly to the airline staff. Upon your pup's arrival, another walk, more water, and a light snack are in order, then life should return to normal as soon as possible. Though flying is the norm for big-time show dogs, I would not personally make it a habit for the family pet.

Boarding Your Dog

A dog's first time at the boarding kennel can be difficult for owners who can't imagine even a few days without their pet. But find a good kennel, and the more you board and witness your dog's excitement at seeing the kennel staff again, the better you'll feel.

Finding a Good Kennel   Your first step when you decide that you will be boarding your pet is to find a good boarding kennel. Ask your veterinarian (whose hospital may even offer pet hotel-like boarding services) and fellow pet owners whose opinions you trust on such matters. It's usually not that difficult to discover which kennels have the best reputations in particular communities. Visit the kennels to start gathering your own information. The good ones will welcome visitors and be sensitive to the trepidation owners often feel at the prospect of leaving their pets with strangers.

Feel free to ask questions. At a good kennel, the staff will be most willing to boast the amenities they offer: feeding choices and schedules, exercise and play programs, sanitation practices, bedding choices, and indoor/outdoor accommodations. I am always comforted by a clean facility with a friendly, animal-loving staff who have a dog's health and comfort foremost in their minds. I appreciate even more staff members who take the time to ask me about my dog's personality, quirks, habits, and special needs. Discovering a kennel that makes that extra effort will make your traveling all the more pleasant, for you'll know that your dog will be safely and contentedly cared for while you are away.

Before You Board As with virtually every aspect of pet ownership, successful boarding begins with proper preparation. First, a well-socialized, well-trained dog will be far more content in a boarding situation and be more a pleasure for the kennel staff. You want your dog to be a favorite, don't you? This quite often occurs when the boarder is a big friendly Golden who willingly does all that is asked of her and showers the staff with affection at the same time.

Also key to successful boarding is keeping your dog current on her vaccines. A good kennel allows only vaccine-protected dogs on their premises and will require your dog's veterinary records to prove it. So keep your pup current on her annual boosters and her vaccine for canine cough, which is typically administered every six months. Bring along all necessary emergency information too, such as where you are staying, the veterinarian's number, or any special circumstances. And finally, make

Did You Know?

The saying "three dog night" is attributed to Australian Aborigines, who would sleep with three dogs (Dingos, actually) to keep from freezing on cold nights.

·your reservations well in advance. How frustrating it can be to find yourself approaching a busy holiday weekend during which you'll be traveling, and realize you forgot to make the necessary arrangements for your dog. You take great pains to find the perfect kennel for your dog—and the good ones fill up quickly—so think ahead and ensure that your dog will always be right where you want her to be. Then drop her off, relax, and enjoy your trip.

Hiring a Pet Sitter

An alternative to boarding these days is the increasingly popular practice of leaving pets at home and hiring a pet sitter to come in (usually twice a day) to feed, exercise, and play with the member of the family who had to stay behind. While cats tend to be ideal candidates for in-home care, sometimes dogs truly believe that they have been abandoned and will never see their family again. This can result in incessant barking and destructive behavior. Plus, dogs—especially large, people-oriented dogs like Golden Retrievers—require more exercise and attention and more frequent bathroom breaks, than do their litter-box trained feline counterparts. The bottom line is that not every dog is cut out to be left in the hands of a pet sitter.

> An alternative to boarding is the increasingly popular practice of leaving pets at home and hiring a pet-sitter to feed, exercise, and play with your dog.

If you would like to try using a pet sitter, you might want to practice first by inviting the pet sitter over to get acquainted. You may also ask the sitter to come over during the day for some practice runs when you are not at home. This will give you an idea of how your dog might tolerate such attention once you have gone. If your dog does prove to be amenable, you are wise to set

Holiday Hazards: Keeping Your Golden Retriever Safe and Healthy

For those times when you decide to stay home and host a holiday gathering, here are precautions you should take to ensure that your pup is not injured or harmed during what can be a crazy time around the household.

○ Resist the temptation to ply your pet with table scraps or other rich holiday treats, and make sure your guests follow this rule. Why ruin your holiday with an acute case of treat-related digestive upset and an emergency trip to the veterinarian?

○ While it is always critical to keep a collar and current identification tag on your dog, now it is even more important. Visitors to your home may inadvertently leave a door or gate open, resulting in a lost dog whose ID tag may be his only chance of getting home safely.

○ If you will be participating in some new athletic activity with your dog—cross-country skiing or snow hiking, for example—prepare your

dog ahead of time with gradual physical conditioning that will help prevent injuries the dog could incur while trying to participate.

○ Make sure your dog has a private place—his own space—to which he can retreat unmolested at any time should noise, crowds, and children become too much for him.

○ Keep breakable items—many of which may be new and interesting to the dog—out of your pet's reach. Even the soft-mouth grip of a Golden Retriever can shatter a glass Christmas ornament or some other fascinating holiday decoration that arouses that insatiable canine curiosity.

up some sort of confined space in which she will stay as she would in a kennel. This will offer security and prevent the dog from destroying the house, which could happen if she is given free run of the place in your absence.

Because pet-sitters come into your home to care for your pet, choose one with good references (check them), who is licensed, bonded, and insured. This will ease your mind while you are away. While I admire pet sitters and simply adore those I have known through the years, I personally prefer a boarding kennel situation for dogs, for the ongoing attention, interaction, and safety that kenneling offers—and most of the dogs I have known agree with me.

A Lifetime of Love and Good Health

In This Chapter

○ Your Aging Golden Retriever—What to Expect
○ How to Keep Your Older Dog Comfortable
○ Saying Goodbye

The time comes in every Golden Retriever's life when her joints begin to stiffen, her senses dull, and she just doesn't have the energy she once had. She has entered her senior years, and so will the relationship you share enter a new stage.

How you approach this stage can make it either a blessed event or a time of sadness and dread. Needless to say, one option is clearly preferable to the other, and it is in your power to determine just how you will spend your Golden's golden years. What follows can help you make them wonderful years indeed, and some of the dearest you share in your life together.

Your Aging Golden Retriever—
What to Expect

A dog is not a puppy forever. Celebrate each age of your dog, and remember that the golden years are to be embraced, not mourned. I have always regarded the dog's older years as the time when owners can repay their companions for all that they have done for (and meant to) their families through the years. Now, with a dog who is not as limber and alert as he once was, we can take up the slack and make his later years some of his best years—a time when he can lean on us, just as we have always leaned on him. Now, let's look at the changes you can expect as your dog enters his geriatric years.

> Celebrate each age of your dog, and remember that the golden years are to be embraced, not mourned.

Changes in Body

When a dog reaches about seven years of age, he enters what we consider the geriatric stage of life. You will probably not notice an outright or drastic change in behavior or action; the only sign may be the sprouting of a few white hairs on your dog's muzzle. But internally, your dog's systems will begin to slow a bit, as will his energy level. It's a gradual process, so you have ample time to prepare for it.

As aging progresses, you may notice that golden muzzle growing increasingly lighter in color. Your dog may not be able to keep up with you on your daily run as easily as he once did (though he will definitely try), and if he is somewhat dysplastic, his hips may begin to cause him more pain and immobility, especially if he begins to develop arthritis. In fact, any health-related problem the dog has suffered through the years, such as epilepsy or hypothy-roidism, may become more pronounced as he ages.

Even without hip dysplasia to complicate matters, arthritis is very common in older dogs. Also common are urinary tract and kid-ney problems, which are evident from the classic signs of increased thirst and urination and/or blood in the urine (either of these should be reported to the veterinarian immediately). Other problems that increase with age include lumps and bumps on the skin (which may require biopsy), incontinence, and constipation. Your dog may also be more prone to respiratory illnesses and gastric upset or disease. With a waning immune system, infectious agents may gain entrance via something as small as an embedded foxtail between the toes or a small injury on the paw pad. Also common in the older dog is a dulling—if not outright loss—of the senses. Your dog may lose his hearing or his sight, or both, but with proper management on the part of his owner, he can get along just fine.

Indeed it is your job to be sensitive to all the physical changes that your dog is experiencing, and adjust your demands on him accordingly. You owe it to him. You know he would do the same for you—in fact, he probably already has. Just think back to all the times you were ill or feeling down. He recognized the change instantly and tended to your needs in your time of vulnerability. Now it's your turn to return the favor.

Changes in Mind

Once, during a radio show on which I was being interviewed, I received a call

Did You Know?

The old rule of multiplying a dog's age by seven to find the equivalent human age is inaccu-rate. A better measure is to count the first year as 15, the sec-ond year as 10, and each year after that as five.

from a woman who was perplexed by the fact that her older dog had suddenly begun to turn aggressive toward her. He would snap at her while she petted him, and at times he seemed not even to recognize the woman who had cared for him for more than a decade. My first suggestion was that she get the dog to the veterinarian immediately—sometimes behavioral changes are the result of an internal medical problem or injury that is causing the animal great pain and discomfort. Although as a rule this is not a common reflex in Golden Retrievers, the dog may react to pain by lashing out. I told the woman that if medical causes for the behavior were ruled out, she would need to accept the fact that dogs, just like people, can experience senility (which, in some cases, may be relieved with medication).

I spoke from experience. At one point, I too had worried when one of my own dogs reached the age of 13 and began to act very strangely. He would begin to shiver uncontrollably, stare at me with a deep intensity, and glue himself to my leg as I moved about the house. He seemed terrified. I finally figured out that the only way I could relax him was to put him in a small, quiet room alone—in a makeshift sensory deprivation tank—where he was not distracted by movements or noise.

I immediately consulted the veterinarian who performed a blood panel and thorough physical examination to rule out any acute health problems as the cause. The veterinarian determined that my dog was probably suffering from small seizures, called auras (the precursors to seizures, which can cause the patient to experience dizziness, blurred vision, or disorientation) which were frightening him. I discovered that other dogs I knew had had similar experiences, all occurring as the dogs aged. After a few days, my dog's behavior mellowed. He would still experience the bouts, but he would actually put himself in his sensory deprivation room. He'd grown accustomed to what was happening to him and was learning how to ease the effects.

The mind alterations of an older dog can be rather fascinating to witness. While senility that leads to aggression is a sad event, the older dog can be a true joy to have around. The older dog may bounce in a single day from one minute wiggling uncontrollably at the sight of a tennis ball, to the next minute lying contentedly on a favorite pillow, watching the kids play. As time goes on, the mellower moments may begin to outnumber the puppyish impulses, and that too is special. The two of you can enjoy time spent together quietly, communicating in that silent way that has always been the cornerstone of your special bond.

How to Keep Your Older Dog Comfortable

A pet Golden Retriever who is deeply bonded to her family and entrenched in the rhythms of the household can go through moments of despair when she realizes that she can't keep up with you like she once could. Believe it or not, she can even become depressed. It's your job to let your companion know that you are there for her, that you will adjust the rhythms of the household in any way you must to accommodate her, and that she remains as important to the family as she has always been. You'll know that she trusts you when you see the understanding in her eyes that, regardless of her age, you are now and always a team.

Exercise and Health Care

Once upon a time, there was no such thing as geriatric veterinary care for dogs, because dogs rarely lived into what we consider the geriatric stage of life. Today, however, dogs commonly live into their teens, precisely because of advancements in canine care and nutrition, and the progressive care they receive as members of the family.

As a dog ages, his aging process speeds up considerably. For a dog who is 11 or 12, one month can equate to as much as a whole year in aging, and detrimental changes can occur rapidly. You must, therefore, keep an even keener eye on your pet than before when looking for signs of developing problems. As is the case in any stage of a dog's life, the quicker treatment is sought, the better the chance of successful and less painful treatment as well as recovery. Here your partnership with your veterinarian really comes into play.

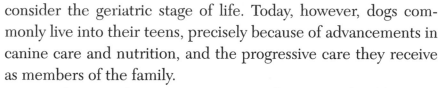

You must keep an even keener eye on your pet than before when looking for signs of developing problems.

The Veterinarian's Role   Once a dog reaches that seven-year mark, you should increase your routine veterinary visits from once to twice a year, so the doctor can keep tabs on your pet's system and its potentially rapid changes. These so-called geriatric visits may now include a blood panel and urinalysis, as well as keeping the vaccinations current and testing for both internal and external parasites.

In addition to keeping up with your twice-yearly appointments, you must report anything unusual to the veterinarian as soon as possible: a strange new lump on the skin, odd behavioral changes, obvious pain, a lack of appetite, changes in bathroom habits, and so forth. You'll quickly understand just why it's so important to work with a veterinarian with whom you are compatible and whose opinions and practices you trust.

At Home   On the home front, you must continue to give your dog all the same diligent care and attention to which you have both become accustomed. Pay close attention to nutrition and resist that impulse to offer your dog a bounty of table scraps and treats (out of pity, perhaps). Now more than ever you'll see just why it's so important to keep a dog svelte and trim. How sad it is to encounter the all-too-common sight of an older Golden with too much weight on his bones. Health problems such as arthritis, respiratory troubles, or hip dysplasia will be dramatically amplified for a dog who is both aging and overweight.

Today there are specially formulated foods designed for older dogs, most of which contain less fat, fewer calories, and less protein (the latter is theoretically designed to prevent urinary problems and a subject of debate). Also available are prescription diets, available from veterinarians, designed to help dogs suffering from such maladies as allergies and urinary tract disorders. Regardless of what you feed your aging dog, it is best to feed him, as you may have always done anyway, several small meals throughout the day, and supplement the meals sporadically with only the healthiest of treats. Your dog will thank you for your restraint—and he'll probably be with you a lot longer, too.

Continuing the Exercise   Exercise will help keep your dog slim and trim, too, and contribute to his all-around contentment. It's time, however, to adjust the regimen. No more marathons or all-day cross-country forays on a secluded mountain trail. Regular walks will usually suffice, perhaps interspersed with a

Did You Know?

The oldest dog ever documented was an Australian cattle dog named Bluey, who was put to sleep at the age of 29 years and 5 months.

moderate game or two of fetch, which will convince the dog that he remains an active member of the family. This time he spends in companionship with his family is also helping keep his joints limber, his muscles toned, his digestive tract stimulated, and his mind sharp. Just remember not to ask too much of your dog, because even if he happens to be in great pain, he will probably try to please you. This is not good for him.

> Exercise will help keep your dog slim and trim, too, and contribute to his all-around contentment. It's time, however, to adjust the regimen.

Ongoing Grooming As for your more hands-on responsibilities, these include routine grooming care, which will keep the dog's coat and skin healthy and his nails under control. It will also provide you with the opportunity to discover signs of budding health problems that may be brewing internally. Keep up with the flea control, too, though steer clear of harsh chemicals that could lead to adverse side effects in the dog's aging system. You may want to consult your veterinarian on what is safest for your dog. Parasite control is increasingly important, since the dog won't be as limber as he once was, and will be less capable of tending to those hard-to-reach spots that are often a flea's favored hiding places.

Pay attention to the teeth, as well. As dogs age, we might be more hesitant to have their teeth cleaned professionally because of the fear of anesthesia (that the dog won't wake up). Your veterinarian can determine if your dog is at risk for complications during such a procedure, which is now far less risky than it was even 10 years ago, with a blood test and thorough physical exam. Whether or not you choose to proceed with professional cleaning, you should do your best to brush your dog's teeth regularly—every day, if possible. Infected gums and teeth can cause a dog great pain. If this condition does occur, it can be remedied by a good cleaning, perhaps some tooth extractions (don't worry; tooth extractions are not unusual for an older dog), and routine follow-up care at home. A dog's dour demeanor can change instantly when his mouth is no longer hurting and infected.

It's also your job to follow the doctor's orders. If your Golden has been prescribed thyroid medication for a hypothyroid condition, make sure you continue to administer it as directed. The same holds true for the medications now available to help treat a dog who is suffering from arthritis. Take advantage of the miracles of medicine we now have available to make our dog's years as pleasant as possible.

Daily Life

Imagine a big, loving Golden Retriever who has been perfectly house-trained since puppyhood—not a single accident in the past 11 years. Then, one day, it happens. She walks into the living room en route to her pillow in the corner, and without even realizing it, she dribbles a trail of urine across the carpet. What do you do? Do you punish her? Heavens no! You know your dog. You know this isn't what she intended. And you know some action must be taken to help alleviate her fear and confusion in the face of a sudden lack of bladder control.

The first step, as is the case with any change in behavior or physical condition, is a trip to the veterinarian to rule out urinary tract problems. If all is well physically, then the dog is just experiencing an all-too-common onset of incontinence, sometimes combined with the mild forgetfulness of senility, that often affects the older dog. Your job is to

accommodate her lack of control so she can maintain her sense of confidence and not feel that she is failing you. You may need to set up a doggie door so she can come and go as needed, or increase the number of times you take her out each day to relieve herself. Your veterinarian might also suggest medications that help control this problem, but some dogs may experience side effects from these.

There is also a strong possibility that as she ages, your dog will begin to lose her sight and/or hearing. Fear not. If you know your dog well, if she has spent her life as an integral member of the household, and if you have built a foundation of mutual trust, you can compensate for her failing senses and she will live just as contentedly as ever. (Your first step, however, is to consult the veterinarian to make sure the sight or hearing loss is not being caused by some type of treatable health problem.)

> In ensuring that your older dog's days remain content and secure, pay close attention to the big picture: her overall comfort and well-being.

You may not even realize that she is losing her hearing until you call her name from behind and she doesn't even twitch an ear. Since this is not a dog to practice the fine art of selective hearing, a Golden Retriever who doesn't leap up at the first hint of attention is probably having trouble hearing the message. You can prepare for hearing loss early on by teaching your dog hand-signal commands while teaching her voice commands. This will provide you with instant communication should her hearing someday fade.

You may not notice that your dog is losing her sight until one day you find her staring right at her favorite toy without really seeing it. If vision loss does occur, it's not a good time to rearrange the furniture. Instead, be sensitive to her needs, try not to startle her, and approach her with a soft voice and a gentle touch. Allow her to smell toys and treats you are offering, and protect her from rough treatment from kids and other animals.

With your older dog, it becomes increasingly important to keep her on a leash whenever you are outdoors. This is even more critical for a dog who is losing or has lost the acuity of her senses. Those senses are her first line of defense when navigating the outside world. Keeping her linked physically to you by way of the leash will provide both safety and security for your dog.

In ensuring that your older dog's days remain content and se-cure, pay close attention to the big picture: her overall comfort and well-being. This means providing her (if you didn't already) with a special corner of the house that is all her own—a quiet, secluded sanctuary where she can retreat whenever the household activity gets to be too much for her. In the rooms where the family typically congregates, you might consider providing her with a selection of comfortable pillows—perhaps a fleecy geriatric model stuffed with an egg-carton pad that helps ease old bones and arthritic joints. This way she remains part of the action, but comfortable, at the same time.

It all boils down to remaining sensi-tive to your dog's limitations—reduced energy levels, stiff joints, faded senses—anything that when taxed can cause the dog physical and emotional pain. You must do your best to prevent that pain and to ease it when its onset is in-evitable. Remember that your dog's love

Did You Know?

Two dogs survived the sinking of the Titanic, a Pomeranian and a Pekingese named Sun Yat Sen.

for and trust in her family will continue to blossom for as long as she lives. Be worthy of those gifts.

Saying Goodbye

We who live with dogs, regardless of those dogs' breeding, all share a communal experience when a dog's life nears its end. Experience this rite of passage once, and it bonds you to every other dog owner who has ever been through it. Discuss it with others, and it evokes universal emotions we all share and we all understand.

It's not every day that a family member passes on. And, if you are faced with the decision to euthanize your dog, you must deal not only with the loss of your beloved pet, but also with determining precisely when she will go. When you lose a dog, you must permit yourself to grieve, to celebrate the dog's life, to allow time for healing, and, when you are ready, to continue on in your relationship with the canine species.

Tough Decisions

If you're lucky, when your dog's time comes, he will drift peacefully away in his sleep. Unfortunately, most of us are not so lucky. Most

of us must, in the face of a dog's severely failing health and perhaps serious illness, make the fateful decision to instigate that peaceful and permanent slumber.

Needless to say, the decision can be devastating, and many owners will grasp at any excuse—any tiny glimmer of possible hope—to delay the decision. The dog knows when his time has come, but it can take time for his family to rise to the occasion. It takes courage, but that courage must be mustered to prevent unnecessary pain and suffering for the dog.

When faced with this decision, you will need to keep a clear head. Speak honestly with your veterinarian to learn all you can about your dog's condition, his prognosis, his level of suffering, and how it might be controlled. Despite that little voice in your head that keeps whispering to you that it really isn't that bad, listen to what the doctor has to say, and reflect honestly on how your dog is feeling both physically and emotionally. The vet may make it easy for you by telling you that the dog's condition is terminal—period. Or she may complicate matters by discussing an expensive treatment with uncertain results that, even were the results guaranteed, you cannot afford. In either case, guilt must not be allowed to enter the decision-making process. As long as you have made your pet's life as fulfilling and joyful as possible, there is no room for guilt as the end of his life nears.

> **W**hen faced with this decision, you will need to keep a clear head. Speak honestly with your veterinarian to learn all you can about your dog's condition.

I will always admire the courage with which one of my friends approached this decision when her Golden reached that threshold. In the wake of her dog's second stroke, even though he could eat and drink and was suffering no physical pain, he could barely stand or walk, and he had to be carried outdoors to relieve himself. This was no life for a formerly robust busybody and athlete. In honor of her dog's dignity and who he wanted to be, my friend made her decision swiftly. Afterward, though her pain of loss was acute, she knew she had done the right thing.

Of course even the knowledge that you are doing the right thing does not make the decision any easier, nor does it relieve the pain. You can, however, take comfort in knowing that you are not alone. All who choose to live with and devote themselves to dogs as family members will at one time or another be faced with this devastating decision. We owe it to the dignity of our pets to approach the challenge with courage. Find that courage in your dog's eyes. As your best friend, he will let you know when his time has come. He will trust that, after all these years, you will continue to act in his best interest. There is no compromise. Be strong.

Coping with the Grief

You never know how or when a dog's end will come. Sometimes, as when a dog's end is the result of a long illness or the gradual decline of age, you have ample time to prepare yourself emotionally for the day when he will be gone. But if the end comes suddenly, perhaps as the result of an acute illness or accident, there is no easing that shock. In either instance, you must allow yourself to grieve, regardless of insensitive comments you may hear from non-pet people who simply don't understand.

We're fortunate these days that the relationship between pet and owner is taken more seriously than it used to be, and so is the grief one experiences over the death of a pet. You're likely to find many sympathetic ears. If you don't find this support among your own circle of friends, there are other sources you may use to seek out kindred spirits. The Internet is filled with pet bereavement sites that enable owners to discuss their pets, their losses, and even pay tribute to their animals who have passed on. Also available are wonderful books on the subject that can help you get through the various and very genuine stages of grief. Grief counselors in many communities also address pet loss, as do support groups dedicated to this subject.

There are also steps you can take, from puppyhood on, to help make coping just a bit easier once the inevitable occurs. A camera can be a great and comforting help. Bring a camera along to every family event and activity, and take lots of pictures of your clan—including its canine members. Videos will accomplish this same goal. Though nothing can replace the real live dog at your feet—how sweet those visual memories can be.

As their dogs age, those who live with only one dog often feel the impulse to get another one. They tell themselves they are considering this for the good of the dog. In truth, it is probably more as an insurance policy for themselves; to make their older dog's passing easier to cope with. I am not really a proponent of this notion. Even though the Golden is ideally an amenable guy, if he has been an only dog throughout his life, he may not enjoy the presence of a spry youngster nipping at him as he settles in to enjoy his older years. So think about this seriously before taking such a plunge. Even if you do decide to add a new dog to the fold, you will discover that her presence won't erase the pain of your older dog's passing when that time comes.

The most positive way of coping with a dog's death is to celebrate his life. Concentrate on what was wonderful about the dog, the special moments you shared, and the ways in which you enriched each other's life. When one friend of mine at last made the difficult decision to euthanize her Golden-mix who had severe, irreversible aggression problems, we grieved together. But I also helped my friend realize how fortunate this poor creature was to have been rescued from a sad existence, and how much they had shared and taught each other during their time together.

Did You Know?

A U.S. Customs Labrador named Snag has made 118 drug seizures worth a canine record $810 million.

Now is the time to leave the guilt and the negative experiences behind. Celebrate what was, and soon maybe you'll be ready to invite a new canine companion into your home and into your heart.

Moving On

I always say that despite the sadness that can shroud the end of your relationship with a beloved pet, the joy that animals bring into our lives far outweighs any pain that ensues at the end. When that sad end comes, you're likely to vow never to have another dog. But once inspired by a legendary dog, it's tough to go through life without a canine partner, and in time you're likely to rethink that vow. Begin this quest when you are ready, not when someone else tells you to. Only you can decide, if, when, and how you will find your next canine companion. It is a most personal decision.

> The most positive way of coping with a dog's death is to celebrate his life. Concentrate on what was wonderful about the dog, the special moments you shared, and the ways in which you enriched each other's life.

If and when you make that decision, you must not head out in search of a Golden with the expectation that you will find a perfect imitation of the dog you recently lost. That's not fair to the new dog, nor is it fair to the memory of the deceased dog to assume she can be so easily replaced. Allow your new addition to carve her own niche and make her own special mark on your life. Allow her to be a unique spirit all her own, who will enrich your life just as profoundly as her predecessor did.

Of course, once smitten by that very infectious Golden Retriever bug, you may find it impossible even to consider life without one of these beautiful dogs by your side. By all means, follow that impulse. The world is rich with these 24-karat dogs, each gifted with the po-

Helping Young Children Say Goodbye

You have to be careful when helping young children cope with the death of a dog they have loved and regarded practically as another sibling. Logical explanations can be misconstrued by a young mind. "Goldie was old," you explain, or "Goldie was sick." The child thus reasons that her parents are "old," and fears that perhaps her parents will soon be passing on, too. Or the next time Mom or Dad are ill could be a terrifying event for the child. As for the ever-popular "We had to put Goldie to sleep," just imagine how that will make the child feel when bedtime rolls around. Encourage your children to ask questions and try to clear up any misconceptions they might have.

Above all, be honest. I've heard the gamut of stories—ranging from telling a child for months that the dog is at the veterinarian, to telling her that the dog ran away. Parents who use the latter story seem to believe that somehow this is easier for the child to handle than the truth. I also know countless adults still haunted by stories fed to them as children about pets allegedly sent off to live on a farm. Many consider their parents' lies about the loss of a pet as some of their earliest, most unpleasant memories.

Be honest about the dog's fate, even though it may be your child's first introduction to the concept of death. Then concentrate together on the dog's life. Allow the child to discuss how she is feeling now that the family dog is no longer in the house. Share your favorite memories about the dog—all the funny things he used to do, the special games you played—and look at photos that bring back those happy memories. Seek out the wonderful books and stories, such as <u>Dog Heaven</u> by Cynthia Rylant, and the now legendary poem "The Rainbow Bridge." These can help soothe both you and your child during this sad time. There is no cure-all method for making the child feel better, but the healing begins with your honesty—and somewhere down the line, when everyone is ready—with a new canine addition to the family.

tential to enhance your life even further. So yes, you can and you will, find what you are looking for. And when you do, be grateful that you have been chosen to be a part of the great circle that encompasses the extraordinary spirit we call the Golden Retriever.

Appendix A: Resources

The following is a list of organizations of interest to those who live with Golden Retrievers, those who would like to live with Golden Retrievers, and those who just plain love these dogs. Where possible, addresses have been supplemented with Internet websites, and vice versa.

Boarding, Pet Sitting, Traveling

books
Dog Lover's Companion series
Guides on traveling with dogs
for several states and cities
Foghorn Press
P.O. Box 2036, Santa Rosa, CA
95405-0036
(800) FOGHORN

Take Your Pet Too!: Fun Things to Do!, Heather MacLean Walters
M.C.E. Publishing
P.O. Box 84
Chester, NJ 07930-0084

Take Your Pet USA, Arthur Frank
Artco Publishing
12 Channel St.
Boston, MA 02210

Traveling with Your Pet 1999: The AAA Petbook, Greg Weeks, Editor
Guide to pet-friendly lodging in the U.S. and Canada

Vacationing With Your Pet!, Eileen Barish
Pet-Friendly Publications
P.O. Box 8459
Scottsdale, AZ 85252
(800) 496-2665

...other resources

The American Boarding Kennels Association
4575 Galley Road, Suite 400-A
Colorado Springs, CO 80915
(719) 591-1113
www.abka.com

Independent Pet and Animal Transportation Association
5521 Greenville Ave., Ste 104-310
Dallas, TX 75206
(903) 769-2267
www.ipata.com

National Association of Professional Pet Sitters
1200 G St. N.W., Suite 760
Washington, DC 20005
(800) 286-PETS
www.petsitters.org

Pet Sitters International
418 East King Street
King, NC 27021-9163
(336)-983-9222
www.petsit.com

Breed Information, Clubs, Registries

American Kennel Club
260 Madison Avenue
New York, NY 10016
(212) 696-8800
Customer Service (919) 233-9769
www.akc.org/

Canadian Kennel Club
89 Skyway Avenue, #100
Etobicoke, Ontario M9W 6R4
CANADA
www.ckc.ca/

Golden Retriever Club of America
http://www.grca.org/
c/o Jolene Carey
P.O. Box 20434
Oklahoma City, OK 73156
OR
Deborah Ascher
P.O. Box 69
Berthoud, CO 80513-0069

Golden Retrievers in Cyberspace
http://www.golden-retriever.com/

InfoPet
P.O. Box 716
Agoura Hills, CA 91376
(800) 858-0248

The Kennel Club
(British equivalent to the American
    Kennel Club)
1-5 Clarges Street
Piccadilly
London W1Y 8AB
ENGLAND
http://www.the-kennel-club.org.uk/

National Dog Registry
Box 116
Woodstock, NY 12498
(800) 637-3647
www.natldogregistry.com/

Tatoo-A-Pet
6571 S.W. 20th Court
Ft. Lauderdale, FL 33317
(800) 828-8667
www.tattoo-a-pet.com

United Kennel Club
100 East Kilgore Rd.
Kalamazoo, MI 49001-5598
(616) 343-9020
http://ukcdogs.com

Dog Publications

AKC Gazette and AKC Events Cal-
    endar
American Kennel Club
51 Madison Avenue
New York, NY 10010
Subscriptions: (919) 233-9767
www.akc.org/gazet.htm
www.akc.org/event.htm

Direct Book Service
(800) 776-2665
www.dogandcatbooks.com/direct-
    book

Dog Fancy
P.O. Box 6050
Mission Viejo, CA 92690
(714) 855-8822
www.dogfancy.com/

Dog World
500 N. Dearborn, Suite 1100
Chicago, IL 60610
(312) 396-0600
www.dogworldmag.com/

Fun, Grooming, Obedience, Training

American Dog Trainers Network
(212) 727-7257
http://www.inch.com/~dogs/index.html

American Grooming Shop Association
(719) 570-7788

American Kennel Club (tracking, agility, obedience, herding)
Performance Events Dept.
5580 Centerview Drive
Raleigh, NC 27606
(919) 854-0199
www.akc.org/

Animal Behavior Society
Susan Foster
Department of Biology
Clark University
950 Main Street
Worcester, MA 01610-1477

Association of Pet Dog Trainers
P.O. Box 385
Davis, CA 95617
(800) PET-DOGS
www.apdt.com/

The Dog Agility Page
http://www.dogpatch.org/agility/

Intergroom
76 Carol Drive
Dedham, MA 02026
www.intergroom.com

National Association of Dog Obedience Instructors
729 Grapevine Highway, #369
Hurst, TX 76054-2085
http://www.nadoi.org/

National Dog Groomers Association of America
P.O. Box 101
Clark, PA 16113
(724) 962-2711

North American Flyball Association
1400 W. Devon Ave, #512
Chicago, IL 60660
(309) 688-9840
http://muskie.fishnet.com/~flyball/

North American Dog Agility Council
HCR 2 Box 277
St. Maries, ID 83861
www.nadac.com

Grooming supplies
Pet Warehouse
P.O. Box 752138
Dayton, OH 45475-2138
(800) 443-1160

United States Canine Combined Training Association
2755 Old Thompson Mill Road
Buford, GA 30519
(770) 932-8604
http://www.siriusweb.com/USCCTA/

United States Dog Agility Association, Inc.
P.O. Box 850955
Richardson, Texas 75085-0955
(972) 231-9700
www.usdaa.com/

Grief Hotlines

Chicago Veterinary Medical Association
(630) 603-3994

Cornell University
(607) 253-3932

Michigan State University
College of Veterinary Medicine
(517) 432-2696

Tufts University (Massachusetts)
School of Veterinary Medicine
(508) 839-7966

University of California, Davis
(530) 752-4200

University of Florida at Gainesville
College of Veterinary Medicine
(352) 392- 4700

Virginia-Maryland Regional College
of Veterinary Medicine
(540) 231-8038

Washington State University
College of Veterinary Medicine
(509) 335-5704

Humane Organizations and Rescue Groups

American Humane Association
63 Inverness Drive East
Englewood, CO 80112-5117
http://www.americanhumane.org/

American Society for the Prevention
of Cruelty to Animals (ASPCA)
424 East 92nd Street
New York, NY 10128-6804
(212) 876-7700
http://www.aspca.org/

Animal Protection Institute of
America
P.O. Box 22505
Sacramento, CA 95822
(916) 731-5521

Golden Retriever Rescue Contacts
(part of Golden Retrievers in Cyberspace website)
http://www.golden-retriever.com/rescue3.html

Golden Retrievers in Cyberspace (abundant information about how and where to rescue and adopt Goldens)
http://www.golden-retriever.com/

Humane Society of the United States
2100 L Street, NW
Washington, DC 20037
http://www.hsus.org

Massachusetts Society for the Prevention of Cruelty to Animals
350 South Huntington Avenue
Boston, MA 02130
(617) 522-7400
http://www.mspca.org/

SPAY/USA
14 Vanderventer Avenue
Port Washington, NY 11050
(516) 944-5025, (203) 377-1116 in Connecticut
(800) 248-SPAY
www.spayusa.org/

Medical and Emergency Information

American Animal Hospital Association
P.O. Box 150899
Denver, CO 80215-0899
(800) 252-2242
www.healthypet.com

American Holistic Veterinary Medicine Association
2214 Old Emmorton Road
Bel Air, MD 21015
(410) 569-2346

American Kennel Club Canine Health Foundation
251 West Garfield Road, Suite 161
Aurora, OH 44202
(888) 682-9696
www.akcchf.org/main.htm

American Veterinary Medical Association
1931 North Meacham Road, Suite 100
Schaumburg, IL 60173-4360
(847) 925-8070
http://www.avma.org/

Canine Eye Registration Foundation (CERF)
Veterinary Medical Data Program
South Campus Courts, Building C
Purdue University
West Lafayette, IN 47907
(765) 494-8179
www.vet.purdue.edu/~yshen/cerf.html

Complementary and Alternative Veterinary Medicine
www.altvetmed.com

Infectious Diseases of the Dog and Cat, Craig E. Greene, Editor
W B Saunders Company

National Animal Poison Control
  Center
1717 S. Philo, Suite 36
Urbana, IL 61802
(888) 426 4435, $45 per case, with as
  many follow-up calls as necessary
  included. Have name, address,
  phone number, dog's breed, age,
  sex, and type of poison ingested, if
  known, available
www.napcc.aspca.org

Orthopedic Foundation for Animals
  (OFA)
2300 E. Nifong Blvd.
Columbia, MO 65201-3856.
(573) 442-0418
www.offa.org/

PennHIP
c/o Synbiotics
11011 Via Frontera
San Diego, CA 92127
(800) 228-4305

Pet First Aid: Cats and Dogs, by
  Bobbi Mammato, D.V.M.
Mosby Year Book

*Skin Diseases of Dogs and Cats: A
  Guide for Pet Owners and Profes-
  sionals,* Dr. Steven A. Melman
Dermapet, Inc.
P.O. Box 59713
Potomac, MD 20859

U.S. Pharmacopeia
vaccine reactions: (800) 487-7776
customer service: (800) 227-8772
www.usp.org

Veterinary Medical Database/Canine
  Eye Registration Foundation
Department of Veterinary Clinical
  Science
School of Veterinary Medicine
Purdue University
West Lafayette, IN 47907
(765) 494-8179
http://www.vet.purdue.edu/~yshen/

Veterinary Pet Insurance (VPI)
4175 E. La Palma Ave., #100
Anaheim, CA 92807-1846
(714) 996-2311
(800) USA PETS, (877) PET
  HEALTH in Texas
www.petplan.net/home.htm

Nutrition and Natural Foods

California Natural, Natural Pet Products
P.O. Box 271
Santa Clara, CA 95052
(800) 532-7261
www.naturapet.com

Home Prepared Dog and Cat Diets,
    Donald R. Strombeck
Iowa State University Press
(515) 292-0140

PHD Products Inc.
P.O. Box 8313
White Plains, NY 10602
(800) 863-3403
www.phdproducts.net/

Sensible Choice, Pet Products Plus
5600 Mexico Road
St. Peters, MO 63376
(800) 592-6687
www.sensiblechoice.com/

Search and Rescue Dogs

National Association for Search and
    Rescue
4500 Southgate Place, Suite 100
Chantilly, VA 20151-1714
(703) 622-6283
http://www.nasar.org/

National Disaster Search Dog Foun-
    dation
323 East Matilija Avenue, #110-245
Ojai, CA 93023-2740
http://www.west.net/~rescue/

Service and Working Dogs

Canine Companions for Indepen-
    dence
P.O. Box 446
Santa Rosa, CA 95402-0446
(800) 572-2275
http://www.caninecompanions.org/

Delta Society National Service Dog
    Center
289 Perimeter Road East
Renton, WA 98055-1329
(800) 869-6898
http://petsforum.com/deltasociety/ds
    b000.htm

Guiding Eyes for the Blind
611 Granite Springs Road
Yorktown Heights, NY 10598
http://www.guiding-eyes.org/

The National Education for Assis-
    tance Dog Services, Inc.
P.O. Box 213
West Boylston, MA 01583
(508) 422-9064
http://chamber.worcester.ma.us/nead
    s/INDEX.HTM

North American Working Dog Asso-
    ciation
Southeast Kreisgruppe
P.O .Box 833
Brunswick, GA 31521

The Seeing Eye
P.O. Box 375
Morristown, NJ 07963-0375
(973) 539-4425
http://www.seeingeye.org/

Therapy Dogs Incorporated
2416 E. Fox Farm Road
Cheyenne, WY 82007
(877) 843-7364
www.therapydogs.com

Therapy Dogs International
6 Hilltop Road
Mendham, NJ 07945
(973) 252-9800
http://www.tdi-dog.org/

Appendix B:
Official Standard for the Golden Retriever

General Appearance

A symmetrical, powerful, active dog, sound and well put together, not clumsy nor long in the leg, displaying a kindly expression and possessing a personality that is eager, alert and self-confident. Primarily a hunting dog, he should be shown in hard working condition. Over-all appearance, balance, gait and purpose to be given more emphasis than any of his component parts. **Faults**—Any departure from the described ideal shall be considered faulty to the degree to which it interferes with the breed's purpose or is contrary to breed character.

Size, Proportion, Substance
Males 23-24 inches in height at withers; females 21½–22½ inches. Dogs up to one inch above or below standard size should be proportionately penalized. Deviation in height of more than one inch from the standard shall disqualify.

Length from breastbone to point of buttocks slightly greater than height at withers in ratio of 12:11. Weight for dogs 65-75 pounds; bitches 55-65 pounds.

Head   Broad in skull, slightly arched laterally and longitudinally without prominence of frontal bones (forehead) or occipital bones. Stop well defined but not abrupt. Foreface deep and wide, nearly as long as skull.

Muzzle straight in profile, blending smoothly and strongly into skull; when viewed in profile or from above, slightly deeper and wider at stop than at tip. No heaviness in flews. Removal of whiskers is permitted but not preferred. **Eyes** friendly and intelligent in expression, medium large with dark, close-fitting rims, set well apart and reasonably deep in sockets. Color preferably dark brown; medium brown acceptable. Slant eyes and narrow, triangular eyes detract from correct expression and are to be faulted. No white or haw visible when looking straight ahead. Dogs showing evidence of functional abnormality of eyelids or eyelashes (such as, but not limited to, trichiasis, entropion, ectropion, or distichiasis) are to be excused from the ring. **Ears** rather short with front edge attached well behind and just above the eye and falling close to cheek. When pulled forward, tip of ear should just cover the eye. Low, hound-like ear set to be faulted. **Nose** black or brownish black, though fading to a lighter shade in cold weather not serious. Pink nose or one seriously lacking in pigmentation to be faulted. **Teeth** scissors bite, in which the outer side of the lower incisors touches the inner side of the upper incisors. Undershot or overshot bite is a **disqualification**. Misalignment of teeth (irregular placement of incisors) or a level bite (incisors, meet each other edge to edge) is undesirable, but not to be confused with undershot or overshot. Full dentition, obvious gaps are **serious faults**.

Neck, Topline, Body   **Neck** medium long, merging gradually into well laid back shoulders, giving sturdy, muscular appearance. Untrimmed natural ruff. No throatiness. **Backline** strong and level from withers to slightly sloping croup, whether standing or moving. Sloping back line, roach or sway back, flat or steep croup to be faulted. **Body** well-balanced, short coupled, deep through the chest.

Chest between forelegs at least as wide as a man's closed hand including thumb, with well developed forechest. Brisket extends to elbow. Ribs long and well sprung but not barrel shaped, extending well towards hindquarters. Loin short, muscular, wide and deep, with very little tuck-up. Slabsidedness, narrow chest, lack of depth in brisket, excessive tuck-up, flat or steep croup to be faulted. **Tail** well set on, thick and muscular at the base, following the natural line of the croup. Tail bones extend to, but not below, the point of hock. Carried with merry action, level or with some moderate upward curve; never curled over back nor between legs.

Forequarters Muscular, well coordinated with hindquarters and capable of free movement. Shoulder blades long and well laid back with upper tips fairly close together at withers. Upper arms appear about the same length as the blades, setting the elbows back beneath the upper tip of the blades, close to the ribs without looseness. Legs, viewed from the front, straight with good bone, but not to the point of coarseness. Pasterns short and strong, sloping slightly with no suggestion of weakness. Dewclaws on forelegs may be removed, but are normally left on. **Feet** medium size, round, compact and well knuckled, with thick pads. Excess hair may be trimmed to show natural size and contour. Splayed or hare feet to be faulted.

Hindquarters Broad and strongly muscled. Profile of croup slopes slightly; the pelvic bone slopes at a slightly greater angle (approximately 30 degrees from horizontal). In a natural stance, the femur joins the pelvis at approximately a 90 degree angle; stifles well bent; hocks well let down with short, strong rear pasterns. Legs straight when viewed from rear. Cow hocks, spread hocks, and sickle hocks to be faulted.

Coat   Dense and water repellent with good undercoat. Outer coat firm and resilient, neither coarse nor silky, lying close to body; may be straight or wavy. Untrimmed natural ruff; moderate feathering on back of forelegs and on under-body; heavier feathering on front of neck, back of thighs and underside of tail.

Coat on head, paws and front of legs is short and even. Excessive length, open coats and limp, soft coats are very undesirable. Feet may be trimmed and stray hairs neatened, but the natural appearance of coat or outline should not be altered by cutting or clipping.

Color   Rich, lustrous golden of various shades. Feathering may be lighter than rest of coat. With the exception of graying or whitening of face or body due to age, any white marking, other than a few white hairs on the chest, should be penalized according to its extent. Allowable light shadings are not to be confused with white markings. Predominant body color which is either extremely pale or extremely dark is undesirable. Some latitude should be given to the light puppy whose coloring shows promise of deepening with maturity. Any noticeable area of black or other off-color hair is a serious fault.

Gait   When trotting, gait is free, smooth, powerful and well co-ordinated, showing good reach. Viewed from any position, legs turn neither in nor out, nor do feet cross or interfere with each other. As speed increases, feet tend to converge toward center line of balance. It is recommended that dogs be shown on a loose lead to reflect true gait.

Temperament   Friendly, reliable and trustworthy. Quarrelsomeness or hostility towards other dogs or people in normal situations, or an unwarranted show of timidity or nervousness, is not in keeping with Golden Retriever character. Such actions should be penalized according to their significance.

DISQUALIFICATIONS

Deviation in height of more than one inch from standard either way. Undershot or overshot bite.

Approved October 13, 1981
Reformatted August 18, 1990

© 1990 Golden Retriever Club of America, Inc.

Index

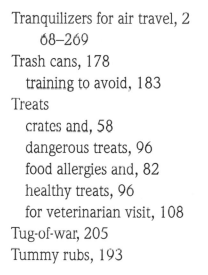

Meet Your Golden Retriever
Care Experts

Author Betsy Sikora Siino is an award-winning author with hundreds of articles and almost 20 books about animals and their care to her credit. Though she specializes in the subjects of dogs and horses, she has written about almost every animal species imaginable and has won acclaim for her work on wildlife species and the many controversial issues surrounding their survival.

Trainer Liz Palika has been teaching classes for dogs and their owners for over twenty years. Her goal is to help people understand why their dogs do what they do so that dogs and owners can live together successfully. Liz says, "If, in each training class, I can increase understanding and ease frustration so that the dog doesn't end up in the local shelter because the owner has given up, then I have accomplished my goal!" She is the author of 23 books and has won awards from both the Dog Writers Association of America and the ASPCA. Liz and her husband, Paul, share their home with three Australian Shepherds: Dax, Kes, and Riker.

Series Editor Joanne Howl, D.V.M. is a graduate of the University of Tennessee College of Veterinary Medicine and has practiced animal medicine for over 10 years. She currently serves as president of the Maryland Veterinary Medical Association and secretary/treasurer of the American Academy on Veterinary Disaster Medicine, and her columns and articles have appeared in a variety of animal-related publications. Dr. Howl presently divides her time between family, small animal medicine, writing, and the company of her two dogs and six cats.